THE COMMONWEALTH AND INTERNATIONAL LIBRARY
Joint Chairmen of the Honorary Editorial Advisory Board
SIR ROBERT ROBINSON, O.M., F.R.S., LONDON
DEAN ATHELSTAN SPILHAUS, MINNESOTA
Publisher: ROBERT MAXWELL, M.C., M.P.

EDUCATION AND EDUCATIONAL RESEARCH DIVISION
General Editor: DR. EDMUND KING

The Upper Secondary School

A COMPARATIVE SURVEY

The Upper Secondary School

A COMPARATIVE SURVEY

by

LEWIS SPOLTON, B.Sc., M.Ed.

Lecturer in Education, University College, Swansea

PERGAMON PRESS

OXFORD · LONDON · EDINBURGH · NEW YORK
TORONTO · SYDNEY · PARIS · BRAUNSCHWEIG

Pergamon Press Ltd., Headington Hill Hall, Oxford
4 & 5 Fitzroy Square, London W.1

Pergamon Press (Scotland) Ltd., 2 & 3 Teviot Place, Edinburgh 1

Pergamon Press Inc., 44–01 21st Street, Long Island City, New York 11101

Pergamon of Canada, Ltd., 6 Adelaide Street East, Toronto, Ontario

Pergamon Press (Aust.) Pty. Ltd., 20–22 Margaret Street,
Sydney, New South Wales

Pergamon Press S.A.R.L., 24 rue des Écoles, Paris 5e

Vieweg & Sohn GmbH, Burgplatz 1, Braunschweig

Copyright © 1967 Pergamon Press Ltd.
First edition 1967
Library of Congress Catalog Card No. 67–21279

Printed in Great Britain by A. Wheaton & Co., Exeter and London

TO THE MEMORY OF MY MOTHER AND FATHER

Contents

Acknowledgements

ACKNOWLEDGEMENT for the reproduction of the extract from *Degrés* by Michel Butor, is due to Editions Gallimard, Paris; Simon and Schuster Inc., New York; and Methuen and Co. Ltd., London. Acknowledgement is made for permission to use the translation, *Not By Calling, But By Duty*, from The Current Digest of the Soviet Press, published weekly at Columbia University, New York, Vol. XVII, No. 1, pp. 29–30; copyright 1965 by the Joint Committee on Slavic Studies.

CHAPTER 1

Stages in Educational Development

UPPER secondary education is not new but, in order to satisfy the demands of what is called variously the second industrial revolution or the cybernetic revolution, it is assuming a different dimension and moving from a restricted base to become an all-inclusive coverage.

In an important chapter entitled the "Sociology of Moral Education" in a book edited by Professor Niblett,* Dr. Halsey looks broadly at the educational process and, after describing what he considers is needed from education in an advanced industrial society, goes on to postulate a sequence of evolutionary stages through which educational systems develop as industrialism advances. He begins by listing four implications of the progress of our society. Each implication has a significance for education.

1. Industrialism necessitates and permits a complex division of labour, and people in different groups who are performing different tasks need experience and education in specialised institutions.
2. Many roles require a long and elaborate training and therefore schooling tends to occupy a longer portion of the life cycle of individuals. The number of such roles is continually increasing.
3. Industrialisation demands an elaborate social organisation in which people tend to fill roles only when they are competent to do so. In place of a system whereby circumstance

* Niblett, W. R. (Ed.), *Moral Education in a Changing Society*, Faber & Faber, 1963, chapter 2.

1

of birth, or wealth, or some other irrelevant factor decides the role a person will assume in society (ascription is the technical term for this process) is substituted a system whereby achievement becomes of first importance.

4. Since an industrial culture is all the time transforming itself, the first three factors are becoming increasingly important.

Halsey then goes on to list three general stages of educational development, at the same time pointing out that variations are possible. His stages are as follows:

Stage I.   A system of universal primary education is achieved.
Stage II.   Secondary education becomes the normal experience of all members of the society.
Stage III. A system of higher education begins to develop for everyone.

He suggests that Great Britain has struggled haltingly through the second stage and "is now engaged in an agony of decision" as to whether to enter stage three. The United States completed the second stage before the onset of World War II and plunged unhesitatingly into the third stage. Nowhere does Halsey suggest the three stages are discrete and obviously approaches begin at one stage before the previous stage is complete. Not everywhere, but in most countries, this book will make clear how incomplete is upper secondary education.

The rate of educational growth brings other changes with it. What were previously terminal institutions become feeder institutions for a later stage in the educational process and the comprehensive principle becomes applicable to higher stages of education. In Europe generally this is the pattern which is emerging with a growing tendency to delay the time of selection. In the United States even the junior college is beginning to be regarded by some as a comprehensive stage leading on to true higher education later. A recent article* denies that common learnings are complete by this stage and states that English, mathematics, the

* Harris, N. C., Redoubled efforts, *Phi delta kappan*, April 1965.

humanities, sciences and social science amounting to one-quarter of the 2-year programme is typically required—"a generous core of common learnings".

However, while Halsey's analysis of the developing educational process is useful, it does tend to be too simple to illuminate sufficiently some of the problems which are involved in the changes made necessary by industrialisation. His first two implications also work to some extent at cross-purposes. He notes firstly the need for education in specialised institutions and secondly the need for a longer schooling generally. A longer general schooling usually means that specialised institutions at a lower level—a level which used to give adequate terminal education but is adequate no longer—need to become less specialised and new institutions at a higher level take on a specialised function which in its turn will become outdated. In France the changes that are now in the process of being implemented can be seen as making the lower secondary school a more general institution feeding specialised institutions at the upper secondary level. Thus Halsey's stages, useful as a starting point, are not sufficiently detailed for a book which is analysing changes at the upper secondary stage.

But by combining Halsey's criteria with a series of educational stages proposed by J. A. Laska* the task facing the upper secondary school can be highlighted more clearly. Laska differs from Halsey in that his analysis includes a preliminary stage in the educational process—a stage which occurs before industrialisation begins. This makes the model more useful because it includes this earlier era which has a long and venerated history in Europe. In including this stage Laska's typology can be made to underline what Halsey's scheme tends to omit—the necessity, not only to provide new institutions, but, also, what may prove more difficult, to change old ones.

As soon as a state becomes organised it requires administrators and professional men who need a higher education. Therefore some system for providing this has to be established and also, as

* Laska, J. A., The stages in educational development, *Comparative Education Review*, vol. 8, no. 3, December 1964.

a preliminary, enough primary and secondary educational provision to feed the higher institutions with an adequate supply of
students is needed. This is the situation prior to Laska's first stage.
In his analysis Laska is thinking particularly in terms of the
developing countries. But the countries of Western Europe were
once developing countries with educational provision of this embryo kind. In England men of quite lowly birth, like Thomas
Becket, whose father was a London official, rose to high administrative office through such an educational system. He passed his
boyhood at home in London attending a city school (perhaps St.
Paul's) and later studied at the University of Paris.* In the twelfth
century the University took students at the age of 13 and gave
them a general education in the arts faculty before they passed on
to specialisation in the faculties of law, theology or medicine.
Upper secondary education at this early period was in the University and, as the chapter on France will briefly indicate, an un-
broken link can be traced between the methods and curriculum
of the medieval university and the modern *lycée*. As the upper
secondary school changes from an *élite* to a mass system it has to
overcome some of the traditions which it has inherited from a long
ancestry. In the United States the lineage is much less venerable
—a mere two to three centuries as against almost a thousand
years. The settlers who left Britain for America were serious-
minded people willing to risk a new life because they were dis-
satisfied with the political, social and religious institutions and
background of the homeland. Once settled, they began to recreate
the institutions of the homeland which they thought would be
valuable. The Latin grammar school was one of these. But because
they were escaping from the past they were willing to treat the old
things with suspicion. (Much later Henry Ford could put it
bluntly—"History is bunk".) The attitude of questioning the past
was reinforced by the experience of the settlers in discovering the
wealth of the new continent. For those willing to work hard there
was a good living to be had apart from any formal education.

* See Jarman, T. L., *Landmarks in the History of Education*, Murray, London,
1963, 2nd edition, p. 80.

There seemed to be illimitable possibilities and this bred the belief that everyone had some talent if he would trouble to find it. So despite the establishment of the old type of Latin grammar school, the gap between the old curriculum and the practical demands required in life was so great that a classical education was seen as largely irrelevant. In the book *Anti-Intellectualism in American Life,** R. Hofstadter has set out the forces working for a school with an ethos very different from the grammar school from which it was derived. To use a metaphor from palaeontology, if in educational institutions, ontogeny recapitulates phylogeny—and schools in the United States were modelled originally on the west European family of schools—then palingenesis has taken place. Stages in evolution have been skipped and hurried over and new developments have put the United States in the van of progress at the upper secondary level. Pre-stage I traditions of *élitism* have not interfered with the flowering of a mass system after the age of 15. But in Europe traditions in this sector have been less easy to change. In fact much of this book will be detailing the arrangements at present being made to extend the traditions and admit beside them new provision necessary because of the changing socio-economic circumstances.

Following the preliminary stage Laska defines three stages and formulates a quantitative basis for them based on the concept of educational completion rate. A completion ratio is obtained by comparing the number of students completing or finishing an educational level with the total population in the age group which corresponds with the average age of those completing that level. The comparison is expressed as a percentage. Thus, for example, at present in England and Wales the primary school completion ratio will be near 100% but the secondary school completion rate is much smaller. In fact for west European countries general secondary completion rates in 1955 were between 5 and 10. The U.S.A. reached the figure of 10 in about 1910 and the U.S.S.R. attained the same figure in 1954. With this definition in mind Laska's stages can be described as follows:

* Hofstadter, R., Knopf, New York, 1963.

Stage I. The first stage requires that sufficient persons to fill the necessary professional and administrative positions shall be educated at secondary and higher levels. Working empirically from advanced countries he suggests a secondary completion ratio of approaching but not exceeding 5% is a suitable criterion. This rate should be obtained with a primary completion rate as low as is consonant with the education of sufficient persons to go forward to secondary and higher levels. Laska distinguishes between the completion of grade 4 of the primary course and completion of the complete primary course, considering that 4 years of primary education are sufficient to ensure literacy and form the basis for secondary education. For Stage I a grade 4 completion rate of 50% is set as a maximum along with the secondary completion rate of not more than 5%.

Stage II is concerned with the provision of universal primary education, i.e. completion rate near 100% with little or no change in the completion rate for secondary education.

Stage III is concerned with increasing educational opportunities at the secondary and higher levels, once universal primary education has been achieved. These educational opportunities are not of one kind: they may be vocational and technical as well as of a more general academic nature. A modern society needs both types and often it is the former type which is in shorter supply. In formulating his criteria Laska has concentrated only on the completion of the general type of education at the secondary level. (Here, too, it may be noted that some countries still include teacher training, usually teachers for the primary level, in secondary education rather than in higher education. For the purposes of this study these teacher-training arrangements have been excluded and attention has concentrated on the various other forms which exist.)

Using Laska's criteria, many west European countries have entered Stage III since World War II and with the extension of opportunity the upper secondary school has begun to feel the wind of change. General secondary school completion ratios for 1955 are as follows:

Sweden	9	Norway	9·5
France	7	Belgium	8·5
Great Britain	4	Netherlands	5
Germany (F.R.)	3·5	Denmark	5

The United States reached the end of Stage II between 1871 and 1890 by which year the secondary completion ratio attained 3·5%. After this rapid progress was made in Stage III giving a ratio of 15 by 1920 and, including all types of secondary school (it is less easy to separate types in the U.S.A. than elsewhere), a ratio of 65 by 1960.

Japan completed Stage II by 1905, but at that date the secondary completion rate was 2·5. Since World War II there has been a rapid increase, and the figure reached 55 by 1958.

In the U.S.S.R. in 1958 only 80% seemed to be completing 7 years of primary education (to 14 years) though the 4-year primary completion ratio reached 100% soon after 1931. In 1950 5% were completing secondary school and by 1959 the ratio was 30. So there, as in Japan, the post-war years are the formative ones for the upper secondary sector.

As this book is describing critically the upper part of the secondary school it is almost entirely concerned with countries developing in Stage III. For Stages I and II Laska lists and describes a number of sub-stages and deviant types but, because he is more concerned with developing countries, goes into little detail concerning Stage III at which stage secondary education proliferates. There is, however, no doubt that Stage III could be subdivided, for, as already shown, and as will be further documented later, the rate of participation varies widely from country to country; and, anyway, secondary education is a term with a wide embrace as was spelled out as long ago as 1895 in that memorable passage in the Bryce Commission report.*

> All education is development . . . by the communication of knowledge. Secondary education may be described as a modification of this general idea. . . . It is a process of intellectual training and personal discipline conducted with special regard to the profession or trade to be followed.

---

* Quoted in *Secondary Education* (the Spens report), H.M.S.O., London, 1938, pp. 58–9.

The passage then goes on to demolish the general–technical dichotomy by showing how technical instruction is comprehended under the term secondary education.

> Technical instruction is secondary i.e., it comes after . . . the rudiments. And secondary instruction is technical i.e., it teaches the boy so to apply the principles he is learning . . . as to perform or produce something, interpret a literature or a science, make a picture or a book, practise a plastic or a manual art, convince a jury or persuade a senate, translate or annotate an author, dye wool, weave cloth, design or construct a machine, navigate a ship or command an army. Secondary education, as inclusive of technical, may be described as education conducted in view of the special life that has to be lived. . . .

At the time of the Bryce Commission and, for half a century later, this country believed that at an early age children could be sorted into categories according to the special life that had to be lived. Nowadays, in the present state of society it is being increasingly realised that common learnings have to be continued to a later age. To give a definition of secondary education, other than the stage that follows primary, becomes more difficult. Laska defines what he means by the beginning of secondary education.

> At the completion of the primary course, those students who are able to continue with the university–preparatory curriculum do so, while the remainder follow various non-university oriented curricula or enter adult roles. The period of schooling which involves differentiated curricula for university and non-university–preparatory students constitutes the secondary level.

He notes that since this definition is functional it may not conform with the terminology employed in any school system. It is here that Halsey's ideas concerning the movement of the point of selection to increasingly higher stages in the educational process, and the progressive application of the comprehensive principle, can be married to those of Laska. Laska's definition would place the commencement of secondary education at the age of 11+ where the tripartite system operates, as in most areas of the United Kingdom; but, using the same definition, as the comprehensive principle is introduced the age of commencement of secondary education would rise. As the chapters on France and Sweden show, plans being implemented there would place the primary–secondary demarcation (by Laska's definition) at 15 years and 16 years respectively. Laska is in fact saying that common learnings are primary, and pressed to its logical conclusion this would bring a great many problems but, nevertheless, Laska's definition is a very useful one, though it seems more satisfactory to accept that secondary education begins at about the age of 11 or 12 after 4, 5 or 6 years of primary schooling, and that upper secondary schooling commences when curricula really begin to differentiate into university-preparatory and non-university oriented sections which is usually also near the point where some students (though it should increasingly be a minority) leave to enter adult roles. Laska's definition can, in fact, be adopted as a suitable one for *upper secondary schooling* as it is being regarded here. No definite age can be laid down for its commencement, but the normal age will be 15 or 16. The completion age will also vary between 17 and 19, and may, in a few cases, be 20, e.g. in German Gymnasien a few students remain to this age.

The idea of a completion ratio has already been explained. Another useful quantitative criterion is the enrolment ratio, which is calculated by comparing the numbers receiving schooling with the total number in the age group, and again expressing the result as a percentage. Such enrolment ratios may be calculated for a single age group or an age range. The choice of age range can introduce complications which must be allowed for in interpretation, so enrolment ratio is less useful in some ways than completion ratio. The most clear-cut example of difficulty is in the enrolment ratio, say for the age range 5–9, because in some countries schooling does not start until 6 or 7 years of age. England and Wales would show a high enrolment ratio for this age range but France, starting at 6, a lower one. At the end of upper secondary schooling the cut-off will not be so clear-cut but it will obviously introduce differences between countries where the normal age of completion is 18 years as in England and the U.S.A., and countries such as Germany and Sweden, where 19 years is the normal for students in the academic courses. With this reservation in mind the list of enrolment ratios (Table 1) illustrates some of the variety which exists.

TABLE 1

Country	Date	15–19-year group enrolment ratio (%)
U.S.A.	1958	66·2
U.S.S.R.	1958	48·6
Japan	1960	38·5
Sweden	1960	32·3
France	1958	30·8
F.R. Germany	1958	17·6
England and Wales	1957	16·8
Spain	1959	13·3

It is worth noting that the disparity in leaving age between Germany and England and Wales already referred to makes the small difference as between these two in the table not diagnostic.

A similar but less useful measure is the secondary enrolment ratio as used in the *UNESCO World Survey of Education,* Vol. III, *Secondary Education,* published in 1961. This ratio compares secondary enrolments (secondary being defined as in any given country) with total population in the 15–19 age group. In these figures England and Wales will show up well because secondary education is defined as starting at 11+ as against 12+ in the U.S.A. for example. By comparing rates of increase of secondary enrolment ratio this difficulty is minimised. The following figures from the *UNESCO World Survey* compare annual rates of increase. In Table 2 are shown side by side increase rates between the averages of the years 1930–4 and the averages of the years 1955–7 and those for a shorter period 1950–4 to 1955–7. The comparison allows some distinction to be drawn between those countries which expanded early and those which have expanded most in the fifties.

TABLE 2. PERCENTAGE INCREASE IN AVERAGE SECONDARY ENROLMENT RATIOS BETWEEN CERTAIN YEARS

Country	1930–4 to 1955–7	1950–4 to 1955–7
U.S.A.	1·6	3·4
U.S.S.R.	—	7·4
Japan	7·8	3·0
Sweden	4·7	3·0
France	5·0	8·7
F.R. Germany	—	decrease
England and Wales	1·5	3·1
Spain	5·4	7·0

The same source suggests a rating scale for secondary enrolment ratios as follows:

under 10	under developed
10–24	developing
25–49	moderately developed
over 50	well developed

It will be noted that this scale is not discriminating at the upper end where anything over 50 is designated well developed. This brings England and Wales into the same bracket as the United States when obviously there is much difference. However, using these categories a square table can be constructed showing alteration in status over a period, and this is done below for the countries described in the chapters which follow.

In interpreting this table not only must the lack of discrimination in the highest category be allowed for; it is important, too, to remember the tremendous rate at which change is proceeding. Gradually gathering pace as the more urgent resettlement difficulties after the war were overcome, the tempo has gone on accelerating and the last 10 years since the figures given in Table 2 and Fig. 1 have witnessed the greatest changes, so that all the

1955–57		Under developed	Developing	Moderately developed	Well developed
	Well developed		Sweden Japan		England and Wales U.S.A.
	Moderately developed	U.S.S.R.	France		
	Developing	Spain			
	Under developed				

Under developed　　Developing　　Moderately developed　　Well developed

1930–4

Fig. 1.

countries included here (except Spain which is a special case) are in the well-developed bracket. It is these latest changes, the background to which this chapter has been explaining, that this book is planned to describe.

This introductory chapter has also called attention to two other factors beside the disparate provision that prevails. They are the inherited patterns and the problem of general versus technical–vocational education.

(a) INHERITED PATTERNS

Most educational systems have inherited a pattern from this formative period which may not be appropriate to the present when a high rate of development and change is needed. How to transform the old to fit the new circumstances and integrate it with the innovations which are necessary is a problem which many countries are trying to solve.

(b) THE GENERAL–VOCATIONAL EDUCATION DICHOTOMY

Pressures on educational systems are twofold. They come from the increase of numbers and from the advances in technology which make necessary an increased number of more educated people. Thus, not only must general education expand: there must be an increase of the technical–vocational too. And, of course, the two types are complementary, for general education is preparatory to the more specialised education necessary for a vocation. One of the special problems is the correct balance which ought to obtain between the two. Different countries deal with the two types of education in different ways. In some countries the two types are mainly given in different institutions, e.g. England and Wales, Germany; some have achieved a good measure of integration, e.g. U.S.S.R. and Japan; other countries are working to give an increased status to the technical–vocational branch, e.g. Sweden, France. Once again it is often a problem of transforming the old pattern to the new circumstances which is difficult.*

In the following chapters the problems of upper secondary education and actual and planned solutions in various countries are described and analysed. First to be considered is the position in England and Wales.

* For a general discussion see Robinson, E. A. G. and Vaizey, J., *The Economics of Education*, especially part V, Macmillan, London, 1966.

CHAPTER 2

The Crowther Report
and the Path Ahead

ANYONE who writes about upper secondary education must be very conscious of the Crowther report which deals in the same field in immense detail. The report itself, entitled simply *Fifteen to Eighteen*, is a volume of over 500 pages and it is buttressed by a second volume which contains the results of three investigations the committee commissioned in areas where it felt short of facts. The whole undertaking is a landmark in British education, and the resulting report is a worthy documentation of the first major inquiry into the educational system, a decade and a half after what has been called the major education act in our history—the 1944 Act. To attempt a brief summary is an almost impossible task for the committee's own summary is 28 pages long. However, since their findings, opinions and forecasts are basic for this study and since chapters 3 and 5 are largely essays in bringing Crowther up to date, it is a task which must be essayed.

The carefully worded remit* which the Central Advisory Council for Education (England) was given largely influenced the shape of the report, which is divided into seven sections. The first section, called "Education in a Changing World", takes a commendably brief, but penetrating, backward glance into history and then concentrates on examining and defining "the

---

* In March 1956 the Minister of Education asked the Council "to consider, in relation to the changing social and industrial needs of our society, and the needs of its individual citizens, the education of boys and girls between 15 and 18, and in particular to consider the balance at various levels of general and specialised studies between these ages and to examine the interrelationship of the various stages of education". Central Advisory Council for Education (England), *Fifteen to Eighteen*, H.M.S.O., London, 1959, vol. 1, Remit.

changing social and industrial needs of society", in which context it was commanded to view its remit. This opening section is one of the strengths of the report. It is commonplace to say an idea, a book or even a philosophy is the product of its time, but for this educational report to begin with a socially and economically oriented discussion was certainly most apposite at a time when much greater attention was being paid to such factors generally. Then follow five sections which investigate how effectively the system is working, and what changes should be recommended to achieve progress in the sector above the compulsory school staying age, which, in the years since 1944, had not received the attention which the Act had adumbrated. The five sections fall into three main parts.

First the modern school and its extension into further education is considered in three sections called "The Development of the Modern School", "Secondary Education for All" and "The Way to County Colleges". In this area the report makes two of its major recommendations—the raising of the age of compulsory schooling to 16, to be implemented in the late sixties when the valley in the demographic curve reaches the secondary school, and the gradual extension of compulsion to further education. Conscious of the economic problems connected with the realisation of these two major advances, it argues and then states the priorities, advocating compulsion in county colleges only after raising the school age has been secured.

Secondly the report looks closely at the sixth form which is the title of its fifth section. It investigates critically, and not uncomplacently the progress that has been achieved, and points out carefully the ways in which the potential of the present system is being under used, and is then content to encourage extension rather than revision. In this area it conducts an inquiry into the balance of general and special studies, mentioned in its remit. Again it is on the whole satisfied with what it sees though it wants a better use of minority time to set right the imbalance which has arisen. It is concerned with both "literacy" for the science side and "numeracy" for those specialising in arts subjects. This debate has gone on with renewed vigour in the period since the report. Only in a short chapter at the end of this section does the report consider possible changes at this level, in what it christens "sixth forms with a difference".

Thirdly the report, in its sixth part, which is called "Technical Challenge and Educational Response", examines carefully the system of further education and, with the help of one of its surveys, is able to document its achievement and also its inefficiencies. Once again it dwells on potential and stresses the need for integration with school at the point of entrance and the need for increased order and rationalisation of the available provision. Economic considerations concerning the growth of the national wealth were much in the Council's thoughts in the preparation of this section, and both at the time of their deliberations and since there has been an increasing amount of attention to this sector of the educational field as Chapter 5 will show.

The fact that these three strands can be distinguished so clearly in the report enables one to suggest that a very brief summary of the report might be: division of the educational system into an hierarchical system below compulsory age is producing sufficient unfilled opportunities in its voluntary extensions at the upper secondary level for a broadly tripartite system to be continued to 18 and beyond.

However, the final clause of its remit asked that it examine the interrelationship of the various stages of education and, at a number of points it does suggest zones of integration. In particular it looks at this more closely in Part 7 where it is concerned with changing patterns in organisation. Many suggestions are here given an airing but at no point is the basic structure strongly questioned.

In its final pre-summary chapter the report considers the problem of providing teachers for the expansion, a problem which has been mentioned time and time again during the report. This is obviously a problem which the Council regarded as vital to the whole issue, and one which must be solved if progress is to be continued. The report—charting progress, illuminating deficiencies and encouraging trends—is filled with good ideas often expressed in apt and memorable phrases. There can be no doubt that it is a major work. But despite these qualities it has been criticised on a number of accounts.

The first criticism is a very general one which has been levelled at other similar educational reports. It calls into question the special committee system of shaping educational policy.* This school of thought insists that the custom of appointing a committee of carefully chosen, and often eminent persons, to investigate a remit is usually vitiated by a lack of real hard facts. The committee invites and collects opinions and information and produces a considered report arrived at by weighing the mass of material, but often the verdict is supported by opinion rather than evidence. In some areas the Crowther Committee realised this limitation and set up three investigations designed to fill obvious gaps in the record. In this way they were able to present important material showing inefficiency in the system. However, in other areas they were less objective and seem to have made a mistake similar to the famous typology of the Norwood report, by accepting rather unquestioningly a situation that had grown up to meet administrative convenience. This mistake was the elevation of subject-mindedness, one of the marks of the sixth form, to the status of a principle. "It is there, whether we like it or not", they wrote. The error in this thinking has been exposed by Peterson in his pamphlet *Arts and Science Sides in the Sixth Form* (1960).

The investigation reported in this pamphlet was being conducted at the same time that the Crowther Committee was sitting. An investigation by questionnaire into the subject preferences of almost 3000 pupils in English schools and over 700 in French *lycées* and German *Gymnasien* provided no evidence of subject-mindedness but showed a clear majority in favour of a curriculum sampling subjects from both the arts and science sides. By a consideration of the history of the growth of the curriculum the pamphlet is able to show there are two main ways of extending the range of subjects covered. The first is an integration of new subjects into the curriculum alongside the old thus preserving

* See Dobinson, C. H., *Schooling 1963–70*, Harrap, London, 1963.

a balance while recognising the worth of the new. The second method is to admit a new subject as an alternative which can be taken instead of, but not as well as, the old. This second method suggests the old, mainly classical, curriculum gives a sufficiently rounded and full education, but gradually admits that other groups of subjects, studied in the appropriate depth, will do the same. Peterson points out that the first alternative is the one that has been accepted on the Continent while England is, to a large extent, the odd man out in accepting the second method, which in accepting "one noble subject" or a group of closely related subjects as the educational material suitable for the upper secondary level, gave rise to the notion of subject-mindedness. It became accepted by the grammar schools after 1902 because their tiny embryo sixth forms were left free by Morant's regulations and so developed along the same lines as the public schools, for they were competing with the products of these institutions for places at the university. Eventually this voluntary imitation was fixed by Board of Education decree and catered for by examination boards. This whole subject of the two cultures and the idea of general studies has been one of the important debates in the post-Crowther era. It is considered in Chapter 3.

Another criticism concerns the general acceptance of the tripartite structure which had grown up since the 1944 Act and has been projected into the upper secondary sector. Some critics have even gone as far as to suggest that the terms of the remit given to the Central Advisory Council tended to over-emphasise the changing social and industrial needs as against the benefit to the individual, which might have been given greater stress. That the committee did take the individual into account cannot be gainsaid, but critics have said that economic considerations were too much in mind, and what some can interpret as a realistic appraisal of the possible, is seen by others as a too-cautious approach, merely suggesting where there is slack to be taken up, and as such is a substitute for a radical forward step. In fact it is suggested that the paramountcy of economic considerations may be short-sighted, in the long run, because it has failed to take into account the possible social consequences on industrial relations of the continuance of a divided system in adolescence. In particular the step-by-step approach to the establishment of a system of further education for the 16–18-year-old, only after the raising of the compulsory school age, is criticised as making the advent of upper secondary education for all too slow a process, unlikely to be implemented before 1980. The substance of this criticism, which can be summarised as concerned with the comprehensiveness of the system, is another of the great post-Crowther debates and will be treated in Chapter 6.

A minor criticism connected with the above is the concept of the county college as envisaged in the report. Here the Crowther report appears to have cast aside, momentarily, economic considerations and endowed the county college idea with the overtones of a disinterested and liberal education divorced from vocation. Here, again, developments since 1959 have tended to stress the vocational incentive much more. Chapter 5 documents this trend.

The public school question, *per se*, gets no consideration in the report: the term is absent from the glossary and the index. Whenever reference is made the much less emotive title independent, efficient or other, is used. One knows, of course, that terminology in this sector is difficult, and to tabulate and extract from Ministry figures makes it necessary to use their classification. However, any consideration of the upper secondary school ought to have something to say on this problem. Chapter 4 attempts to investigate some of the difficulties.

For a final criticism the report itself can be quoted because it is being self-critical. In its final summing up it states: "Other countries are wrestling with the same problems as ourselves and, some of them, finding interesting solutions to them; but our knowledge of what they are doing rests far too much on the subjective basis of returning travellers' tales." The second part of this sentence may be a striving after a memorable phrase. If it is intended as a serious criticism it shows a lack of appreciation of the state of comparative education and the insights it can give.

For over a century educationists have been looking at other people's schools. Travellers' tales belong to a very early stage which has long been superseded by careful description, but this is still only a basis and must be followed by analysis to give a clear apprehension and then by juxtaposition of data from several areas to build up a comparison. A further step would be the study in depth of a small part of the total field. The Crowther Committee were given just such a problem—the education of boys and girls between the ages of 15 and 18. Did their naïve approach to comparative education quoted above lead them to neglect the insights which a study of other systems might have provided? To some extent their attitude was ambivalent. For technical education and vocational training they undertook a study of arrangements in France, the West German Federal Republic and the Netherlands and reported their findings in Appendix 3 to the report. This section concludes with a general comparison with English practice and suggests some lessons which can be learned from the exercise. Apart from Appendix 3 the report makes a few, usually very minor, references to practice abroad. One of these concerns the problem of sixth-form specialisation, and it deals in two paragraphs with the broad outlines of American and continental European practice which while differing from each other also differ from our own. As already described a few pages earlier, Peterson had made an objective assessment of this problem in contrast to the report's subjective conclusion.

The Robbins Committee studying Higher Education appeared to agree with the Crowther report's statement "other countries are wrestling with the same problems as ourselves and, some of them, finding interesting solutions", but instead of dismissing the comparative approach took the trouble to make a careful survey. Chapter 5 in their report, entitled "International Comparisons", is an excellent example of comparative writing based on knowledge, and in Appendix 5 to the Robbins report is provided the descriptive and analytical studies which are its background. This appendix, "Higher Education in Other Countries", really covers more than its title implies, for it supplies for each of the ten countries studied a brief sketch of the arrangements for secondary education on which higher education depends. Hence Appendix 5 is apposite to this study. Its coverage of countries forms a good cross-section. It consists of the two giants, U.S.A. and U.S.S.R.; two countries important historically as well as contemporaneously, France and West Germany; those smaller European countries, Sweden, Switzerland and the Netherlands, which exemplify different viewpoints; and the three important Commonwealth countries of Australia, Canada and New Zealand. Though all fit into the overall plan which is used in the report, the treatment brings out the variety which they contain—variety which led the Committee to write "to look at systems very different in structure brings into the open assumptions implicit in the British pattern". This is the view held here and the selection of countries for comparative study has been made for this purpose.

CHAPTER 3

Traditional English Sixth Forms— The Maintained System

BETWEEN 1947 and 1964 the number of sixth-formers increased threefold. In 1947 there were 32,000 17-year-olds in sixth forms, by 1964 the bulge in the birth rate and the trend to stay on had resulted in just over 100,000 17-year-olds being in school. 1965 is certain to produce a higher figure, but the valley in the secondary age groups in the late sixties may then produce some levelling of the graph before a further and steeper climb in the seventies. Can this change in magnitude, this explosion in the sixth form, still leave the sixth form unchanged? It has already been noted that the Crowther report emphasised the extension that it was possible for the maintained school to achieve by extrapolation without much change. It admired what it saw and argued for a continuation. Miss Frances Stevens was working on an intrinsic study of the social and educational assumptions of the grammar school at the same time as the Crowther committee and calling her book, which came out in 1960, *The Living Tradition*, she indicated a desire for a programme of minimum change. However, a man of 50 watching his own family follow their path through the university-oriented sixth form cannot but be struck by the differences a quarter of a century has brought. How much greater must these be on the periphery? This chapter will examine how far the tradition has continued: Chapter 6 will look at the extent of the changes.

The Ministry of Education Pamphlet 9 (1947) is famous for the blueprint it sketched for the secondary modern school, but it also took a brief glance at the other types of secondary provision. Of the grammar school it suggested that its ethos and aims were so well known there was really little that could be usefully said though it might prove there was perhaps too much provision! Evidently what had gone before was meant to continue. Secondary school regulations after 1902 ensured a 4-year course to 16 with a wide range of subjects, and later this pattern was continued by the group examination requiring English, Latin or mathematics, a science, a foreign language and another subject for a certificate. For the few who stayed after 16 and worked for the second school examination the course was entirely different based on the alternative rather than the integrative principle. Instead of new subjects being introduced alongside the old they were introduced as equal (or fairly equal) alternatives and very small groups at the upper secondary level studied either the classics or the sciences or the humanities to an increasingly advanced stage. Higher school certificate began to carry exemption from "intermediate", and increasingly the first year of university work began to be studied in school. University courses which had been of 4 years' duration were more and more frequently reduced to 3 years. This was essentially the pattern which continued in the years immediately after 1944.

During the war years the Norwood Committee had been considering the curriculum and examinations and they produced their report in 1943. They argued that secondary schools had reached a suitable maturity in the years before the war, and were now at a stage when they could dispense with the prop of external examinations, which had been useful in fixing a standard but had largely outlived their nursemaid function and were preventing schools from really growing up and reaching their full stature. In 1950 school examinations were reorganised in such a way that there was more freedom and at about the same time the Ministry brought out the pamphlet *The Road to the Sixth Form* (1951) as a guide for action. Its theme was the continuous course to 18. It asked for a reconsideration of the normal grammar school curriculum to encourage more pupils to stay on. It is filled with thoughts like those in the following sentences:

No magic break occurs at 15 or 16 which can justify a complete alteration in studies at that point. Up to the present the course has been thought of as consisting of two unequal parts but the time has come to change this. At sixteen there should be no illusion of a completed examination. Ordinary level is a false climax for those who will go on to advanced level. Although it would have been unthinkable twenty years ago, the grammar school today need not fear organising work on a continuous course to eighteen.

The introduction of the pamphlet had prepared the way for these suggestions by saying "nor can it be supposed that in a changing world the education of the gifted majority has reached any final stage of perfection". They pointed out that an academic course could hardly be expected to pay much dividend before 17 or 18 and thought it wrong that a boy should reach the sixth completely unprepared for the kind of work he would find there. They wanted ordinary level to be by-passed in advanced level subjects and wanted the curriculum to taper in the fifth form rather than present a blunt rectangular base for sixth-form work. The pamphlet also suggested there were two kinds of subjects and by using them properly more variety could be brought into the curriculum. Some subjects such as mathematics and languages need to be pursued steadily and evenly but others can be looked upon as non-continuous and can be left off and taken up again more readily. Geography, history, English literature and even some science subjects are susceptible to this treatment. This suggestion has been used little in British schools.

The Road to the Sixth Form was quickly followed by an investigation into the length of school life of the 1946 intake into grammar schools, and the facts discovered were given in the report of the Gurney-Dixon Committee significantly entitled *Early Leaving*. Working from a sample they found that of the grammar school intake only about one-quarter were still at school in the seventh year. There were a variety of reasons for leaving and many of them were socio-economic although it was surprising how much schools in similar circumstances differed showing that such problems were not insurmountable. Petty irritation with school was much commoner in the case of girls than boys. The report re-iterated the idea of removing the clean break at 16, contending, as had *The Road to the Sixth Form*, that a gradual transition to the sixth form meant that more would stay on. They pointed out the new G.C.E. examination was sufficiently flexible to make this reorganisation possible. The new examination also gave an opportunity to the secondary modern school. Few modern school pupils could successfully tackle a group examination, but a certificate with one or even several subjects was within their powers. Schools began to use this incentive. The report asked for transfers from modern to grammar schools—its investigation showed how much placement in the grammar school intake varied in a few years with some pupils migrating up, and some down, the rank order— and also for the provision in both modern and grammar schools of courses for pupils of similar ability. In this way were sown the seeds for an eventual upper secondary harvest in the secondary modern school.

In particular the report called for an increased entry into advanced courses in grammar schools but it also anticipated Crowther's "sixth forms with a difference" when it advocated more general sixth-form courses, and an altered career structure for the trades and professions putting the age of entry at 18 and encouraging more vocational courses in the sixth forms of both grammar and technical schools. It also advocated special attention to the weaker grammar school pupils in the early years with the object of fostering a greater interest and an increased likelihood of a longer school life.

The Gurney-Dixon Committee had been given their remit at the end of 1952 when the actual size of the sixth form for the last 5 years had been stationary or had even decreased slightly. But, in 1953, before the report was ready an improvement began and has continued. The Crowther Committee, although advocating still greater expansion, was able to chronicle a considerable growth and give good grounds for an optimistic forecast of continued expansion. The "trend" had begun.

The Crowther Committee analysed the position carefully, not only in general terms taking 17-year-olds as a measure of the growth, but also comparing different types of school and showing that what the direct grant and independent efficient were doing in 1957 the maintained grammar could emulate. As already noticed, helped by the "bulge" and the "trend" the figures have gone on increasing, and a few of Crowther's tables brought up to date reveal what a mere 7 years have achieved. The report used 1947 as a base and this has been continued so the tables show the growth since the end of the war.

First, in Table 3, are the numbers of 17-year-olds in all types of school (except independent schools not recognised as efficient).

TABLE 3. NUMBERS OF PUPILS AGED 17 IN ALL TYPES OF SCHOOL
(ENGLAND AND WALES)

	Boys (000's)	% increase over 1947	Girls (000's)	% increase over 1947	All (000's)	% increase over 1947
1947	18·0	—	14·0	—	32·0	—
1958	28·8	60	22·5	61	51·3	60
1964	57·6	220	42·8	205	100·4	213

In round numbers this shows the actual numbers have doubled since 1957 and increased threefold since 1947.

The contribution made to this total by the three main types of school is shown in Table 4.

TABLE 4. RELATIVE INCREASE OF NUMBERS IN DIFFERENT TYPES OF
SCHOOL (ENGLAND AND WALES) 17-YEAR-OLD PUPILS

	Maintained grammar		Direct grant		Independent recognised efficient	
	Boys	Girls	Boys	Girls	Boys	Girls
1947 (000's)	10·8	9·8	1·8	1·5	5·1	2·4
% increase over 1947:						
1957	53	52	66	79	54	54
1964	210	153	183	187	96	121

Table 4 shows that the maintained grammar is increasing at a more rapid rate than the other types of school. As the Crowther report noted, there was no reason to suppose the maintained grammar could not approach the independent efficient schools in its holding power in the sixth form and this it is doing with increasing success. Another way of showing this is to express the figures as shown in Table 5.

TABLE 5. PUPILS AGED 17 AS A PROPORTION OF THE PUPILS IN THE SAME SCHOOLS AGE 14 THREE YEARS EARLIER

Age 14 in	Age 17 in	Maintained grammar		Direct grant		Independent recognised efficient	
		Boys	Girls	Boys	Girls	Boys	Girls
1947	1950	26·5	24·6	38·8	34·0	58·6	36·1
1954	1957	33·9	30·1	48·8	42·0	58·3	30·6
1961	1964	52·6	41·0	68·9	56·6	62·0	32·0

In Table 5 the strong position of the direct grant school is evident. The figures for independent schools show only a slight increase, but of boys in the maintained grammar schools while just over a quarter stayed on to 17 in 1950, this fraction was one-third in 1957 and a half in 1964.

However, this relatively improved position in the grammar schools—and it must be remembered that selection for grammar education ought to mean the ability for a full 7-year course, i.e. the figures for the percentage of 14-year-olds staying on to 17 ought to approach 90–100%—must be kept in perspective by considering Table 6.

Table 6 underlines how many 17-year-olds have yet to be persuaded to stay at school. Enrolment ratio for 17-year-olds for Sweden in 1960 is 23·5: France (in *lycées* only) in 1961–2 is 15·6% and Germany in 1963 12·4% may be noted in comparison.

Also worthy of note is the increased contribution at 17 years

TABLE 6. PUPILS AGE 17 IN ALL SCHOOLS AS A PER-
CENTAGE OF ALL 17-YEAR-OLDS (ENGLAND AND WALES)

	Boys	Girls	Boys and girls
1947	6·2	4·8	5·5
1957	10·0	8·0	9·0
1964	14·7	11·5	13·2

(Table 11 in Chapter 5 showing those following courses
elsewhere should also be consulted.)

being made by schools other than the three types quoted in the
tables so far. Table 7 makes this clear.

TABLE 7. NUMBER OF PUPILS AGED 15 AND 17 IN VARIOUS TYPES OF
SCHOOL (ENGLAND AND WALES) (000's)

	1958		1964	
	15	17	15	17
Maintained:				
Modern	33	—	185	3
Grammar	96	32	120	61
Technical	19	2	17	4
Bi- and multilateral	2	—	7	1
Comprehensive	7	1	28	5
Other Secondary	14	—	17	2
	171	35	374	76
Direct grant	14	6	16	9
Independent recognised efficient	26	11	32	15
Other independent	9	1	10	2
Totals	220	53	432	102

The approximate doubling in the number of 17-year-olds in
school between 1958 and 1964 has been noted. As there were
53,000 in 1958 and 102,000 in 1964 it is easy to calculate rough
percentages—take the 1964 figures as percentages and double the
1958 figures. This gives the relative proportions for the 17-year-

olds in school and shows the relatively decreasing position of the direct grant and independent schools.

Crowther was able to write about the "swing"—the well-marked tendency for the sixth-formers to specialise in science which was being manifest when their report was in preparation. This swing appears to have continued until 1960 since when a reverse trend has appeared. Examination entries and passes are one objective way of measuring this. Expansion at O- and A-level has been so great that all subjects show a relative increase of actual entries and passes; it is only when relative proportions are considered that the breakaway becomes evident.

Tables 8 and 9* make the position clear for A-level though at O-level there is still a slight swing to science. This could be due to pupils taking more science subjects rather than more pupils taking the same number. To particularise, the A-level counter-swing seems to be away from physics, chemistry and mathematics as a specialist subject but not from the biological sciences and mathematics as a general subject. All arts subjects except Latin show a proportionate increase with the highest percentage increases in economics, geography, history and English literature.

It is, of course, relatively easy to show a large percentage increase in a subject like economics which starts from a small base, but Table 9, which deals with the twelve numerically most important subjects at A-level, shows its position as compared with other subjects. Despite the swing and counter-swing the table shows the unchanged order of the twelve subjects between Crowther and the present. However, extrapolation indicates that economics may already be more important numerically than Latin and that it may soon overtake applied mathematics. The reason for the counter-swing is not too readily apparent. Several possibilities have been suggested. In the case of boys, science may have reached a saturation point with all those really capable now engaged. Lack of science staff may have an effect, as may the relatively lower qualifications of science as compared with arts staff.

* Phillips, C., Science and arts subjects at G.C.E. level, *T.E.S.*, 19 November 1965.

TABLE 8. AVERAGE PERCENTAGE INCREASE PER
YEAR IN THE NUMBER OF ENTRIES AT A-LEVEL

	1957–60	1960–3
Physics	9·9	7·0
Chemistry	9·1	4·1
Pure mathematics	13·5	9·1
Applied mathematics	6·9	2·9
Biology and zoology	7·3	9·8
English literature	8·7	11·9
History	7·1	12·9
Geography	9·4	13·1
Economics	19·1	31·8
French	8·2	10·3
German	10·9	9·4
Latin	1·9	0·4

TABLE 9. PASSES AT A-LEVEL (BOYS AND GIRLS)
IN THE TWELVE NUMERICALLY MOST IMPORTANT
SUBJECTS GIVEN AS PERCENTAGE OF ALL PASSES
IN ALL THESE SUBJECTS

	1957	1960	1963
Physics	15·3	16·2	15·6
Pure mathematics	14·0	15·7[a]	15·2[a]
Chemistry	12·9	13·1	12·2
English literature	12·0	11·5	11·9
History	9·6	8·9	9·7
French	8·3	8·1	8·3
Biology and zoology	6·9	6·4	7·0
Geography	6·3	6·0	6·4
Applied mathematics	5·5	5·2	4·2
Latin	3·7	3·9	3·8
Economics	2·7	2·4	3·2
German	2·2	2·4	2·4

[a] Pure and applied mathematics.

The sixth-formers may be choosing teachers rather than subjects. The humanities, it has been suggested, offer a more attractive course than an overloaded syllabus and time-table in the sciences. Others note that the subjects with the largest increases are those associated with the social sciences, and this may be part of the trend to pay more attention to sociological factors. It is worth noting that Sir Charles Snow in his addendum to the Rede lecture on the two cultures, which he called *A Second Look*, suggested the social sciences might bridge the gap and afford a way out of the dilemma of the divided curriculum.

It is this problem of the two cultures, the division between the arts and the sciences, that has been the most important debate on the sixth form since Crowther.

C. P. Snow's *The Two Cultures* was published in 1959 and Peterson's *Arts and Science Sides in the Sixth Form* appeared in 1960. In 1959 the Crowther report endorsed the principle of specialisation but showed a real concern for the literacy of the science sixth-former and the numeracy of his arts associate. Peterson's work led to conferences on sixth-form work and through the agreement to broaden the curriculum brought the General Studies Association into existence. In 1961 a Leverhulme Study Group published an inquiry into the problem of achieving breadth in the education at school and university of scientists, engineers and technologists.* In 1962 the Incorporated Association of Assistant Masters published a survey of replies from 300 schools which they called *General Education in Grammar Schools*. The Vice-Chancellors' Committee also made some proposals concerning the sixth-form curriculum aimed in the same direction, and experiments and investigations concerned with the examination of general studies have continued during the period. One of the difficulties in the sixth form is the growth of knowledge—the sheer bulk of material in the syllabus. This has increased the demand for specialist time with a consequent lessening of time for the compensatory subjects. Currently the sixth-form syllabuses in physics, chemistry, mathematics and biology are being subject to a thorough appraisal in an

* Leverhulme Study Group, *The Complete Scientist*, O.U.P., London, 1961.

attempt to prune the old and introduce newer material. A formidable amount of content must remain, but the result may be a better distribution of time and a specialisation which will contribute more breadth. The attack, then, is on two fronts, and it is worth analysing in more detail.

The Complete Scientist examined the time-table for science specialists in the 3 years below the sixth form and found an increasing percentage of the time given to mathematics and science. Even below the sixth form they found half the boys' schools and one-quarter of the girls' schools had some pupils spending more than half the lesson time (excluding religious instruction) in mathematics and science. In the sixth form this percentage naturally increased sharply. What was alarming though was the concentration of study time on mathematics and science and the perfunctory attention given to non-science. The group estimated that for boys 94% of study time (free periods and homework) was spent in mathematics and science. The figure for girls was 90%. The Tables 10 and 10A show the findings.

TABLE 10. PERCENTAGE OF TIME TO VARIOUS BRANCHES

	Fifth form		Upper and lower sixth		Third-year sixth	
	Boys	Girls	Boys	Girls	Boys	Girls
Mathematics and science	41	38	68	63	58	44
Non-science	51	51	19	15	18	16
Study	0	3	8	14	19	32
Physical education and games	8	8	5	8	5	8
	100	100	100	100	100	100

The group concluded that while the basic system of specialisation was sound it had become distorted in practice and suggested a fairer division of the time would be as shown in Table 10A.

As for the third-year sixth they recognised its utility but

TABLE 10A

	Fifth form %	Lower sixth %	Upper sixth %
Mathematics and science	37	54	59
Non-science	55	25	20
Study	0	16	16
Physical education and games	8	5	5

deplored its narrowness and recommended that it should not continue at its present lack of breadth nor should the aim be to include everyone. They stressed that what was really required to improve education were:

(a) well-conceived and well-taught syllabuses;
(b) ample out-of-school activities;
(c) cultural interests outside school catered for in the locality.

While the Leverhulme group were studying the scientists, the I.A.A.M. were examining the whole of the sixth form and particularly the offerings in general studies. They noted the growth in size of sixth forms and especially the third-year sixth, though they remark that size can vary with the policy in the lower school. If express routes are organised pupils reach the sixth earlier and because of age stay longer. Joint-Four policy is that one-third of the time should be given to studies and activities outside A-level subjects but laboratory work in science means that especially on the science side this objective often remains unrealised. The figures collected from schools showed the following modes for non-specialist offerings.

	1st mode (periods)	2nd mode (periods)
Religious instruction and physical education together	4	3
General study periods	3	—
Private study periods	4	6

The arts specialists usually had more free time than the scientists, and in the general study periods the curve was a low one with many schools having less than the mode.

In addition to A-level work they found a good deal of sixth-form O-level work which was not merely repetition of unsuccessful subjects. There were five categories:

(a) arts students taking Latin;
(b) pupils taking O-level in a new subject on the way to A-level, e.g. economics, geology;
(c) a science to supplement general science;
(d) an additional modern language;
(e) pass in a subject not taken to O-level.

Considering the general study periods proper they found that the most usual use of time was for civics or current affairs followed by an arrangement for music and art. The third claimant for general study time was in the attempt to counter specialisation. From a group of 100 maintained schools 48 were offering English for science or general English. Fewer seem to offer science for the arts side though there are some outstanding exceptions. Some schools considered the proper use of the library was of first importance and more useful than most teaching. Other schools regarded three A-level subjects properly taught as sufficient discipline. The book also mentions those schools puzzled by the questionnaire on general education because they were making no special effort to do anything they had not always done—for them a general education had always been important. As might have been expected, the inquiry revealed a wide range of attitudes towards general education. In our system, at any rate in theory, schools are free to choose their own curriculum. Often, of course, they are at the mercy of outside forces which are strong enough to determine what schools shall do. Entry requirements to universities have been one of the factors at work here and some schools have given perfunctory attention to what is not examined and this has led pupils to neglect it.

As a result of his arts—science inquiry already referred to,

Peterson called a series of conferences at Oxford. He hoped to broaden the sixth-form curriculum by reducing the syllabuses at A-level by about one-third and introduce four A-levels of which at least one must be chosen from the alternative side—either arts or science. This proposal would have made a really serious attempt at bridging the gap between the cultures because the offerings would all have been examined and what is examinable in sixth forms is treated seriously. However, Peterson's proposals never got off the ground, but in 1961 360 headmasters signed the agreement to broaden the curriculum (and became known as the A.B.C. Schools). Another 270 agreed in principle. (Four times this number of schools have sixth forms.) The signatories pledged that not later than September 1963 their schools would devote not less than one-third of the sixth-form time-table (other than physical education and private study) to non-specialist work. Universities were to have copies of the list of schools so due allowance could be made when entry lists were being drawn up. Despite illustrious names the idea was not very enthusiastically received, but to form a rallying point in 1962 the General Studies Association was formed. This Association favoured an approach through the existing time-table by a better use of minority time and hoped that progress in the areas where some work was already being done would be more efficacious than the more radical approaches which always seemed to fail.

One point of contention was the question of an examination for general studies. It has already been noted that what is examinable is treated seriously. Nevertheless, there were those who spoke of external examinations of general studies as attempts to "imprison moonbeams" and less poetical critics pointed out that the best general studies grew out of the interests of the staff which could themselves change as the staff of the school could change too. But some examinations were available. Northern Universities Joint Matriculation Board had been setting a general paper at O-level since 1951 and set a paper at A-level in 1955 and later this was regularised in 1959. It contained sections on current affairs, the fine arts, general science and English literature. It was intended that this paper should be taken with only the very broadest of syllabuses. However, in 1962 of 5700 students only about two-fifths were successful, so its usefulness can be called to question. Other boards have provided general papers and the use of English paper in the sixth form is now mandatory for entrance to some universities. No clear-cut opinion on these examinations has crystallised so far.

Conscious that university entrance requirements had much effect on the sixth-form curriculum, the Committee of Vice-Chancellors and Principals in 1962 put forward a suggested sixth-form scheme of study and examination. The curriculum they looked at in two parts:

(a) a course requirement of two A-levels on the present standard;

(b) a general requirement replacing O-level which required passes to be gained in papers taken not before January in the second year of the sixth-form course.

The intention was to keep general studies going until a late stage. This general requirement was in three parts:

(i) a use of English paper;

(ii) a general paper;

(iii) a use of foreign language paper.

This suggestion was decisively rejected by the schools not only because they were suspicious of more examinations and of examinations as capricious as general studies (e.g. N.U.J.M.B. 1962) but also because the foreign-language requirement would mean keeping up the language already taken and inhibit the taking up of a fresh language. Caution, they felt, would always prevail.

To sum up, it is possible to say that since Crowther general studies have made progress but on a very uneven front and still many schools give little time to anything outside the main examinable course.

The other line of attack on the overloaded specialist syllabus is by a reappraisal, and the Nuffield projects are undertaking this in some fields. Some good teachers are saying that the Nuffield approach is not new. They have been attempting it for years but they can see that its implementation on Nuffield lines will need increased laboratory space and increased technical help.

A recent suggestion concerning the sixth-form curriculum has emanated from the Schools Council* which shows itself concerned to construct curricula suitable for a widening range of individual needs as, in addition to the traditional clientele, sixth forms attract students with lower examination qualifications and varied career intentions. In particular they aim to give greater flexibility to the sixth-form time-table, and while keeping some study in depth, to combine with it the possibility of more breadth. They suggest this could be attained by a general pattern of major–minor–general studies courses as follows:

(a) major courses, very similar to the present A-level courses, requiring about eight periods (including private study) per week;

(b) minor courses requiring about four periods per week;

(c) general studies requiring about six periods per week but not subject to assessment.

Traditional sixth-form students would take two major and two minor courses taking up 24 periods out of a 35-period week leaving 11 periods for the general studies course and physical education and religious instruction. Other sixth-formers could take one major and several minors and other arrangements are possible.

These ideas are developed further in two more recent publications from the Schools Council. In Working Paper No. 5† the pattern is laid out in models suitable for two differing schools and in Working Paper No. 4‡ the resulting discussions on the new ideas are made available. The latter pamphlet also presents a number of arguments in favour of amalgamations of parts of "subjects" as conceived in the sixth form at present. It considers "the structure

* The Schools Council, *Change and Response*, H.M.S.O., London, 1965.

† The Schools Council, *Sixth Form: Curriculum and Examinations*, H.M.S.O., London, 1966.

‡ The Schools Council, *Science in the Sixth Form*, H.M.S.O., London, 1966.

and properties of matter" containing material and ideas from physics and chemistry, biology as a single subject, mathematics as a single subject, and elsewhere an amalgam called "engineering studies". A danger here may be the difficulty of reducing the syllabus in a joint subject and a three-subject major of mathematics, structure and properties of matter and biology envisaged in Working Paper No. 4 could be an exceedingly heavy load. The Schools Council appear strongly attracted to subject combinations for in Working Paper No. 2, *Raising the School Leaving Age*, they argue for a very broad combination (see Chapter 10 for a detailed discussion of this). There was a strong movement for integration in the thirties and some analysis of the reasons for its lack of success might be useful as a pointer to the likely advance of the Schools Council's ideas, though that is outside our scope. What is of importance is the new ideas which are coming forward.

Another sixth-form topic recently brought into prominence and currently causing concern is the position of applied science. For long it has been felt that insufficient able boys choose to study applied science. The Spens Committee reporting in 1938 made suggestions aimed at mitigating the problem but after 1944 the number of technical schools was so small that our system was never really a tripartite one in the sense of three equal parts and for a variety of reasons the number of technical schools has gone on decreasing (see Chapter 9 for a general discussion of this problem). However, partly because of the better post-war image of technical jobs, some grammar schools have been more ready to introduce practical subjects. Nevertheless, there is still a good deal of prejudice as an investigation in 1961 revealed.* A survey among almost 1500 boys in 121 schools showed that sixth-formers had very hazy ideas about the professions and scientific and technical careers. Asked to rank a number of professional jobs for prestige and intelligence the technologist and engineer did not come in the first six in either category. The words "pure" (as applied to science) and "research" seemed to possess some magical and idealistic connotation. When the boys in the survey were

* Oxford University Department of Education, *Technology and the Sixth Form Boy*.

divided into six grades on their results at A-level the following was found with regard to choice of university subject:

Top two grades	Pure science was chosen three times as often as technology.
Middle two grades	Pure science was chosen twice as often as technology.
Lower two grades	Technology was chosen three times as often as pure science.

The results of the survey suggested that there was a lack of adequate counselling in school.

The professional institutions of engineers have known of these problems for some time and with the news of more and more schools becoming interested in engineering activities filtering through, the Institution of Mechanical Engineers decided to initiate an inquiry to ascertain the facts about applied science and engineering activities in grammar and public schools. The inquiry* revealed a variety of approaches and with one or two exceptions (e.g. Oundle) most of the school activities were of very recent development—"sometimes within only the last two or three years"—indicating an upsurge of activity. Provision varied: it might be an engineering sixth form or a formal engineering sixth-form activity, or an engineering department or a special examination syllabus in engineering (three schools) or an examined engineering project or a close relationship with the engineering department of a technical college. Many of those who followed the metalwork approach stigmatised it as boring and the activity idea was held up in contrast.

The idea that engineering is creative and can provide realistic open-ended projects is an interesting point showing how ill-conceived is the sixth-former's idea of connecting only pure science with research.

The technical activities centre at Sevenoaks School† gives an

* Page, G. T., *Engineering Among the Schools*, Institution of Mechanical Engineers, London, 1965.
† Taylor, L. C., *Experiments in Education at Sevenoaks*, London, 1965.

idea of what can be achieved with the right people in charge. Here is a laboratory with facilities for spare-time creative and technical interests. After a programme of training courses on a Dalton system, boys state their targets and the master provides ladders for them to climb to reach them. This activity started in a modern pre-fabricated building in September 1963. At Dauntsey's School project activity is not a great deal older.

Engineering, applied science, technology—seems to be a growth point. Whether this activity is consonant with the grounding in basic sciences necessary for applied science at university is a question that will have to be answered but not all will be going to university, so however that question is answered development will proceed.

This chapter, called "Traditional Sixth Forms", has been analysing some of the trends making for change—trends that have become more insistent during the last decade. The Crowther report, only published in 1959, listed five distinguishing marks of the sixth form: close links with the university, specialisation, intellectual discipleship, independent work and social responsibility; and wondered whether they could survive.

A study of time-tables indicates that independent work is on the decrease. Increased numbers, despite the Robbins' expansion in higher education, mean that sixth forms must look elsewhere than the universities—a university-oriented course will not be satisfactory for all. Increased numbers, too, have their effects on intellectual discipleship. How many real disciples can one teacher nourish? Can social responsibility be spread over the augmented sixth form? Chapter 6 examines some of the changes which seem inherent in the sixth-form explosion.

CHAPTER 4

Traditional English Sixth Forms— The Private System

THE sixth form has long been an important feature of the independent system and many practices now common in the maintained system originated in the public schools. Although relative to the school population as a whole, the enrolment in independent schools is small, at the level of the 17-year-old, the boys' schools have always made a sizeable contribution to the total. In 1947 there were about half as many 17-year-old boys in the independent schools recognised as efficient as in the maintained grammar schools (5100 as compared with 10,800). However, by 1958 the fraction had been reduced to about one-third and by 1964 to one-quarter. Because other types of schools were, by this time, making an increased contribution, the total contribution of the independent sector to the total 17-year-olds (boys and girls) was 15%. In 1947 it was almost 24%.

Fifteen per cent is still a significant fraction of the total provision and, because of the high socio-economic level of the families who use the private schools, they exercise an influence far greater than mere figures would suggest. Because of their importance and the feelings they engender—of unfair privilege on the one hand and a sense of superiority on the other—they are worthy of separate consideration here.

A foreign observer can sometimes illuminate facets of an educational system from a new angle, presenting us, as it were, with comparative insights in reverse.

One of the most thorough and discerning commentators on the

public school question is Edward Mack* who, working in the States, produced a monumental two-volume work on *Public Schools and British Opinion*. He was completing the second massive volume at the outbreak of World War II. The conclusions he reached then are still important even though their roots are well back in history. In fact to understand this, as for almost any problem in English education, it is necessary to take a backward historical glance. Mack takes 1870 as a kind of watershed. Before this date the public schools reformed themselves because a new social class —the bourgeoisie— gained admittance to the schools and changed them to suit their needs and the needs of the time. But, says Mack, since 1870 the reforms have been marginal. During this period Labour has played the part that the middle classes played in the earlier period, but Labour never gained a substantial foothold in the public schools which thus became an institution representing only one of the two dominant classes in English life.

Because the public school has not accommodated itself to a class which can no longer be ignored as it could in the early period, Mack believes that it has also failed to open its doors to new policies and changes. To summarise Mack very briefly: since 1870 the public school has become an institution serving a limited class and has shown conservative tendencies. Mack was writing these conclusions in 1940. Have the events of the last 25 years invalidated his analysis?

Even as Mack was completing his book the public schools were asking how their ties with the state system of education could be strengthened. Some commentators have seen this as high-minded concern based perhaps on an analysis of events broadly similar to Mack's, while others have characterised it as a life-saving action against a fear for the future. Certainly fees were not easily paid in the thirties and no one could be certain what the outcome of the war would be. So the initiative for a change came from the schools and in 1942 the Fleming Committee was set up to consider the

* Mack, E. C., *Public Schools and British Opinion since 1860*, Columbia, New York, 1941.

means of extending and developing the relationship between the public schools and the general educational system.

The report of the committee was published in 1944. It reviewed the history of the public schools; undertook an analysis of the education given in various schools; and made some proposals designed to fulfil its brief.

The gist of the main proposal was that boys who had been at state primary schools for a period of at least 2 years should be awarded bursaries at public schools. The scheme was to be reviewed every 5 years but initially it would cover a minimum of 25% of the places available. Argument naturally followed. There were three main points of contention; the number of places which should be made available; the method of selection and the age at which transfer should be made.

Many argued that 25% was too high a proportion. To admit one-quarter of boys with scholarships from the state system would cause a break with the traditions of the past and result in changes in the schools which would alter them so radically that their distinctive features, which it was intended to spread more widely, would be destroyed. Others argued that this figure was too low. While it would certainly give a much-needed injection of new blood into an institution which was dying, it would mean only that the scholarship boys were lost to their old way of life and would become subordinated to a system which was outdated.

Although this argument is now 20 years old it is by no means historical. "Flemingism", as it has become unfortunately termed, is continually being revived as, for example, in a recent article "Making public schools public" by Dr. Hamilton, headmaster of Rugby and chairman of the Headmasters' Conference.*

In 1944 the Fleming report had to compete with the Butler Education Act and the implementation of this took time and energy. By abolishing fees in the state system the Act gave a fillip to the private system. It was the grammar schools who felt themselves isolated at this time. Mr. Rée in his book *The Essential Grammar School* wrote of the grammar schools, as it were, bemoaning

* *The Guardian,* 1965.

their fate caught between the lower millstone of the new secondary modern school, which was attracting the attention of L.E.A.s, and the rejuvenated independent system which before the war had been feeling difficulties over fees. Grammar schools, too, were apprehensive over possible methods of selection of any recruits from the state system to the public schools. In the psychological climate of the time one certainty seemed to be the predictive value of the I.Q., and in any competition for a limited number of places the grammar schools had no wish to lose their potentially most academically able entrants. With neither L.E.A.s, nor grammar schools, nor independent schools enthusiastic the Fleming scheme languished although a limited number of scholarships were made available in some areas. They mainly served to show that state pupils could easily be absorbed into the system although, of course, the public schools could say these experiments served to show that selective procedures could be carried out and the problem of age of transfer—13 in the public schools and 11+ in the state system—could be overcome. For a number of years the ideas which led to the setting up of the Fleming Committee and recommendations which emanated from it, were both alike largely forgotten in a period of expansion, and have only comparatively recently been revived.

During the intervening years it is suggested the public schools reorganised themselves very thoroughly. *Public Schools in a New Age** by George Snow gives a very rosy picture, but perhaps the Headmaster of Marlborough, J. H. Dancy in his book *The Public Schools and the Future,*† gives a more balanced view. He also suggests a line of rapprochement with the state system. Before looking at his scheme it is instructive to look briefly at the post-war changes and also how the grammar and independent schools worked together in this same period and the effect this had on the problem.

A cynic has categorised the product of the public schools as having "a well developed body, a fairly well developed mind and

* Snow, G., Bles, London, 1959.
† Dancy, J. H., Faber, London, 1963.

an underdeveloped heart". While this can be rejected as nothing more than a cheap gibe it suggests a threefold way of looking at what the public school is attempting to do. The three facets can be considered in the reverse order.

A public school education is accused of narrowness because of the segregation involved in grouping in a secluded institution. Similar enclosed communities, it is suggested, are monasteries, prisons and borstals. In a public school there is segregation by class and by sex, and segregation from family. The last 25 years have seen much of a breakdown in the term-time segregation from the family. Longer weekends and improved transport have played their part. The growth of a teenage culture has ameliorated the segregation from society but has not removed it. The high fees ensure that only a selected section of our community can be represented. Over 20 weeks of holiday each year ensure that segregation by sex is not complete. The schools claim that term-time segregation is a definite advantage in that it encourages identification with one's own sex and so makes for uncomplicated relationships in the future. This claim is, of course, not un-challenged. Dr. Armstrong, in his series of case histories which he has called *The Mortar Board Spartans*,* has presented an opposite view, written to show the unhappiness which stems from a segregated society of this kind.

Leadership has long been claimed as an attribute of public school education. A recent study, *The Prefects*, has shown how the type of leadership based on subordination as a "fag" in the early school years followed by the privileges as a prefect later may have been suitable for the period 1850–1914. Bronowski has remembered the battle of Waterloo was won on the playing fields of Eton and suggested that Suez was lost in the same place. Certainly a different kind of leadership is required today. Mr. Wilkinson's analysis in *The Prefects: British Leadership and the Public School Tradition*† suggests the pattern is so stylised that it can hardly be expected to evolve. There are, of course, those who would contest this

* Armstrong, A., pseudonym, Muller, London, 1963.
† Wilkinson, R., O.U.P., London, 1964.

viewpoint. They emphasise that responsibility is what is being inculcated rather than leadership and no greater aid to this end than community living can be envisaged.

In his work Mack made many analyses of works of fiction and used them as a clue to contemporary opinion. What would he have made of *The Fourth of June*?* This is a story of Eton and particularly of a group of boys containing one who may almost be called a "Fleming" boy. It may not be intentional but it seems significant that this boy's father is a factory farmer involved in rearing battery chickens and veal in slatted pens—producing a standard product under artificial conditions. The laziness, the beatings, the sexual misunderstandings described in the book cannot possibly be real and must be vividly overdrawn, but it is difficult to rid oneself of the idea of a grain of wheat in a bushel of chaff. Dancy in his factual book says that it is a bad term when 5% of the boys are beaten and gives 3% as a more average figure. The word "beaten" may be a perjorative word, meaning different things to different people, but with three terms in the year and 5 years in the public school even 3% per term multiplies to a horrible percentage in a school lifetime. Considerations such as these lead to the belief that if hearts are not undeveloped they are at any rate developed one-sidedly.

Public schools have always had academic successes and there is no doubt that many boys from public schools do exceedingly well by any academic rating. There have been suggestions, too, that a public school type of education can do much for boys in the second quarter of the ability range—that boys of secondary modern school A-stream quality do better under public school conditions.

A study reported in *The Times Educational Supplement* in May 1963 showed that of rather over 1000 boys in independent schools who failed the 11+ but later passed common entrance, 70% obtained 5 or more O-level passes before they left public schools. The spread of I.Q. at 11+ is not reported, presumably because the information could not be collected, nor is the seriousness of the

* Benedictus, D., A. Blond, London, 1962.

11+ attempt. Preparatory schools really taking the 11+ seriously might be expected to have I.Q. figures for their entrants. In any case it is significant that all the sample carried on at H.M.C. schools. The maintained system has many examples of later success of failed 11+ candidates. Croydon found success at G.C.E. O-level was possible with an I.Q. at 11+ not much above average. In 1954 Bournemouth admitted 18% of the age group to grammar schools and the next 13% to four-stream secondary modern schools with a G.C.E. course. During the 5 years to G.C.E. heads in these schools added a further 13% of late developers to their G.C.E. streams. This 13% achieved similar success in O-level to the 13% chosen at 11+, and some individual results were better than those of individuals in the 18% who went to grammar school. So the state system with a more adverse staffing ratio can do quite well for the second quarter too. All the results may perhaps be better interpreted as showing the invalidity of hard-and-fast predictions from the 11+.

The Robbins Committee have also uncovered some interesting evidence regarding the percentage of entrants from different types of secondary schools who left universities (in 1958) without gaining a degree.

Type of school	Oxford and Cambridge	London	Civic
Maintained grammar	3	14	10
Other day	3	9	8
Boarding	6	29	25

These two sets of facts—

(a) good results from the "second quarter" of the ability range; and

(b) the greater failure rate at university,

could be explained by one cause—the greater amount of individual attention available in public schools (in classroom *and* in preparation time) because of the greater number of staff and the better qualified staff attracted by better pay and conditions.

At one time the curriculum was predominantly classical but there are now strong science sides. Laboratory accommodation has been brought up to date with the aid of grants from the Industrial Fund. £3 million is the quoted figure.

The critics of the public school have always pointed to the emphasis on games and particularly on compulsory team games. Supporters have mentioned the character-building propensities of team games but there have always been suggestions that games are necessary in the school because "Satan finds some mischief still for idle hands to do". There is still much attention given to team games but there has doubtless been much diversification and individualisation of activity. The ideas of Kurt Hahn, put into practice at Gordonstoun and at the many Outward Bound Schools, have had an effect on attitudes to athletics generally and the dissemination of these ideas has no doubt been helped and hastened by the interest and enthusiasm of the Duke of Edinburgh who came up through this regimen. A greater variety of activities is now acceptable. There has been progress here as on the other fronts.

While everyone has a clear general image of a public school, compounded from the attributes of a few of the better-known schools, the difficulty experienced by the Minister of Education in October 1961 when he said "I do not know what a Public School is. No one has been able to provide me with a satisfactory definition", still remains. As already mentioned, the period immediately after the war saw the grammar school on the defensive, but as the advantages accruing to them from the Act became apparent, especially the intellectual calibre of the intake, they began to take a more positive position in educational arguments. Many of their interests interlocked with the interests of the public schools, and while the difference between an ancient foundation and a new county grammar school may be very great, there is a wide borderland at the edges of the H.M.C. and in the direct grant country where distinctions are not easy to draw, and interests in defending

the *status quo* and opposing evolutionary ideas are not easily distinguished. As a result the grammar schools and the independent schools have often ranged themselves side by side. This tendency has been helped by the appointment of assistant masters from public schools to the headships of grammar schools, a process explained very adequately in the book *The Boys' Grammar School.**
A more honest book than this can seldom have been written. The author, head of a grammar school, shows how a well-run school giving satisfaction to parents, governors, and staff falls far short of providing a really worthwhile education. "Beneath the efficient and prosperous surface [is] the disappointing reality of the education to be obtained in a particular grammar school." He is equally critical of headmasters. "The divine right of headmasters is a conception which has spread through secondary education to its great disadvantage." "The autocratic rule of a headmaster is capable of producing more unhappiness among the boys and more frustration among the staff than any other single factor in school life." The degree of autocracy allowed to a headmaster is one of the factors which determines admittance to and removal from the H.M.C. list. *The Boys' Grammar School* goes on to explain how the aspirations of grammar schools and public schools become interwoven in a passage typical of the straight speaking which occurs throughout the book.

> A still more important consideration emerges when the prestige of Public Schools is taken into account. Many assistant masters on the staffs of the inferior Public Schools seem to have decided that it is a legitimate outlet for their ambitions to apply for the headship of a grammar school. They do this, in many cases, very conscious of the superiority of the school which they wish to leave, but unhappily quite unconscious of their supreme ignorance of the type of school to which they wish to go. When a governing body, impressed by the name of candidate's Public School, has appointed him, he sets about the reform of his new school on Public School lines. The governors who appointed such a headmaster presumably support him, and the result is that a day school is turned into an inferior imitation of a boarding school, although its needs and traditions are fundamentally different. Its prestige may rise, but its educational value is much more likely to sink. Such are the schools which compel a chosen few of their pupils to become

---

* Davies, H., Methuen, London, 1945.

classical specialists with a view to University Scholarships, which put down their names on the waiting list for a J.T.C., which decide to play rugger in order to obtain fixtures with "superior" schools, which take up the cult of athletics, house activities, and cups, which adopt school uniforms in order that the boys shall at least look like gentlemen, which strive in every way to make their pupils behave as members of a class apart, apart unfortunately in many cases from their elementary schools and even from their own homes. The dead hand of Public School tradition must be lifted from the grammar school, which should exist to educate a democracy in a different and happier world.

There are, of course, some notable recruits to the grammar school in this way. But even Guy Boas could write in *A Teacher's Story*:* "After eight industrious years at St. Paul's I felt ready for a change. When therefore the Headship of Sloane Grammar School was advertised, I applied and was appointed. I knew nothing of municipal Grammar Schools . . . ." However, not all attain his standard.

One of the first issues on which the public and grammar schools acted in unison can be presented as an attack on "this divine right of headmasters". It concerned the reform of the examination system. The Norwood report had suggested that grammar schools had profited from the helping hand of school certificate standards through a sufficiently long adolescence to be mature enough to need the prop no longer. This change they did not expect to come at one fell swoop. However, the replacement of the old school certificate, a group examination, by the new general certificate of education, a subject examination, was seen as an opportunity to take a step on the way from a rigid dependence on external examinations. The idea was to encourage a 7-year course to A-level instead of a split course either 5–2 or 4–3. O-level was to be omitted by those proceeding to A-level and, in order to keep a general course in school for a reasonable time, O-level was not to be taken before the age of 16. Schools were being given an opportunity to free themselves from what had been regarded by the reformers as shackles. Quickly the schools showed themselves as wanting to struggle back into their chains. Great was the outcry which went up protesting against the iniquity of the suggested

* Boas, G., Macmillan, London, 1963.

system with its age limit. Headmasters were the best judges of the boys' interests, and the Ministry capitulated to pressure. Heads were allowed to enter under-age candidates who had a good chance of success which meant in fact that there was no age limit. O-levels could now be "got out of the way" at any age and often earlier than previously since this was a subject and not a group examination. This was more important to the public schools which, with smaller groups, more often run express courses into the sixth form giving 3 years for most and 4 years for some in the sixth form. Specialisation has been driven further down the school. At an increasingly early age pupils choose their future side—Lord Bowden has pointed out the logical consequence of this—the structure of our university expansion is being decided by the choices of our 13–14-year-olds in the schools. Here is an example of a well-thought-out reform which was never allowed to operate. A regulation of this kind fixing a minimum, and not a maximum age, would be one way of keeping the maintained and independent systems in step. It is regulations of this nature which make the independent school system much less divisive in other countries than it is in our own. In the early 1950's the public schools were quick to scent the danger offered by the new examination system to their prestige—offsetting as it would have done some of the advantages of smaller groups and express courses. In their campaign against the introduction of the system they were supported by the grammar schools who were, on the whole, much less affected as the age was nearer their normal age for taking the first school examination.

In 1954, as a result of a careful study of their examination results, the Croydon L.E.A. prepared a scheme to make all their secondary schools carry a non-selective intake to first examination standard and to concentrate all work over the sixth form in one institution, Addington College (see Chapter 6). This, again a well-thought-out plan, was opposed by the grammar schools though supported by the secondary modern schools. The H.M.C. also pronounced themselves in support of the grammar school line. Eventually the Croydon Committee had to shelve their scheme and the country was denied a knowledge of what such a scheme of reorganisation could achieve.

The scholarship results at Oxford and Cambridge obtained by large day schools, quoted in Chapter 6, show how good sixth-form colleges could challenge the independent schools. The chairman of the H.M.C. in the article already quoted, "Making public schools public" canvasses the idea of some sixth-form level transfers of pupils to public schools. He says:

> Such transfers might be particularly suitable for pupils from schools, comprehensive or otherwise, which have a difficulty in providing a wide range of sixth-form teaching. But it must be emphasised that transfers at this level are not by any means the same thing as the establishment of sixth-form colleges to which the Headmasters' Conference is strongly opposed on educational grounds.

Meanwhile Welbeck College and Atlantic College give a lead which the H.M.C. would like to resist. "The arguments which seem valid against sixth-form colleges in general would apply to boarding sixth forms in an exceptional degree", writes Dr. Hamilton.

These two reforms—the age limit for examinations and the setting up of sixth-form colleges—would have given the maintained state system a good opportunity to really challenge the independent schools. A further possibility was connected with curriculum reform. The freedom of the school to determine the curriculum has become a fetish in British schools. Acting from the seemingly laudable base that freedom can only come from full knowledge, Sir David Eccles, when Minister of Education, expressed a desire to enter "the secret garden of the curriculum" and set up the Curriculum Study Group. Again this action was assailed from all sides and again it has been necessary to beat a retreat, though a very broadly based body, the Schools Council, has been instituted to do a somewhat similar job.

Recently, with the growth of support for the Labour party, there has been an upsurge of interest in ways of integrating the public schools in the state system.

First there is Mr. Dancy's solution as outlined in *The Public*

Schools and the Future. He really appears to welcome the Fleming idea and sees 25% as only a step on the way. Gradually he would wish to see the intake of scholarship boys from primary schools further increased until 50% is attained. Then he suggests the public schools should be prepared to take over direct-grant status which he regards as an eminently suitable administrative arrangement for a school. Whether all independent schools could hope for direct-grant status is not certain. Direct-grant schools are a variable but generally highly privileged minority, and their retention unchanged or strengthened in a truly comprehensive educational system would be anomalous. The wholesale addition of schools to the direct-grant list might have unfortunate effects on L.E.A. schools and also on preparatory schools. Those who argue that direct-grant schools are not competitive with maintained schools and can well exist side by side are not helped in their advocacy of this viewpoint by the willingness of the Headmaster of Marlborough to grasp the direct-grant nettle. On the other hand, Mr. Dancy's change would not be sufficiently radical to satisfy many people.

Various educationists have suggested restrictions which would remove some of the grosser inequalities and allow the maintained and independent systems to compete on more equal terms. Dr. Pedley, Director of the Exeter Institute of Education, is one of these. He finds the staffing ratio the greatest anomaly. The state system has to operate on a quota laid down by the central administration but public schools are free to employ all the staff they wish. In 1959 the independent system had 6·5% of all pupils but 9% of all the staff. Pedley wants public schools to be restricted to the same pupil–staff ratio as schools in their own area with appropriate allowance for boarding duties. In addition he wants payments above Burnham to be discontinued with safeguards for extra duties which boarding entails but with due allowance made for accommodation on school premises. There are rates for these in the maintained system which could be applied. This, coupled with advance in the maintained system on comprehensive lines, would be a satisfactory start towards a solution.

The Director of Education for the West Riding (Sir Alec Clegg) has gone a little further than this. In the Presidential address to the Association of Chief Education Officers in January 1965, in addition to advocating the teaching quota for all schools, he said it was indefensible that 7% of pupils in public schools should have access to 50% of places at Oxford and Cambridge especially as wastage is higher. The main support of the older universities comes from government grants and he wanted 80% of places in the older universities for pupils from maintained schools. Again given these reforms with progress on comprehensive lines in the maintained system he believes the public school question could be allowed to solve itself. The Franks report on Oxford published in May 1966 advocates the abolition of closed awards.

Other more radical opponents have merely suggested that the public schools should be abolished. But the Labour administration has chosen neither the Fleming line advocated by Dancy; nor the abolish line of the extreme Left; nor the wither-away line of Pedley and Clegg. Instead another Commission has been set up with a number of tasks and objectives giving it the dual function of:

(a) advising the Government on the best way of integrating the public schools (it is interesting to note that *Hansard* (22 December 1965) in printing the terms for the Commission uses the small "p" for public schools throughout) into the state system; and also

(b) of initiating, subject to government approval, experimental schemes.

In the first instance they have been asked to consider certain schools in membership with three bodies—the Headmasters' Conference, the Governing Bodies' Association and the Governing Bodies of Girls' Schools Association—a total of 277 schools in all. Questioned concerning this the Secretary of State said these were the main socially divisive schools and a scheme for them would be worked out first. Later it could be extended to other independent schools. Direct-grant schools are also excluded from consideration.

This exclusion may well be on the divide-and-rule basis for direct-grant schools are explicitly included in Circular 10/65 (see Chapter 15) in which the hope is expressed that co-operation between L.E.A. and direct-grant school governors will be maintained and developed in the context of the new policy of comprehensive education. In the arrangements for the Public Schools Commission the actual word "comprehensive" is not used, but paragraph (c) under objectives (see below) makes the intention to pursue this line crystal clear. So many facets have to be included that the remit becomes a very complicated statement as follows:

The main function of the Commission will be to advise on the best way of integrating the public schools with the State system of education. For the immediate purpose of the Commission public schools are defined as those independent schools now in membership of H.M.C., G.B.A., and G.B. of G.S.A.

The Commission will be expected to carry out the following tasks:

(a) to collect and assess information about the public schools and about the need and existing provision for boarding education: forms of collaboration between the schools (in the first instance the boarding schools) and the maintained system;

(b) to work out the role which individual schools might play in national and local schemes of integration;

(c) if it so wishes, and subject to the approval of the Secretary of State, to initiate experimental schemes matching existing provision with existing need;

(d) to recommend a national plan for integrating the schools with the maintained sector of education;

(e) to recommend whether any action is need [*sic*] in respect of other individual schools, whether secondary or primary.

In carrying out its tasks, the Commission will be expected (while respecting the denominational character of the schools) to pay special attention to the following objectives:

(a) to ensure the public schools should make their maximum contribution to meeting national educational needs and, in the first instance, any unsatisfied need for boarding education in the light of the Martin and Newsom reports;

(b) to create a socially mixed entry into the schools in order both to achieve (a) above and to reduce the divisive influence which they now exert;

(c) to move towards a progressively wider range of academic attainment among public school pupils so that the public school sector may increasingly conform with the national policy for the maintained sector;

(d) to co-operate closely with LEA's in seeking to match provision with need for boarding education;

(e) to ensure the progressive application of the principle that the public schools, like other parts of the educational system, should be open to boys and girls irrespective of the income of their parents.

This is a formidable remit and lays down very clearly lines of operation. Of interest is the way in which it connects with the working party report (Martin report) which defined the groups in need of boarding education and with the Newsom report which advocated an extension of part-time boarding provision for those of average and less than average ability. Continuity in this objective should be assured as Sir John Newsom chairs this new body.

The 277 schools involved have about 90,000 places of which two-thirds are for boarders. At present L.E.A.s are supporting about 9000 boarders but, using the criteria of the Martin report as a yardstick, Dr. Lambert, who has made a close study of the problem, suggests the number requiring boarding education may be five times this—a figure of 45,000.

The Commission have begun their deliberations and, even if their report takes 2 years, there should be time for action with this present Government still in office.

This chapter begins and ends with an inquiry. By the time the second Newsom report is ready there will also be more experience with new forms of upper secondary schooling.

CHAPTER 5

Further Education for 15–18-year-olds in Britain

NEGLECTED educational territory is how the Crowther report described the field of the upper secondary sector which this chapter seeks to describe and define. The title they chose for their section—"Technical Challenge and Educational Response"— usefully indicates the broad limits. In charting the ground they were to cover they were able to delimit the field by pointing out that about half the 15-year-olds, on reaching the compulsory age, leave school and take no further significant part in education. As the cricket commentators say of batsmen who make a duck— "they do not trouble the scorers". Of the other half who do trouble the scorers, about 50%, representing one-quarter of the total, stay on at school for at least a year and some for much longer. They have been dealt with in detail in Chapter 3. The remaining quarter, though leaving school, do take some part in further educational activities. Below the age of 15 our educational system has often been accused of neglecting the second quarter of the ability range. Independent schools have claimed they can do more for these adolescents in school than the maintained system usually attempts. Chapter 4 has examined this claim. However, here after the age of 15 it appears they have to be satisfied with limited provision. The recent figures given in Table 11 make more precise these simple fractions of one-quarter in school, one-quarter in further education and one-half opting out of the system, but these easily memorable proportions from a survey in the late fifties make a satisfactory framework into which detail can be built.

Although the Crowther report called it neglected territory, it was already coming under cultivation while the Committee were making their survey and writing their report. This renewed activity was triggered off by the white paper called *Technical Education* published in 1956. It drew attention to the pyramid in technical education, estimating that one technologist requires to be supported by six technicians with lower layers of craftsmen and then operatives, each containing increasing numbers. At the upper secondary level most technologists and a good many of the future technicians are still at school full-time, but operatives, craftsmen and some technicians are catered for by the provisions to be described here. Among the committees whose reports were contemporaries of Crowther can be listed:

1. The Willis Jackson report (1957). It deals with the recruitment and training of teaching staff for the technical colleges.

2. The Carr report (1958) dealing with Training for Skill—the recruitment and subsequent training of young workers in industry. This committee worked quickly to bring out their recommendations before the bulge left school in 1962. They recommended the institution of group apprenticeship schemes, joint training centres, pre-apprenticeship courses and block release schemes.

3. The McMeeking report (1959). It examines further education for commerce and asks for an increase of day release in this area as well as the wider development of apprenticeships in commerce based on combined systematic practical training and commercial education.

Since the publication of the Crowther report, the opening up of the territory has continued, and a summary of the main items can be continued as follows:

4. *Better Opportunities in Technical Education* (1961). This white paper contained proposals for a major reconstruction of the system of courses for operatives, craftsmen and technicians in technical colleges with five objectives in mind:

(a) to broaden the education at this level;

(b) to provide more continuity between school and technical college;

(c) to meet better the needs of industry;

(d) to increase the variety of courses available;

(e) to reduce the wastage by enabling more students to complete their courses successfully.

5. *Forward from School* (1962). This government publication dealt with the links between school and further education, hoping to show, by a description of achievements in various localities, the successful arrangements which could be copied elsewhere.

6. *From School to Further Education* (1963). This report, now usually called after its chairman, the Brunton report, comes from the Scottish Education Department and deals with the links between secondary and further education. While dealing specifically with the Scottish situation, many of its arguments and recommendations are entirely relevant south of the border and, once again, education in England and Wales can be grateful for work done by a Scottish team (cf. *Secondary Education*, 1947).

7. *Day Release*—the Henniker-Heaton report (1964). This committee was set up to report on steps to bring about the maximum practicable increase in day release from employment for young persons under 18 years of age to attend technical and other courses of further education.

It pointed out that all young people need day release, and asked that further educational provision should be made on a broad and balanced front and not be merely vocational or technical. As a realistic target for advance it suggested a further quarter of a million adolescents should be getting day release by 1969–70. To attain this would require an increase of 50,000 each year, which means the existing rate of increase must be much accelerated. If priorities had to be established the report suggested that young people in occupations requiring knowledge and skills had the first claim, and second priority should go to those taking vocational classes by evening study only. Here an approach should be made for day release to be granted on an individual basis. The report also asked for development work to proceed on courses for those who get little educational training through work, and whose work cannot be said to require vocational education. It also suggested the problems involved in day release for all should be studied. (Twenty years earlier provision for day release for all had been put in the 1944 Act.)

8. The Industrial Training Act (1964). This act was intended to make further provision for industrial and commercial educa- tion and give better training for persons over compulsory school age for employment in any industrial and commercial activities. It legislated for the setting up of Industrial Training Boards for each industry in order to ensure:

(a) sufficient people are trained for the industry;
(b) the courses have the correct content and proper standards are maintained;
(c) the financial burdens are fairly spread among all firms, large, medium and small in the industry. On each a levy, depending on the size of the wages bill, is imposed.

The Act came into force in March 1965 and before the end of the year nine boards were in existence, viz.: engineering, con- struction, iron and steel, wool textiles, shipbuilding, gas, water supply, ceramics, and glass and mineral products. Man-made fibres, furniture and timber, knitting, lace, and net and carpets were added in the first 3 months of 1966. Under the terms of the Act, training may be given by the firm itself or in a Ministry of Labour training establishment without any attendance at a true educational establishment. It has been pointed out that this may mean a narrow training with hearts and imaginations not in- volved, and it may neglect to counteract the influence human inadequacies have on industrial progress.

Additional to these official documents there has been much valuable description and comment from individuals and organisa- tions. Most active have been the British Association for Com- mercial and Industrial Education (B.A.C.I.E.) and the City and

Guilds of London Institute, both producing many useful documents concerning methods at home and also sponsoring valuable comparative studies.

From these preliminaries it is now useful to turn to a consideration of the developments in this sector since 1944. The Education Act of that year reorganised education in three stages—primary, secondary and further. Primary education for all had long been achieved, the Act granted secondary education for all, and envisaged the time when everyone would have further education, if not full time, then at any rate part time, to 18 years of age. It laid down that it should be the duty of every local education authority "to secure the provision for their area of adequate facilities for further education" and it specified two types of provision.

(a) full-time and part-time education for persons over compulsory school age;
(b) leisure-time occupation, cultural and recreational, for any persons over compulsory school age who are able and willing to profit by the facilities provided.

These two types are obviously very different but they are not mutually exclusive as far as age goes. The first, for persons over compulsory school age, looks like continuing provision, while leisure-time activities are more episodic in character. Obviously further education is a generic name covering many types, but it is perhaps easiest to think of the first as further education, in the strict sense, and the second as adult education. Higher education is another species of the genus further. It is further education in its more restricted sense that is the province of this chapter, though of course, this whole book is looking at the provision to 18 or 19 years of age as upper secondary education.

The Act went on to ask for schemes for further education to be submitted to the Minister, and it also requested, as it were in advance, that local education authorities should establish and maintain county colleges for providing young persons not in full-time attendance at any school, with "such further education, including physical, practical and vocational training as will enable them to develop their various aptitudes and capacities and will prepare them for the responsibilities of citizenship". As a requirement this was to come into force at a later date, when provision was to be made for all young persons aged 15 up to 18 not undergoing full-time education to attend on one whole day, or 2 half-days in each of 44 weeks in each year or for one continuous period of 8 weeks or two periods of 4 weeks. This was, and still is, the Plan, but unhappily further education in county colleges has not materialised, as the continuation schools of the Fisher Act did not materialise. However, the impetus of the Act has caused irreversible progress towards the goal to be made. In our society it appears that legislation cannot operate too far in advance of performance. This can be illustrated from the Hadow report which advocated the establishment of separate schools for senior pupils. Reorganisation already begun even before the Hadow Committee met was accelerated after 1926, so that by 1944 it was possible to make secondary a stage in all education. But even in 1966 some all-age schools still remain and, as they are designated primary some pupils, despite "secondary education for all" and all that, still never attend a secondary school. Similarly, 22 years after 1944 the country is still not ready for day release on a compulsory basis, but the necessary groundwork is gradually being established.

Whether an adolescent has any further education depends very largely on his own interest or ambition and on the attitude of his employer and the type of job he is doing. As a result some have no interest in further education and leave it strictly alone; others have to pursue courses in their own time in the evening either in technical colleges or, if they are less fortunate, in evening institutes, while others are granted day release from their employment to follow a course. Many of these are required to supplement this day release by a further evening session from their own time. There are also some adolescents who leave school and transfer to full-time courses in technical colleges. The progress made in each of these types of provision can be reviewed in turn. Table 11 shows the quantitative picture.

TABLE 11. 1963–4. PERCENTAGE 15–17 INCLUSIVE
RECEIVING EDUCATION

Type	Men	Women	All
Full-time and sandwich			
schools	21·3	19·8	20·6
Non-advanced F.E.	3·1	4·3	3·7
Sub-total (full time)	24·4	24·1	24·3
Part-time in F.E.:			
Part-time day	18·3	5·1	11·8
Evening only			
Major establishments	5·5	7·5	6·5
Evening institutes	9·2	9·7	9·5
Sub-total (part time)	33·0	22·3	27·8
Total (all methods)	57·4	46·4	52·1
Not involved	42·6	53·6	47·9
	100·0	100·0	100·0

From Table 11 it can be noted that the simple fractions quoted by the Crowther report for 15-year-old leavers now apply, in the round, to this 3-year age group from 15 to 17 years inclusive. There is little variation between the sexes for full-time participation, but in part-time classes, especially in day release, men are in preponderance. Obviously this represents good progress since Crowther's analysis as is seen more clearly if a single age group is taken. As the figures for 15-year-olds are complicated by the

TABLE 12. 1963–4. PERCENTAGE
AGED 16 RECEIVING EDUCATION

	Males	Females
Full time	29·5	28·4
Part time	36·1	24·1
Total	65·6	52·5

leaving regulations it is useful to look at the 16-year-old group where there is no legal compulsion (except for a few pupils in special education).

Immediately the difference in part-time attendance between the sexes is seen. Very roughly for women of 16 the proportion of one-quarter full time, one-quarter part time and one-half out of contact applies, but for men of the same age almost two-thirds are still in contact and very roughly it can be thought of as one-third full time, one-third part time and one-third no time.

As this chapter now proceeds to consider full-time further education, day release and evening work separately, it must be remembered that the whole system is very complex, and if needless repetition is to be avoided some cross-reference is essential.

FULL-TIME STUDENTS

In 1963–4 the overall percentage of the 15, 16 and 17 years in full-time further education of a non-advanced character was $3 \cdot 7\%$ which is made up of $3 \cdot 1\%$ of the boys and $4 \cdot 3\%$ of the girls. These figures represent a general all-round increase of 1% in 6 years. Even when allowance is made for the larger age group due to the bulge in the birth-rate curve reaching the age of 16 in 1963–4, this cannot be regarded as spectacular progress though it must be remembered also that school enrolment increased during the period at a rate of 1% per year. The actual courses followed are many and varied.

First there is a broad group of subjects of general education including English, modern languages, mathematics, physics, chemistry, history, geography—all the usual "school" subjects—which are taken to obtain passes at the O-level of the G.C.E., and at A-level too, with a wide spread of subjects including economics. The O-level courses cater for many boys and girls from modern schools and at A-level they are joined by others; some from grammar schools who are finding school discipline too irksome; some from the lower ranges of the independent sector who find their schools have no suitable provision.

There are also many courses in commercial education, mainly the province of girls. Many courses may be of one year's duration and contain a sizeable content of general subjects, though they are followed chiefly for the large element of typewriting, shorthand and office routine included. Since the McMeeking report (1959) there have been many measures taken to promote the growth of further education in commerce or, as it has since 1959 been increasingly called, business studies. Ten years earlier, in 1949, the Carr-Saunders Committee had made many recommendations for improving the quality of commercial education, but, as is brought out again later, the emphasis at this time had to be on technical and scientific requirements, so it is only in this decade that much progress has been possible. New general courses for business have been established, starting with the certificate in office studies for the beginner in an office. It was introduced in 1963 to meet the needs of those who start work in offices without the O-level passes needed to enter a course for a national certificate. The course is for 2 years part time, and the curriculum includes English and general studies, business calculations and office routines. Not only is it a worth-while qualification on its own; if it is passed with credit it qualifies for admission to either the ordinary national diploma or certificate in business studies. These two qualifications were introduced in 1961 to replace the old national certificates in commerce. The O.N.D. in business studies is a 2-year full-time course, while the O.N.C. is a 2-year part-time course. The subjects studied include commerce and economics in all cases, and a number of options which may be accounting, elements of statistics, principles of law, economic history, economic geography, and modern languages. Obviously the full-time diploma allows for deeper study and also gives time to become really proficient in typing and shorthand at the same time. The diploma and certificate give access to work at the higher national level, and if passed with credit, to a number of other more advanced courses, all of which are outside the limits of this study. The numbers following these courses in 1963–4 were as follows:

Certificate in office studies	3,360
O.N.C. in business studies	12,195
O.N.D. in business studies	4,084
Other non-advanced courses	48,153
Total	67,792

Broadly fitting into this group of commercial courses are the many full-time and part-time modern language courses which may lead to examinations or may use language laboratory and other modern techniques to give oral proficiency.

Third are the many craft courses which form a very important part of many departments. As the courses lead to the City and Guilds of London Institute examinations which can be taken in over 150 subjects, they are very varied, depending often on the locality, though some are less specific. Engineering and building, both with many subdivisions, catering, typography, hairdressing, paint technology are only a few from the long list. Only some of the students take these courses full time: there is a much larger part-time participation.

Fourthly, there are some students who are embarking on technician's courses which demand a higher academic background and a longer school course with more and more often some success at O-level standard, though good grades in the certificate of secondary education (C.S.E.) from 1965 onwards will be increasingly acceptable. Some with better results at O-level pass into O.N.D. classes at 16 years and eventually they work through to technologist level. Once again all these courses but with different names, i.e. certificate instead of diploma, are going on part time alongside the full-time study, and increasingly sandwich courses which make the best of both worlds are being introduced at these ages. The pattern of courses is set out in Fig. 2, but the reality is more complex than any diagram can indicate. While a rigid well-demarcated system might be administratively convenient, it would not allow for transfer between courses as abilities blossom, or, less happily, fade, or as new ambitions motivate greater efforts resulting in better achievement.

A fifth strand in the full-time provision is art education. Some courses start at 16, training designers to serve industry and

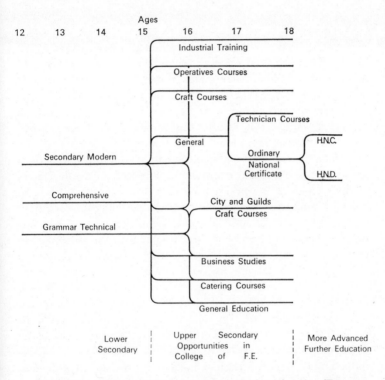

FIG. 2. Some of the varied opportunities in further education (England and Wales).

commerce through such subjects as illustration and commercial design, embroidery, wallpaper design, modelling, display work and photography. Since 1963 courses in art education have been rationalised by the Summerson Committee. The number of colleges granting diplomas has been reduced to 39, but many others carry on with commercial and vocational courses and also teach the pre-diploma course. Soon this is to be renamed the foundation course and it will be taken before passing on to the diploma in art and design at the minimum age of 18.

DAY RELEASE

By 1963 about one-third of one million adolescents aged 15–18 inclusively (i.e. four age groups) were taking day-release courses in the ratio of almost four males to one female. Day release is largely a post World War II phenomenon which has gained its impetus from the still long-delayed promise of the 1944 Act. In 1938 only 42,000 students of all ages, not merely in the restricted age group here being considered, were granted day release, so the 1963 figure represents a tenfold increase in the upper secondary sector achieved without compulsion. The idea of employers releasing employees in working hours has a considerable history. In 1893 a Manchester engineering firm was affording this facility to its apprentices, and, a little later, a London dressmaking firm was doing the same for girls. For these occupations the advantage to employers as well as to employees is fairly readily evident, but the gain is less clear (though obviously apparent to the enlightened) in the case of Rowntrees, who gave their girls domestic science in the firm's time, and Cadbury's who started on the road by giving time for swimming and gymnastics to promote physical well-being. There were these, and other, experiments to encourage the 1918 Act to include its continuation school provisions, and although by 1920 six L.E.A.s had made some provision, resettlement difficulties after World War I caused retrenchment in 1921 when a total of 95,000 participants had been reached. Rugby alone continued with attendance on a district basis, but a number of enlightened firms kept the spark kindled.

After World War II the promise of the 1944 Act caused a renewed interest, and by 1948 enrolments had reached five times the pre-war figure. Again there were resettlement difficulties and other post-war problems, but the request for a development plan of further education to include the provision of county colleges, and the arrival at county offices of circulars from the Ministry of Education kept the idea alive. First came the cheerfully titled Pamphlet 3—*Youth's Opportunity—Further Education in County Colleges* (1945). As an introduction it analysed the reasons for the failure of the Fisher Act, in the spirit that this was history which could not be repeated, and then went on to reiterate that young people needed to be kept in touch with the life, discipline, teaching and outlook of an educational institution so that their lives could be enriched and their share of personal happiness increased. The reverse side of the picture was also revealed—the best educated make the best workers (really many provisos are needed at this point). Pamphlet 8—*Further Education* (1947)—put the county college idea in its complete setting, pointing out still that its provision would come in due course. However, history was not to be entirely denied, and difficulties quickly began to appear. There were problems of lack of buildings and staff, and these logistic difficulties led to an emphasis on voluntary methods which by 1950 were producing all the students that could be coped with. The necessity to expand technical education and build up a skilled labour force which became so apparent at this same time meant that new building had to be earmarked for vocational education only. In 1951 the further education projects which were sanctioned were for mining, building, textiles and engineering while commerce, catering, art and printing had to wait. Where there was accommodation which could be switched to the priority occupations, this was done. Separation into sheep and goats on this basis led to misgivings and inevitably slowed progress. Even when in 1954 restrictions were eased the emphasis on vocational provision remained. In the following year the speech from the throne at the opening of Parliament promised remedies to help to make up the deficiencies in technical and scientific manpower. The promise was redeemed by the appearance of the white paper on *Technical Education* (1956) already noted. Its chief concern was with plans for full-time educational provision and it sketched out the organisational structure with colleges of advanced technology (C.A.T.s) at the peak, underlain successively by regional colleges, area colleges and local colleges. These last formed the base of the system.

The list for 1964 (Table 13) illustrates the size of the layers of the pyramid and includes the numbers of other institutions:

TABLE 13. NOVEMBER 1964. GRANT-AIDED
FURTHER EDUCATION ESTABLISHMENTS

Type	Number
The Pyramid:	
Colleges of advanced technology	10
Regional colleges	25
Other major establishments	514
Other Institutions:	
Agricultural colleges	5
Farm institutes	40
Art establishments	148
Evening institutes	7784

No mention was made of proceeding eventually to county colleges. The main effects of the white paper were felt at higher levels than our age range, but as reorganisation proceeded a further white paper, much more relevant to this study followed. Already briefly noted near the beginning of this chapter—*Better Opportunities in Technical Education*—appeared very early in 1961. It deals with the lower ranges of technical education and defines the three broad categories for which provision is necessary:

(a) *Technicians.* These people are employed in a wide range of responsible jobs, under the direction of technologists. They can be employed in a wide range of designing, constructional, testing and inspectional capacities, freeing scientists and technologists for tasks more appropriate to their capacities.

(b) *Craftsmen.* This is a well-defined range of occupations already well catered for in further education, but rising standards and the need for broader courses to give greater adaptability under modern conditions make continued replanning of provision necessary.

(c) *Operatives.* The white paper introduced this as a convenient term for the many more-or-less skilled workers who carry out specific operations involving machinery and plant. Previously often trained inside industry they showed a growing need for further vocational education courses to supplement and broaden the practical training given on-the-job.

Better Opportunities suggested changes in organisation were needed for a number of reasons. In industry conditions were altering at an accelerated pace: in schools progress was resulting in students being basically better prepared to begin courses than had been the case previously: in further education itself the present system was not sufficiently flexible and streamlined resulting, as the Crowther report had so clearly documented, in a very high rate of "wastage"—courses started and not completed—and retardation—whole years repeated, sometimes because of a failure in only a small section of the course. Thus of 100 students entering the first year of an O.N.C. course, 11 passed in a minimum of 3 years, and 24 eventually after various resits. Passing to H.N.C., 3 of the original 100 were successful in minimum time and only 9 passed after many delays. Craft courses were very similar, showing the difficulties inherent in the part-time system.

Besides a thorough overhaul of the structure of the courses and the provision of new courses for technicians and operatives it urged as its chief proposals:

1. Students should begin courses at the technical college immediately after leaving school and discontinue the practice of taking preliminary courses in evening institutes.

2. Experiments should be made with full-time induction courses, instead of one-day-per-week courses, to give a good start and a firm basis for progress. Tutorial methods should also be tried.

3. More time should be provided under day-release schemes (e.g. the "county college" year of 330 hours) and no one should need to rely on evening study wholly.

4. There should be an increasing development of block release to replace day release and more sandwich courses should be organised for technicians.

In 1959 about 450,000 students enrolled in major establishments of further education were taking the type of course covered by the white paper. This figure included students to the age of 21. About one-quarter of a million were in the 15–18 range. A small proportion were taking full-time courses and the rest were divided between day release (or in a few cases block release) and evening-only in the proportions of 2 to 1. In addition a large number of young students were following courses in evening institutes. Before the white paper the organisation was as follows:

(a) *Preliminary courses.* These were part-time courses often given in evening institutes and intended for the pupil who leaves school at 15 as a preparation for a craft or other technical college course at 16.

(b) *Courses for craftsmen and technicians.* A wide variety of courses leading to examinations, mainly City and Guilds, starting normally at 16 and leading after 3 years' part-time work to an intermediate certificate and from there (but outside our scope) to the final. Of the 200,000 students enrolled in craft courses in 1959, many were beyond 18.

(c) *National certificate courses.* These, again part time, had a higher academic content than craft courses and led, given steady progress, to the ordinary national level after 3 years and from then onwards. Students taking these courses successfully became technicians or even technologists eventually.

(d) *Diploma courses.* These were full-time or sandwich courses, starting at 16, for better qualified students. After 2 years O.N.D. standard was reached and the course then continued to a higher standard. In 1958–9 1600 students were enrolled in O.N.D. courses.

The new pattern of courses suggested in 1961* allows for more transfer between courses, and by widening the range of courses offered makes more suitable placing possible. The opportunities open to boys and girls under the new scheme at different ages of entry can be summarised from the white paper. All courses are part time except where specifically stated full time.

A 15-year-old leaver granted day release may pursue:

(a) an operatives course;
(b) a craft course of 2 years' duration. The syllabus will cover what a 16-year-old will usually complete in 1 year;
(c) if he shows promise of reaching technician standard, a general course of 2 years' duration with three possibilities:
    (i) either after 1 year, to the first year of a technician course, or, after 2 years,
    (ii) to the second year of a technician course, or
    (iii) the first year of a 2-year O.N.C. course or a full-time O.N.D. course.

A 16-year-old leaver granted day release may pursue:

(a) and (b) operative and craft courses as above;
(c) the first year of a technician course;
(d) a 1-year general course leading to either.
    (i) the second year of a technician course, or
    (ii) the first year of an O.N.D. (full-time) or O.N.C. course;
(e) with four appropriate O-level passes direct entry to O.N.C. or O.N.D. (full-time) courses.

By November 1964 over 70,000 were taking O.N.C. courses as detailed in Table 14. Engineering leads the field. New syllabuses were introduced in 1962, combining mechanical and electrical engineering but providing more options, and other amalgamations and alterations are planned to improve the other courses. The numbers of students continues to increase.

* H.M.S.O., *Better Opportunities in Technical Education*, 1961, p. 16.

TABLE 14. NUMBERS OF STUDENTS IN GRANT-AIDED ESTABLISHMENTS
TAKING O.N.C. AND O.N.D. IN NOVEMBER 1964

	Certificate (O.N.C.)	Diploma (O.N.D.)
Building	9,558	1404
Business studies	12,734	5188
Engineering (all)	36,687	2670
Metallurgy	1,357	—
Mining	1,733	—
Textiles	441	37
Chemistry	7,677	—
Physics	1,456	—
Total	71,643	9299

EVENING INSTITUTES

In 1963–4 just over 9% of both girls and boys in our age group
still obtained their further education through evening institutes.
In actual numbers this represents about 150,000 students and
about one-sixth of all the adolescents who trouble the scorers of
education beyond the compulsory age. It will, of course, take
time for the proposals in *Better Opportunities* to take effect, and for
schools to feed directly to technical colleges. In some cases the
necessary technical colleges are not yet in existence. Even when
the proposals are fully implemented (the all-age school has been
an unconscionable long time a-dying) the 15–18 age group will
still use the evening institute for some purposes, often recreational.

The evening institute today is a composite organisation which
falls with some blurring of the edges into two sections—junior and
adult. The adult section is almost wholly a leisure time, recreational or sometimes cultural, system and hardly concerns us here
though a few of our group may use it.

Under the age of 18 is the junior section with, in 1963–4, about
one-quarter of all the enrolments. In the early years after World
War II the proportion was higher. Boys and girls of 15, and
often of 14 years of age and in their last term at school, enrolled

in large numbers though their rate of re-enrolment in succeeding years showed a marked diminution. The boys enrolled
for the preliminary technical course following a syllabus of English, science, mathematics and technical drawing which entailed
attendance on two nights per week. Girls (and a few boys) followed a commercial course paying chief attention to typewriting,
shorthand, English and calculations. From September to June
they attended two or three evenings a week and then took the
examinations offered by one of the regional institutes. For long
this part-time course, staffed in the main by principals and staff
from the schools, themselves working part time, has been the
bridge from school to technical college. Since 1944 direct entry,
always possible at 16, has grown, and now, of course, since *Better
Opportunities* the bridge is officially closed, or it might be better to
say is being gradually dismantled for old arrangements linger
until new structures, adumbrated by the new ideas, materialise.
In 1959 42% of 15-year-old leavers enrolled at evening institutes.
As abler boys and girls go straight to technical college so others
seem to take their place at evening institute. As the apprentice
gets his day release, so the would-be apprentice joins the evening
institute in the hope that the technical course certificate will help
him in his search for a better job. As more operative courses
become available the source of supply will eventually dry up
and the evening institute will finally lose its further education
(*sensu stricto*) and become an establishment for adult education
only.

The junior evening institute has had in the main a short-term
vocational aim. Established usually in school buildings, it has
remained largely in the orbit of the school-teacher (though full-
time principals have been appointed in increasing numbers
recently) with its discipline and work habits not unlike school.
Many students have given up very soon after enrolment; many
have entered for examinations and failed to pass. While it has not
yet finished, it is on a decline which must be hastened by extended
courses in modern schools, the C.S.E., and the eventual raising of
the leaving age to 16.

INDUSTRIAL TRAINING

Apprenticeship has a very long history and though it has been an important source of education it has failed to change sufficiently with the passage of time. One of the most knowledgeable critics is Professor Lady Williams. She has argued cogently for changes* and since 1964 the way has been cleared for progress. Until 1963 Lady Williams was still able to write that the responsibility for training its workers had been left entirely to industry. The Ministry of Labour since 1945 has played a part in giving advice and encouragement but apprenticeship schemes depend on arrangements between employers' organisations and trade unions. In all apprenticeship schemes training begins at 16 and ends at 21, lasting the same length of time whatever the skill involved. Provision for day release for those under 18 is made but there are no sanctions against those employers who do not grant it. In particular the criticisms of the system have been:

(a) the invariable 5-year training scheme;
(b) the rigid age and demarcation lines;
(c) the lack of outside supervision of the quality of training;
(d) the methods of training, because often there is little actual instruction. Methods are picked up watching. "Sitting by Nelly" is one way of describing it. Other countries have the same problem. In the U.S.S.R., critics of the productive work programme have christened the people who learn in this way "backwatchers".

The Carr report in 1958 spoke of flexibility towards age and length of training and the possibility of examinations. Discussions on the white paper and the Bill leading to the Industrial Training Act have aired the problems and now the situation holds the possibility of change. Speaking about the Act, the Minister sketched out the elements which industrial training might include. They were:

(a) actual experience on the job should be retained;

* Williams, G., *Apprenticeship in Europe: A Lesson for Britain*, Chapman & Hall, London, 1963.

(b) full-time initial training off-the-job probably for 1 year, i.e. induction courses;
(c) planned progression on a series of jobs in actual industry;
(d) an analysis of skills required in order to set a content;
(e) the change from a fixed period to one fixed by the necessities of the skilled involved;
(f) a further education element because diagnostic as well as manipulative skills will be increasingly necessary;
(g) proficiency tests at stages throughout the training.

The way forward to some of these desiderata has already been demonstrated. Since 1960 Government Training Centres have run full-time first-year courses to help, in particular, the smaller firms. By mid-1962 55 L.E.A.s had similar schemes with students taking full-time initial courses while they are indentured to firms who pay for the training. What has happened at Crawley College of Further Education is an example.* Crawley, in Sussex, is a new town with much light industry in firms which are too small to support their own apprentice training schools. Eleven apprentices took the first 1-year course in 1959. Firms were very doubtful of the efficiency of industrial training away from the factory, but results showed that the 1-year course was the equivalent of $2–2\frac{1}{2}$ years training in industry. In 1962 an apprentice training centre, with 42 engineering apprentices on the course, was opened. It is administered by the local education authority but the firms pay £50 per apprentice, and the four training officers are employed on an industrial basis. When it is desirable these men can be taken back to their firms and so training can be kept closely relevant to current needs and practices. The apprentices attend the college of further education one day per week on day release and take a variety of City and Guilds courses. However, schemes like this cannot involve all the levels of training. The semi-skilled and unskilled need attention too. In 1959 one-third of young persons below the age of 18 years entering employment went to apprenticeships

* Sikbo, J., *Partnership Incorporated—A Joint Effort to solve Apprentice Training*, London, 1963.

or learnerships in skilled occupations while over one-half went to occupations with no systematic training. Even though the dividing line between craft workers and operative (or skilled and unskilled) is becoming increasingly blurred, it seems likely that this general proportion of 2–3 at present will persist. Training for the non-apprentice is usually unplanned learning on the job and is slow, inefficient and wasteful. There ought to be a planned training schedule at the place of work, including an introduction to the firm and systematic instruction in a range of jobs with some general vocational education on the day of release to a college of further education.

Boots (Cash Chemists) of Nottingham are one firm which has worked on these lines. Boys have a $2\frac{1}{2}$-day residential initiation course within the first few weeks of joining the firm. They then work 4–6-month periods in two factories and two warehouses and get normal day release to Boots College. After 2 years with the firm, a placing is made and for another year more specialised training is continued in this post with day release still operative. Through schemes of this nature training can be extended to all.

FARM INSTITUTES

Agricultural education has also undergone its reorganisation in keeping with the other technical subjects. On 1 April 1959 responsibility, including the provision of farm institutes, passed to the Ministry of Education. A committee chaired by Earl de la Warr reported on the pattern of courses, the facilities which ought to be made available and the routes of access for students. Following this the Lampard-Vachell Committee cleared up some other details in two reports. Enrolments have increased and by 1964 the number of farm institutes had increased to forty with 6429 students, mostly in non-advanced courses, though courses are available at various levels. Because day release can cause difficulties, courses are better taken full time after a period of actual work on a farm. The nomenclature of courses is different. The national certificate course is a full-time 1-year course taken after farming experience and with three O-levels or the equivalent as the entrance qualification. It should be completed at 18+. The diploma course starts at 18 and takes 2 years full time and is outside our age range. However, in 1964 only thirteen students were following advanced courses. Farm institutes provide other courses of varying duration for both boys and girls between the ages of 16 and 18.

THE YOUTH SERVICE

Until World War II this was an entirely voluntary service but late in 1939 the Board of Education circular *Service of Youth* intimated that responsibility for the welfare of youth was to become a part of the national system of education. It was expected that there would develop a partnership with the voluntary organisations and gaps would be filled and this has, by and large, been the method by which progress has been attained. By the provisions of the 1944 Act it became obligatory for local authorities to ensure adequate facilities. Then in 1958 a committee chaired by the Countess of Albemarle was set up to review the contribution the youth service could make to assist young people to play their part in the life of the community. This review was to take place in the light of social and industrial conditions and current trends in other branches of education. Teenage culture was becoming increasingly self-conscious at this time and sub-cultures were evolving, and against this background expansion of the service has continued. More buildings have been provided, more leaders have been trained and some interesting programmes have been devised. For the less purposeful members of the age group the service still seems to be lacking in attraction, perhaps because it is trying too hard. The Ministry of Education have in fact written concerning this group, "It may not yet be widely enough recognised that it is a proper function of the service if it simply tries to meet these young people's wants. It seems that this aspect of the development of the service has not matched development on more traditional lines."[*]

[*] Ministry of Education, *Reports on Education—The Youth Service*, H.M.S.O., 1963.

INFORMAL EDUCATION

Obviously the educative function of the environment must not be neglected. The effect of the mass media, too, is of increasing importance and they certainly widen horizons particularly for the less privileged. The provision of more sophisticated programmes for the age group, e.g. "The Whole Scene Going",* introduced on B.B.C. television in the autumn of 1965 combining entertainment with serious discussion of teenage topics is worth noting, but the field is too wide to be discussed here.

So far this chapter has reviewed, section by section, the provision of further education for the upper secondary age group. Carrying out a similar task, the Crowther Committee found it taxing and summed up the difficulty by writing: "To our sorrow, there is hardly a single generalisation that can be made about further education that does not require an array of reservations and exceptions before it is accurate". Despite the regularisation that has gone on since, further education still presents an exceedingly complex picture, and because of the different needs at this age it seems likely that it must always continue to manifest a great variety. It is noteworthy that among all the present turmoil of change in this field, there is nothing emerging that clearly corresponds with what the Crowther report sketched out as a county college.

In the layout of *15 to 18* the section on county colleges is separated from the considerations of further education by a long section on the sixth form. This divide is symptomatic of the Committee's thinking, as is evinced by their definition. In the glossary they write under County College:

> An institution to be provided by a local education authority under the 1944 Act and attended part-time on a compulsory basis by young people under 18 not in full-time attendance at a school, or other educational institution. The term is sometimes used to cover any institution which might be attended by young people receiving compulsory part-time education, and sometimes to refer only to an institution designed to provide for

* The title is from a phrase in *Absolute Beginners*, by Colin MacInnes, Penguin edition, 1964, p. 88.

those whose education at this stage will not be mainly vocational. Except where otherwise stated we use the term in a more restricted sense.

They obviously envisage a clear break between the curriculum of the county college and that in further education generally, following closely the lead given in earlier statements from the Ministry. Pamphlet 3, already mentioned, looked forward to a kind of charismatic education in county colleges, exuding sweetness and light. In rural areas it might share facilities with a school but it was not to be a school. Village colleges on the Cambridgeshire pattern were probably the prototype here. The curriculum was sketched out in terms of an eight-period day with three periods to be given to practical work, two to general studies and one and a half each to physical education and elective subjects. This is definitely a recipe for a liberal education. Two years later, in 1947, Pamphlet 8 still preserved the distinction between county colleges and vocational education. It saw in further education a tripartite division consisting of:

(a) full-time and part-time courses for occupations;
(b) provision, in due course, of county colleges for part-time day education;
(c) the development of varied opportunities for young and old.

County colleges it was expected would have contacts with the youth service and with secondary schools providing for the same ages and would cater for vocational interests and leisure-time interests and activities. The introduction of a vocational element represents some change from previous thought but the curriculum was still aiming chiefly at a liberal education.

The Crowther report was in favour of a very liberal approach indeed. It distinguished four strands:

(a) aids to good citizenship (it is always possible to argue that the first requirement of a good citizen is that he shall be a good worker but the report was not thinking of this aspect);
(b) moral education;
(c) a continuation from school of physical and aesthetic pursuits;

(d) strictly educational tasks in the narrower sense, since many county college students will have grave deficiencies in their formal education.

Developments since Crowther seem to have gone in a diametrically opposite direction to this idea of a continued liberal approach for a group who have never done very well at "school" tasks anyway. Provision through the Industrial Training Act for the apprentice and widening opportunities for the non-apprentice (or trainee as some would have him called) with increasing blurring of the distinction between the two is in marked contrast. The Newsom report (1963) called for a vocational, practical, realistic education at the middle secondary level for the lower half of the ability range, with the student given some choice in part of his course. This hardly accords with the liberal ideal at the post-school day-release stage. The Brunton report (1963), while still maintaining a distinction between vocational further education as the province of the education service, with the aim of giving the broad background needed for any skill, and industrial training as the province of the employer, pointed out there was no hard and fast line. The two should not be entirely separated but rather a joint enterprise based on sound vocational guidance at school, where the courses followed should already be related to the future lives of the pupils. The vocational impulse, introduced into schools, should, they think, have a favourable result on general education without needing to commit anyone to a narrow vocation.

Here then in further education can be seen a parallel with developments in the secondary modern school where early pamphlets from the Ministry encouraged an unfettered approach to a very liberal curriculum. Recoiling from a surfeit of freedom, the schools began a search for a sense of purpose which a few found in vocational courses but most are finding in external examinations. *Youth's Opportunity* can be equated with the *New Secondary Education*—both appeared in 1947. Nowadays staff in the field are doubtful of the willingness of students to attend for an education that is not clearly vocational in character, and are sceptical of the success of courses in general education. Students' reactions to the courses provided *at present* seem to confirm this view. How they would react to better courses is not known, but so far developments are not in line with idealist hopes.

Is there another parallel to draw with secondary education which started from a tripartite basis and is now becoming more comprehensive? The Crowther Committee sketched out the education of the 15–18 age group on essentially tripartite lines—full-time academic in school; full-time and part-time vocational in technical colleges; and day-release liberal in the county colleges of the future. In their final chapter which looks forward to possible changing patterns in organisation, they toy with the idea of junior colleges running parallel with, but not replacing, sixth forms. Even these institutions will only cater for full-time students: part-time students will be outside in other institutions. Events since Crowther have tended to add a further strand—industrial training—rather than make an approach to integration. Even more separate tracks have been identified at this stage. In 1960, summing up at a B.A.C.I.E. Conference held to survey policy recommendations in the field of education and training, an Under-Secretary from the Ministry (Mr. T. R. Weaver) was able to identify six groups.* Using the analogy of the high fliers he coined a series of terms, all connected with movement because he believed that progress was discernible at all stages, to describe the educational levels as follows:

(a) *The plodders.* They provide a challenge to industry and education. At present there is little provision for them apart from the youth service, and one can only look forward to the future, to county colleges, and industrial training for the non-apprentice.

(b) *The pedestrians.* These will be provided for by courses in industrial training.

(c) *The runners.* This group, increasingly having qualifications

* B.A.C.I.E., *Policy in Perspective*, London, 1960.

in C.S.E., will be making their way into craft, and sometimes technician, courses.

(d) *The hurdlers.* Having jumped the G.C.E. O-level hurdle,
these have many opportunities on the technical side but,
despite the importance of tertiary activities, still find a lack
of preparation for commercial activities.

(e) *The fliers* and (f) *the high fliers.* Both these groups are still at
school while in our age range but will differentiate at 18
into those finding a place in H.N.C. and H.N.D. courses
and those going on to higher, rather than advanced further
education.

Thus when the Circular 10/65 has been implemented and comprehensive education has been established to 16 years, the upper
secondary level will still be operating on a system of parallel
tracks. Already, long before it is achieved, there are critics who
want a fully comprehensive system to operate much longer. Some
even believe that a comprehensive pattern to 18 is already present
in embryo in the colleges of further education. Proponents have
joined in the debate to point out they are really the first in the
field to be catering for students at all levels from day release for
industrial trainees to full-time A-level work for university entrance. As an example can be cited a college of further education
in a county borough with a population of over 160,000, which also
supports a college of art and a college of technology. With 45 full-
time and 100 part-time staff it offers a whole gamut of courses to
500 full-time students, 900 students with day release (36 days per
year) or block release (three blocks of 20 days) and 1200 evening
students. It offers:

1. Academic courses to O-level in twenty-one subjects including commerce and accounts. These subjects are arranged in
groups which cater for commerce or engineering students
who want suitable O-levels to start on their course. A-level
can also be taken in the same number of subjects in both day
and evening classes. Courses for first M.B., veterinary, dental
and preliminary pharmacy examinations are also available.

2. Pre-apprenticeship courses for 15-year-olds with the local certificate of education, leading to later courses in engineering, building, commerce and catering.

3. National courses in construction leading eventually to O.N.C. Entry for these is at 16.

4. A variety of craft courses on City and Guilds syllabuses.

5. A general engineering course intended to be useful for orienting students into suitable courses at either technician or craftsman level. It is a basic course for both potential mechanical and electrical engineers or for a craft course in electrical installation. There are many problems of guidance involved in correct choice of course at this level.

6. Courses for laboratory technicians and also a telecommunications for the Post Office employees and for British Rail.

7. Some general mining courses.

8. Courses in business studies at several levels from an introductory course leading to the national certificate, to the certificate in office studies and to secretarial training.

9. Courses in horticulture for Parks' staff.

10. Courses in the retail trades, e.g. meat.

11. Various courses in housecraft, domestic science, needlework and millinery.

This adds up to a quite comprehensive provision. Arguing from this point of view the Fabian tract *Educating for Uncertainty** advocates an evolution from provision of this kind to "local colleges for all".

Earlier, but approaching the problem from the extension of the grammar school, Pedley† had come to a similar conclusion: "the comprehensive county college for all . . . would be a development of the process for which I have reasoned already; the transformation of the grammar school into a school or college for older adolescents, at first perhaps from 13 to 14, later from fifteen or sixteen, to eighteen plus".

---

* Downes, D. and Flower, F., Fabian Tract 364, London, 1965.
† Pedley, R., *The Comprehensive School*, Penguin, London, 1963, p. 189.

These idealistic projections for the future are referred to again in Chapter 6 on new developments in upper secondary schools and in the final chapter on the form of upper secondary education for all. Here they receive a mention, though the main concern has been to chart the recent progress in the further education field. What emerges is a picture of advance along many avenues with, as yet, no integration in view. It has been mentioned earlier that successful legislation seems unable to run too far ahead of current practice and so much more pragmatic expansion can be expected before a synthesising effort materialises. When it is expansion that is required it is perhaps well that plans should not be too rigid for while plans presage opportunities, rigidity may lead to loss of opportunities which only flexibility can provide. In a recent article* "The demand for technical education in the United Kingdom" Sir Peter Venables is making the same general point when he writes:

> The history of the teaching of skills shows a reluctant widening of their base from the specific requirements of firms to the general principles underlying them, a change which has been slowly established over a long period, facilitated by the transfer of the teaching process from industry to the colleges able to exercise the broader educational function. Despite the long sustained trend, the Industrial Training Act leaves the implementation to industry and makes no explicit provision for the expansion and reorientation of the work of technical colleges.

Sir Peter Venables goes on to juxtapose the Robbins report and the Industrial Training Act, which as he reiterates, covers all levels from operatives to technologists and managers. All the young people affected by the arrangements stemming from these two contemporaneous manifestations of the need for more education (used in the broadest sense) will be involved in the upper secondary sector. The extent of the required growth in the full-time academic sector is large, but figures quoted in the same chapter of the *Year Book* show the massive turnover required throughout this decade at the lower levels of manpower. It is estimated that a *net annual* addition of 153,000 craftsmen to the labour force is necessary while at the same time there is a redundancy of

* *World Year Book of Education 1965*, Section II, chapter II, p. 235.

151,000 unskilled workers. At intermediate levels the additions, though important, are much smaller. Alongside these figures must be placed the numbers in the age group. In 1965 there were about 380,000 17-year-old boys and 365,000 17-year-old girls (1000 of each sex for each day of the year is a useful mnemonic). About 80,000 to 90,000 of these have day release and about 100,000 are at school full time. Quantitative estimates of this nature underline the tasks ahead and show that effort at the level of the plodders, the pedestrians and the runners, with which this chapter has been mainly concerned, is of vital concern.

CHAPTER 6

New Sixth-form Patterns

THE statistics from the Department of Education and Science for 1965 show the following types and numbers of secondary maintained schools.

TABLE 15

Type	Number of schools 1965
Modern	3727
Grammar	1285
Technical	172
Comprehensive	262
Other secondary schools	417

Many of the comprehensive and other secondary schools are large and have more pupils on roll than the more orthodox modern, grammar and technical schools, but their sixth forms are no larger and may well be smaller than the grammar schools. Comprehensive schools, and others like them, have, quite understandably, been concerned to show that they are able to do everything that grammar schools can do just as well as the traditional school (as well as doing other things besides) so the traditions of the sixth form can be seen in them, writ quite as large as in the grammar school. In addition they have developed, or are in the process of developing, courses more suitable for less academically inclined pupils at the upper secondary level. However, this chapter is interested in examining patterns of education in which the upper secondary sector is physically separate from the lower school. The number of schools with this restricted age range is small. Sixth-form colleges at Welbeck College and Atlantic College are very special institutions. At Mexborough the sixth-form college is separate, yet shares facilities with the lower school on the same site. Some other schools are separating the sixth form on a pragmatical basis, making a sixth-form centre where the older pupils can have some kind of semi-private life in their own domain, so combining to some extent the advantages of having a sixth form as an integral part of the school and the freedom which would come with a sixth-form college. Other areas have plans for sixth-form colleges and Luton is starting in September 1966. But actual experience of this type of organisation is very limited and plans and ideas must figure more largely in the discussion than actualities.

With a different age range there is more experience. Leicestershire has upper schools from 14 to 18 years operating in several areas, and other counties are adopting a similar system. The uppermost portion of these schools, catering for a wide self-selected ability range, brings experience which is a useful guide.

A brief recapitulatory glance is useful. The maintained grammar school course was, at first, of 4 years' duration, and was extended as a few bright pupils stayed on after 16. Originally these first sixth formers were a tiny atypical proportion of the whole school but they set the pattern for the future upper school. After 1944, when there was a desire from above for a change to a continuous course, the pattern was so rigid that change would not come. Many schools found the course satisfactory and had no desire to change. Today the vast majority of schools are organised on a 5–2 basis or, if they have an express route to the sixth form, have a minority 4–3 organisation. Because the course falls into two parts—and almost every school does emphasise the difference between the sixth form and the lower school—there have been many suggestions for separating the upper school and establishing a new institution catering only for senior pupils. Some of the arguments have been on strictly educational grounds, some on the

D

economical use of staff, some are based on sociological considerations and some grow out of other reorganisation schemes. Some schemes would include only academic work in the sixth-form college but other schemes aim to include a wider provision embracing a broader band of ability and in distinction are called junior colleges (see Chapter 15). Already many colleges of further education are demonstrating how even now they are filling this latter role and claiming that evolutionary steps should be based on the expertise they have been able to garner.

Although Croydon was the first authority to suggest the establishment of a sixth-form college, Preston has used a series of general arguments in its booklet on the organisation of secondary education.* Preston, a county borough with a fairly low proportion of selective provision, envisaged its original development in terms of 7-year schools and 5-year schools. The 7-year course was thought of as catering for not less than 15% of the age group who would remain at school until the age of 18. Experience showed, however, that even in 1960 40% of entrants left the 7-year school after 5 years and only 11% proceeded to universities and 14% to other full-time further education. On the other hand, 25% of pupils stayed on for a fifth year in the "5-year schools". Considerable overlap between the types of school developed, and experience showed that the 5-year course in the 7-year school was less responsive to individual need than the 5-year course in the 5-year school. Five-year schools began to develop upper schools because pupils were unwilling to transfer to 7-year schools which offered opportunities limited almost exclusively to the academic side. Preston therefore argue that in place of two parallel systems an end-on system should be established. They want a high school offering 5-year courses for all pupils from the ages of 11–16. There would be general, technical, commercial and academic courses culminating where appropriate in G.C.E., or C.S.E. No pupil would be channelled too early into a course. No longer would it be assumed that "not only is the man pre-destined in the 11-year-old boy but

* Preston Education Committee, *Organisation of Secondary Education—A Reappraisal,* Preston, 1964.

also that he may then be recognised". Instead schools would be responsive to developing individual needs. Following the high school would be the sixth-form college which would accept all youngsters wishing to enter after completing the 5-year course. No formal qualifications would be necessary, so, in the strict sense, Preston are suggesting a junior college which would offer courses of 2 or 3 years' duration designed to have regard to the abilities and aptitudes of individuals, together with their need to qualify for entrance to further full-time education or a profession or a career in industry. In addition to traditional sixth-form courses the college would offer liberal courses suitable for pupils entering teacher training, technology, business, social service or full-time study in music and art. The high school (for the 11–16 age group) would encourage teachers qualified, but not already teaching to O-level, to do so, and the sixth-form college would concentrate suitable qualified teachers on advanced work. It is envisaged that the Preston colleges of further education would still offer part-time courses but full-time courses at the upper secondary level would be in the sixth-form college. Preston's is a well-argued and comprehensive plan, but one must question whether the separation of full-time from part-time work in this sector is the right decision. It would seem to be uneconomical in equipment and, perhaps, staffing and it could make transfers from full-time to part-time courses, which is a natural progression for many in this age group, difficult to achieve.

Early in the 1950's the Croydon L.E.A. were keeping records of 11 + performance and subsequent O-level results and finding that many selected for grammar school by the former did less well at O-level than some pupils left behind in the secondary modern schools. These findings were consonant with those from similar investigations elsewhere, despite the tests at the age of 11 being as good as could be devised. Arguing from this demonstrable fact and the uneconomic size of many sixth forms, the Croydon L.E.A. suggested that apart from the small numbers (5%) going to independent and direct-grant schools, all sixth forms should be collected in one college (Addington College) and other schools should cater for the whole of the age range from 11 to 16. This division, they contended, would remove the weak link in the chain of maintained education—the small sixth form—which is quite unable to compete with the independent and direct-grant schools. About thirty different subjects can be taken at A-level and to teach anything like this number in viable groups needs a larger sixth form than most grammar schools are able to attract. A large sixth-form college, properly equipped and staffed, would be able to challenge the independent sector. Weight is added to this argument when the top schools in the list of those gaining scholarships at Oxford and Cambridge is examined.

TABLE 16. AWARDS AT OXFORD AND CAMBRIDGE
1957–62 (6-YEAR PERIOD)

	Number	Type
Manchester Grammar School	195	Day
Winchester College	161	Boarding
Dulwich College	153	Day
St. Paul's School	105	Day
Bradford Grammar School	100	Day

This list suggests that it is not boarding *per se* which is important, as only one of the top five is a boarding institution. The others are day schools with a wide and densely populated catchment area. Academically there appears no reason why sixth-form colleges should not be extremely successful.

The headmaster of Sevenoaks School* makes the same point, in a more general way, at the beginning of his book. He believes the accident of boarding last century led to power being attributed to schools when they were only partially instrumental in achieving the ends. Four factors influence the growing boy—home, society in general, the boy himself and the school. All the boarders came from a broadly similar background of society with well-to-do and literate homes. This common background was not so much

* Taylor, L. C., *Experiments in Education at Sevenoaks*, London, 1965.

discounted as not considered when a balance sheet was being drawn up, and public schools were credited with much that springs from home and society. Hence, according to Taylor, much of the power attributed to boarding becomes a plausible delusion.

A further line of argument favouring a concentration of sixth-formers can be developed from an article* by Dr. Hudson of the Cambridge Psychological Laboratory, who, over the years since 1957, has tested a number of fifth-form and lower sixth-form boys from English public and grammar schools with a high grade intelligence test. The sample he built up had a range corresponding closely to the spread for grammar school boys as a whole, ranging from I.Q.s of 110–139. Not working with raw I.Q.s but grading the whole of his sample on a scale from A to E in the following proportions:

A	B	C	D	E
1	2	4	2	1

he was able to show that there was scarcely any relation between winning a scholarship or exhibition at Oxbridge and I.Q. score—of course, as long as you are sufficiently good to be in the sample in the first place. The results he gives are as follows:

	E	D	C	B	A	*n*
Scholars and exhibitioners	3	6	12	13	3	37
Commoners at Oxbridge	1	11	15	7	6	40
Other universities	7	13	26	15	9	70
No university	10	10	19	6	3	48
	21	40	72	41	21	

Dr. Hudson reports a similar pattern of scores holds good for a number of other tests and measures—verbal intelligence, vocabulary, general knowledge—and so suggests a future open scholar is

* Hudson, L., Future open scholars, *Nature*, vol. 202, no. 4934, 23 May 1964.

indistinguishable from his form mates by I.Q. It is not the gifts but what he makes of them that is important. This certainly suggests that a large school with students in this range (and a sixth-form college would be this) able to give both wide and specialised opportunities would be of great benefit and afford genuine possibilities of rivalling the large independent schools.

Others have concentrated on social arguments and suggested that a separate institution at the upper secondary level could be more easily organised as a democratic community than a school with a wider age range. The young adults could share the responsibilities with their elders, while enjoying the social conditions appropriate to their status. Instead of having an autocratic relationship with pupils much younger than themselves, they would be operating within a peer group. It has been pointed out that leadership among equals is what is required today, as opposed to hierarchical arrangements appropriate to previous times.

An arrangement showing some of the possibilities is the sixth-form international centre at Sevenoaks which has been operating since 1962.* Adolescents of a minimum age of 16 live together for 1, 2 or 3 years in a self-governing boarding house. Sevenoaks is a part-boarding, part-day school. The sixth-form boarders come from various countries and English boys transfer from ordinary boarding houses. The intake is so arranged that never more than half or less than one-third of the forty boys is English. In the centre no school ranks apply, and boys who are prefects in the school have no more authority in the house than newcomers from overseas. A three-man committee consisting of not more than one member of a previous committee, and with always, at least, one English and one foreign representative, runs the centre. This committee must obtain willing co-operation, for it has no powers of coercion, but it has to organise a number of "chores" such as serving meals, washing up and tidying the grounds. All the boys have examinations in view, and know they must do well, so all the self-made rules are found to be relevant ones. Already it has been

* Taylor, L. C., *Experiments in Education at Sevenoaks*, London, 1965.

shown that boys with a great variety of temperament can take initiative, and the critical self-help principle operating in the centre has spilled over into the school causing new looks to be levelled at arrangements there and fixed ideas are now constantly being challenged. A functioning adolescent society has been produced.

Sixth-form attitudes have recently been investigated and reported under the rather journalistic title "The sixth-form myth".* The author worked with a sample, in a college of education, just fresh from the sixth form. In general their academic results were below or border-line university standard. Working on the basis of a set of essays entitled "A critical review of my own education", Mr. Child worked out a questionnaire which was then completed by a group of 150 students. Various attitudes had to be rated on a scale from 1—fully satisfying, to 5— most unsatisfactory. Here are some of the findings:

> 56% said they had little opportunity to discuss social problems with teachers.
>
> 60% said they were treated as individuals but not as adults.
>
> 60% said the prefect system was artificial. They found trivial tasks such as turning juniors out at break soon became boring and they did not really like looking after juniors.
>
> 57% said there was lack of help in choosing a career.
>
> 70% said that teachers only stressed the value of passing examinations.

A few were very complimentary concerning the efforts to supply a mature atmosphere and there were no complaints about the academic efforts of the schools. On the five-point scale the schools came out at 2 on the rating for academic sufficiency but at 4 (i.e. unsatisfactory) for social education.

Sir Geoffrey Crowther (of the report) in a letter,† thought that a new institution at the sixth-form level would give a positive reaction instead of the diminishing returns supplied by a larger

* Child, D., in *Education,* 3 December 1965.
† *Times Educational Supplement,* March 1965.

school. If education cannot be continuous from 5 to 22 breaks must occur somewhere. Reasons have been suggested for almost any and every age, but since the end of compulsory schooling is a break for the majority why, if it is good for some, should it not be so for all. Dr. Miller, working at the Tavistock Clinic, argued against the 15–16 break on psychological grounds but, it has been suggested, he was only considering the aberrant cases.

Leicestershire, working for a comprehensive system in existing buildings, have established, on a largely pragmatical basis, a two-tier system with a break at 14, giving a 4-year upper school, which in 1964 took about 45% of the age group, for, at least, the first 2 years.* The upper schools find this intake falls into three broad bands of ability but not in equal proportions (tripartism again, or is three still a magic number?). Three or four streams take G.C.E. courses, a middle band C.S.E., and a lower band take no examinations. There is no evidence that the academically-minded child has suffered from the break at 14, and the grammar (upper) schools agree that transferred children have reached appropriate standards. G.C.E. results at O-level in 1963 and 1964 reached roughly the national average with a larger percentage entry. It is suggested that although transfer to the upper school is attractive for the brighter child, offering, as it does, entrance to the examinations to which our educational system is geared, and the prospect of an adult community, it may act less favourably for those of lower ability who see no chance to rise in the upper school. However, already the curriculum has been widened beyond that of the traditional sixth form and when the school staying age is raised all will transfer to the upper school.

An argument used against the sixth-form college has been the short 2-year course (for many, even most) that transfer at 16 years of age entails. Too long will be spent in settling down and the course will be half over before coherence is gained. With proper liaison between schools much preparatory work is possible. Pupils themselves settle in very quickly as anyone who has worked to

* Special Correspondent, A look at Leicestershire, *Times Educational Supplement*, 12 February 1965.

integrate new entrants into a school knows. Welbeck and Atlantic Colleges have shown that 2-year institutions can work successfully, though these are very special cases. In the present pattern of education generally there is already a good deal of transfer at the post O-level stage for reasons of internal migration or the wish for a different course, and 2 years proves to be a viable unit. When it becomes a planned change for all it should be a stimulus and not a burden.

A full discussion of the problem of where our educational system should be articulated has been attempted recently. Professor Elvin* eventually concludes that 15 years is the best age to start the upper secondary school and this age, he thinks, should become operative as soon as our system of external examinations has been altered to fit this. He argues for a common school to 15, with 3 years in a sixth-form college for those who wish to stay on: or 1 year full time followed by 2 years of related part time for the others. Besides giving a variety of social advantages, he also lists the following:

> First, we should have eliminated selection at too early an age and have turned it largely into self-selection. Second, we should have concentrated high level upper secondary education where the need for concentration is serious and the argument for segregation strongest. We should have fused the last year at school for those who left at sixteen with continued part-time education and young adult interests in work and leisure.

Some people argue that the advantages of the sixth-form college can be combined with the advantages from the present continuous course by establishing contiguous institutions for sixth-formers. The headmistress of Wycombe High School is one of these.† She says it is quite true that some girls need a freer atmosphere at 16 and this is being met by changing attitudes which allow an enfranchised sixth form which is much preferable to a 2-year course *directed by* strangers (my italics: staff in a school would not be strangers for long). Her sixth form has no formal class organisation: the girls sign in and each is assigned to an individual tutor.

* Elvin, H. L., *Education and Contemporary Society*, Watts, London, 1965, chapter 7.
† Letter in *Times Educational Supplement*, 2 April 1965.

No uniform is worn—the guide being what is appropriate for any young member of staff. The group hold their own morning assembly which they conduct for themselves. The Head conducts it only when asked to do so. Prefects and school officers are recruited not from the sixth but from other forms. If they wish, sixth-formers can enter into the activities of the school proper, and many do so on an entirely voluntary basis, helping with school societies, organising junior choirs, and working as deputy form mistresses. Although it is a new venture, the headmistress reports the wonderful zest and loyalty which the granting of freedom and treatment as adults has engendered. She regards it, not only as meeting the mood of the times, but also as building a bridge between school, college and life. This upper secondary department draws from a lower school of about 1000 girls.

A more comprehensive type of institution, still organised in close conjunction with the main school, is the sixth-form college at Mexborough, Yorkshire, claiming to be the first sixth-form college.* There new buildings give a separate upper school block, out of bounds for the main school. The sixth, however, share laboratories, workshops, gymnasia and playing field with the remainder of the school. Entry is not merely restricted to the pupils of the lower school but is open for anyone who wishes to continue full-time education to 18. The headmaster believes that earlier maturation, much greater affluence and a vastly changed public opinion make it imperative to treat the sixth form as an adult group. Ensuring this entails problems of two kinds. Academically the sixth-form college must provide a very wide range of courses of varying standards, and on the social side its discipline and *mores* must be acceptable to its clients. The academic arrangements are probably easier to achieve. Subjects are offered at different levels:

1. Advanced level with 8 periods per week.
2. Cultural level of a similar standard but not tied to examinations, 8 periods per week.

* Shields, G. W., The first sixth-form college, *Education*, 6 November 1964.

3. Vocational level leading to various professional qualifications—also 8 periods.

4. Ordinary level—4 periods.

TABLE 17. MEXBOROUGH SIXTH-FORM COLLEGE
Lower VI time-table 1964–5 (eight periods in each group)

Level	Group I	Group II	Group III	Group IV
Advanced and scholarship	Mathematics Further maths. Biology Botany History (1) German English (1) R.I.	Further maths. Chemistry Economics Latin English (11) Domestic sciences Woodwork Metalwork Art	Physics Maths. (with statistics) Zoology History (11) French Geography Craft and design Further art	General studies course
Cultural level	Drama Housecraft Woodwork Metalwork	Art	Mathematics Music (instrumental and vocal)	
Vocational level	Accountancy	Shorthand	Typing	
Ordinary level (four periods)	Biology Agriculture Physiology and hygiene English Physics	Domestic science Art Chemistry R.I.	History Geography Mathematics Commercial mathematics	French English Latin (6) Spanish (6)

The whole time-table (see Table 17) consists of four groups of setted alternatives which allow a wide choice including mixed arts–science courses. General studies is also available for most students.

Socially all the sixth-formers belong to the college society which

76231

elects a council which subdivides into committees covering various aspects. Life centres on a large general common room available during the day and the evening. Freedom is not absolute as there is a no-smoking rule and various prohibitions connected with the care of the building. Attendance at daily prayers for all, except those with a conscientious objection, is obligatory. The daily life is largely separate from the lower school which appoints prefects from the fifth form, organised by the deputy head boy and girl. The sixth form help with school societies, and a house system runs through the two sections of the school. Separate dining facilities are provided for the sixth-formers, with a cafeteria system, giving some choice of menu and no regimentation.

It is evident that where experiments have been tried secondary groups from 16 upwards function well. As yet, though, the home evidence is slight and, in the appraisal, the Hawthorne effect must be allowed for. Most of the arguments are conducted on a theoretical basis.

Opponents of the idea point out that a truly comprehensive school should not segregate by age any more than by ability and there should be continuous and gradual change in status rather than a saltative progression. Emancipation of the sixth form should be within a framework of responsibility. Such people also argue that staff are better when involved with the complete age range (whatever that may mean), which ensures continuity of teaching. Younger pupils benefit from their contacts with sixth-form staff. Teachers are usually the people who can persuade pupils to stay on. A forced move to a new institution, they say, may induce the alternative choice and school education may be terminated.

Every one of these points can be challenged by a similar, but opposite, kind of testimony, which is easy enough to work out. Advocates point out a sixth-form community can be a bridge between school and university and an institution at this level with a homogeneous age group allows for social development in an adult setting and time also becomes available for attention to methods of learning rather than merely teaching.

More concretely this break removes the necessity for the large size of the comprehensive school, but yet can give a sixth form of between 300 and 600 students, which is economical and can be a real community giving every kind of opportunity. A separate institution at this level can also forge better links with a college of further education and lead eventually to total comprehensiveness in the upper secondary sector. Certainly at this level all opportunities need expanding, and it is better that proper liaison should exist if integration is not feasible.

Decision in this debate must wait upon events, but in the meantime experience from abroad is worth exploring.

CHAPTER 7

The United States of America—
General Education: A Search for Standards

In the United States there is a full flowering of upper secondary education. During the last decade of the last century the percentage of students completing secondary school rose quickly to reach 5% by about 1900. Using Laska's criteria, this is the entry point to Stage III of the educational process. By 1920 the secondary level completion ratio was 15%; by 1950, 50%. For the entry of 1953 to the senior high school (pupils born in 1938) the Robbins report in Appendix V gives the following percentages:

	Total	Boys
High school graduates	63	59
Entrants to college	29	33
Entrants to junior year	20	25

This represents progress through Stage III at an average rate of 1% per year throughout this century so far. Will it level off or will it reach virtually 100% by the year 2000 are questions which are open to speculation.

At this point it is useful to spell out a warning. Generalisations, like Laska's, concerning educational expansion are very helpful but are not without their pitfalls. As other countries have followed the U.S.A. and begun to make progress through Stage III and have, almost inevitably, become more comprehensive in the process, it has been assumed by some that the pattern set in the States would be imitated very closely elsewhere. In particular comprehensive developments in the United Kingdom have been opposed by many on these grounds. The great comparative educationist, I. Kandel, in particular, has been unimpressed by the American comprehensive system and warned against the spread of comprehensiveness here. Others have quoted him or followed his example. It cannot be stated too clearly that stages are generalisations and not detailed blueprints. While broad lines of progress will be matched elsewhere, the details will show great variety depending on the history and the outlook of the country concerned. So, although the U.S.A. has been in the van in educational provision and is still evolving a system which suits her needs, there is no likelihood that other systems will develop in any but the broadest similarity.

The fact of continuing evolution is important as the chapter will reveal. The table already quoted from the Robbins report is interesting in this evolutionary context. It shows the percentages of students entering college and then proceeding with their education 2 years later. One school of thought already regards the 2 years after high school when given in a junior college as secondary education. These people see the preferred pattern of American education as 6–3–3–2, with 8 years of secondary education.

> The American secondary school, from one point of view, might be considered of eight years' duration—the junior high school (grades seven through nine), the senior high school (grades ten through twelve), and the junior college (grades thirteen and fourteen). Although all educators will not agree on this (many arguing for the higher educational status of the junior college), the fact remains that the total secondary school corresponds approximately to the time and content of the standard secondary school in European countries.*

The official contribution to Volume III of the *UNESCO World Survey of Education* revised to November 1959 notes that "the present trend in public education is for local communities to provide tax-supported and publicly-directed schooling for all from the age of five to the age of twenty". Important words here are "publicly-directed schooling" which tend to suggest the real break

* Brickman, W. W., *Educational Systems in the United States*, New York, 1964.

follows the age of 20. Before the chapter ends this trend will be set
in perspective. It will require the erection of a further stage in
Laska's classification.

The division of secondary education into two 3-year periods
following on from 6 years of elementary education became the
preferred pattern in about 1910, and reorganisation to this end
has gone on since, but is far from complete as Table 18 shows,
and Fig. 3 can only be regarded as a stylised presentation. The
variety of arrangements remain for a number of reasons. Some
school districts have insufficient enrolments for a senior high

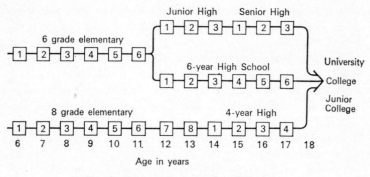

FIG. 3. Patterns of schooling in the U.S.A.

school, and so a 6-year high school remains. Some areas have
separate administrative districts for the 4 years of secondary education (e.g. Arizona, Illinois, California) and so continue with a
4-year plan, either 8–4 or 6–2–4. Because of problems posed by
existing buildings there are a few aberrant patterns such as 5–3–4
and even 7–5. (Table 18 with its variety of pattern is interesting
in view of the Department of Education and Science circular
on comprehensive reorganisation 1965, which lists six possible
comprehensive patterns. It is one effective answer to those who
denigrate the circular because it is not more dogmatic.)

The requirement for graduation from high school and college
entrance still tends to be based on sixteen units collected over the

TABLE 18. HIGH SCHOOL PATTERNS IN 1959

Type of high school	Number of schools	%	Enrolment (000's)	%
Combined (6–6)	10,130	41·9	3537	32·0
Separate junior	4,996	20·6	2750	24·9
Separate senior	1,642	6·8	1625	14·7
Reorganised 4 year (6–2–4)	1,396	5·8	1194	10·8
Unreorganised 4 year (8–4)	6,023	24·9	1939	17·6

last 4 years of high school. A unit consists of the satisfactory attendance and completion of work (an approved average mark in tests and for homework) for a course of at least 120 clock hours per year. Periods may be short (40–45 minutes) or long (50–55 minutes) so 120 clock hours would be 180 40-minute periods or 140 50-minute periods. The former would require a class to be scheduled everyday the school met in the year. This system of reckoning units tends to perpetuate the idea of 4 years of senior high school and often the first year of senior high school proper is looked upon as a sophomore year. The last 4 years of high school are usually called freshman, sophomore, junior and senior years as are the 4 years at college and university.

This wide provision of upper secondary education has a long history. A useful summary of the development in one sentence has been given by Martin Trow.* "Our secondary system began as an élite preparatory system: became a mass terminal system in the years of its great growth, and is now making a painful transition to a mass preparatory system." The transition from mass terminal to mass preparatory is the one that this chapter is attempting to summarise. World War II which is the starting point here is an important watershed.

In the years from 1890 to 1940 when enrolment in the high schools was doubling every decade the role of the school was to

* Quoted in Hofstadter, R., *Anti-intellectualism in American Life.*

Americanise the wave of immigrants and the view which stressed the development of discipline through academic studies was being successfully challenged by the idea of a school adapted to general needs, laying the foundations of good citizenship and helping in a wise choice of vocation. Progressive education and activity methods, with John Dewey providing both the theoretical drive and some of the practical methods, were in the ascendant. But by World War II the wave of immigration was over; the nation had been knit together and was no longer merely content to turn its back on Europe. In fact prosperity and easier travel made it possible for more administrators, teachers and laymen to travel and see other cultures at first hand. The war, too, finally made the Americans conscious of their role of the prime supporters of democracy and the free society. After 1945 she found herself committed to playing a major part as supporter of the world organisation for welfare and peace. In keeping with this mood 1945 saw the publication of the Harvard report *General Education in a Free Society*. This report suggested that the idea of general education had been lost in the eruptive expansion of schools at a time when society was becoming increasingly complex and knowledge was accumulating at an ever accelerating pace. Instead of an increasing load of elective subjects, it said that education required a new unifying purpose and idea. As a basic plan for the schools it outlined the following:

1. General education should take up half the total time with offerings in three major fields:

   (a) the humanities giving a view of man's inner visions and standards;
   (b) the social sciences giving an insight into corporate living;
   (c) the natural sciences giving a background to the physical world.

There was thus to be no dichotomy between the two cultures.

2. The general school atmosphere and extra-curricular activities would be the same for all and act as a further unifying agent.

(In the U.S. extra-curricular activities are generally called co-curricular activities.)

3. The remainder of the time would be occupied with different courses for pupils with different abilities. These elective subjects were thus to have a limited place.

The common core of subjects would take up about half the available time but the possibility of some specialisation on one of the three sides would increase this to about two-thirds of the total leaving the remaining one-third for special training and vocational education. The idea of a core curriculum has had a good deal of influence on the offerings in secondary education since the Harvard report.

The true core curriculum is a large block of time, common to all pupils, planned on problem-oriented or guidance-oriented lines and largely ignoring subject matter boundaries and dealing with the problems of youth. Skills are taught as they are required and allowance for individual differences is made by method rather than through content. However, not many schools use a true core approach covering a wide area of knowledge. Much the most usual integration includes English and the social studies. In 1952 of all schools reporting the use of a core curriculum less than 25% were using the true core approach and by 1958 this figure had dropped to less than 12%. More use is made of the core in the junior than the senior high school. A variation of the core curriculum is the block-of-time approach by which more than one teaching period is allotted to a subject, thus allowing for discovery and activity methods, but again this is found predominantly in the junior high. A census of block-of-time classes in New Jersey schools in 1958 showed that although 51% of schools had such arrangements in grades 7 and 8, only 14% were carrying on with the arrangement in grade 9. A recent book* on the curriculum in the United States summing up the position of progressive versus traditional education points out that secondary schools follow both approaches with a leaning towards the conservative. Truly progressive and

* Douglass, H. R., *Trends and Issues in Secondary Education*, New York, 1962.

truly traditional schools are almost all private institutions of which there are about 10% of the total school provision. The public system is more eclectic but on the whole the core curriculum, activity movement, the problem approach and life adjustment have made little impact in their extreme forms although they have affected method. On the whole the curriculum remains subject-centred with courses common to all pupils in grades 7 and 8, and more differentiated curricula in grade 9 and in the senior high school but everywhere subject matter courses predominate.

Another movement in the after-war period has been the life-adjustment idea, calling for an education "which better equips American youth to live democratically with satisfaction to themselves and profit to society as home members, workers and citizens". Educators in favour of this approach began by suggesting that 20% of pupils should be prepared for college, 20% would go to skilled occupations while the remaining 60% would best be catered for by life-adjustment courses. These percentages are reminiscent of the tripartite suggestion of the Ministry of Education immediately after the war (15% grammar, 15% technical and 70% secondary modern) and the life-adjustment aims were not too dissimilar to the Ministry intentions as expressed in the famous pamphlet 9. Soon life-adjustment educators were suggesting their courses were suitable for all pupils not merely for the lower 60% and until the Russians put their first Sputnik into orbit in 1957 there was a lack of concentration on, some would say, a definite neglect of the gifted pupil, though others have written of the "happy plight of the gifted child" and given figures for 1959 of 10,000 high school pupils taking college courses while still at school. The Sputniks in 1957 and 1958 certainly gave edge to an outcry for a reappraisal, but they did not initiate it. Already in 1955 the association for progressive education had been wound up and two years later its journal ceased publication.* The reason was that by the end of World War II progressive education had become conventional wisdom. The application of the promise of American life to the new society which had been evolving,

* See Cremin, L. A., *The Transformation of the School*, Knopf, New York, 1961.

had, by a great educational effort, been in the main successful. It had:

(a) broadened schooling to include matters connected with health and vocation and infused it with something of the qualities of family and community life;
(b) succeeded in applying successfully in the classroom research findings from psychology and sociology and so made learning a happier process;
(c) altered classroom approaches and the materials of instruction and adapted them for different kinds and classes of children.

In many ways the time when the ideas of good education and progressive education had become synonymous had been reached and so there was less to be struggled for. The very atmosphere in the schools had been changed. The last phase of the progressive movement was the movement to life adjustment and this ran down because it failed to keep pace with the changes in American society.

The period of the great immigrations was over. It was no longer necessary to strive for a homogeneous culture—an American way of life had been established. The burgeoning economy was being harnessed to vast new sources of energy and the age of automation was on its way. A new outlook and new teaching was required for a new age. Once again it was necessary to delineate what only the school could do; what must be done because nothing else could do it. This had been the attack that the essentialist school had made on the progressive movement in the early 1950's. Education they categorised as intellectual training given through academic disciplines and true education as learning to think in the academic disciplines. The schools they said were trying to do too much and were thereby neglecting their essential tasks. Russian space successes gave fuel to these critical fires and a renewed impetus for a reassessment of the academic tasks of the school at both elementary and secondary levels. As early as 1950 a report from the National Education Association called *The Education of the*

Gifted pointed out that a democracy had a responsibility for providing the best possible service for its academically gifted members. International events in space accelerated work on the lines it advocated. Then in 1958 the National Defense Education Act made available from federal sources funds for the training and retraining of teachers and the equipping and re-equipping of schools for the teaching of science and languages. But for some this new orientation was insufficient. The diehards wanted the end of the comprehensive idea with instead a separate provision for gifted pupils in a way entirely alien to the American tradition.

At this point came Dr. J. B. Conant with his series of reports:

> *The American High School Today* (1959)
> *Education in the Junior High School Years* (1960)
> *Slums and Suburbs* (1961)
> *The Education of American Teachers* (1963)

It is not invalid, despite the different provenance, to compare these reports with those from the Central Advisory Council, especially for this study the reports connected with the names of Crowther and Newsom. What should be noted is the unimpeachable academic background which the author—first Professor of Chemistry and later President at Harvard for 20 years until 1953, and then for a time ambassador in West Germany—brought to his appraisal of the educational system, in a country where there has sometimes been a lack of respect between educationists and academics. The books are in fact pieces of operational research carried out by a team headed by Conant. Because he is solely responsible the findings and recommendations are expressed more forthrightly than a committee document is always able to do. Some researchers have tried to measure the effects of Conant's work and it has been suggested they have not been very influential. Thirty-three high school principals in East Massachusetts were circulated concerning Conant's proposals. Of the 726 possible responses, 487 were positive indicating the suggestion was already implemented, 287 were negative and only 14 answers attributed an introduction due to Conant's advocacy.

Nevertheless, it is remarkable, as the sequel shows, how many of his recommendations are being implemented. Charged with being prophetic John Dewey claimed that he was merely sensitive to changes that were occurring in education, and when he proclaimed them was credited with bringing them into existence. Could it be that Conant has the same kind of feeling at the organisational level?

For the upper secondary school the books *The American High School Today* and *Slums and Suburbs* are the most relevant. Really they are a pair of complementary studies for in the first Conant was considering the high school in the small-sized independent communities where, because of size, the institution was necessarily comprehensive, while in the second and later report he looked at the variety of high schools in the major urban areas. His first study led him to a statement of faith in the high school. "If all high schools functioned as well as some, the education of American youth would be satisfactory except for the study of foreign languages and the guidance of the more able girls." This testimony was accompanied by a series of twenty-two recommendations aimed at increasing the efficiency of the schools and the efficacy of the education they give. Before considering these proposals it is useful to look at some factual records showing *What High School Pupils Study**—the results of a national survey of pupils graduating from high school in 1958.

Seventy per cent of all pupils graduated with at least $16\frac{1}{2}$ units and 9% of the upper quartile had more than $20\frac{1}{2}$ Carnegie units.

The typical pupil in the upper quartile had 80% of the credits in the five main academic fields of English, social studies, foreign languages, mathematics and science, and in the lower quartile the typical pupil had 66% of credits in the same areas.

The median pupil had the following list of credits:

English	$3\frac{1}{4}$–4	Foreign languages	0 –1
Social studies	$2\frac{1}{4}$–3	Business studies	$\frac{1}{4}$–1
Mathematics	$1\frac{1}{4}$–2	Physical education	$\frac{1}{4}$–1
Science	$1\frac{1}{4}$–2		

* U.S. Office of Health, Education and Welfare, 1962.

with others in elective subjects. Health education and art were subjects earning credit for both sexes, while home economics and industrial arts were often included in the list for girls and boys respectively. (It is useful to remember that the median pupil in England and Wales would have attended a modern school and would be unlikely to be still a pupil. This median pupil is one expected to obtain grade 4 in the C.S.E. examination at 16. Here have been listed his counterpart's achievements in the U.S. 1 or 2 years later.)

Of all pupils:

> 81% had some credits in business studies.
> 18% had 3 credits in business studies.
> 60% had some credits in physical education.
> 38% had some credits in home economics.
> 33% had some credits in industrial arts.
> 43% had some credits in music.
> 25% had some credits in art.
> 24% had some credits in health education.
> 7% had some credits in driver education.

The last figure is surprisingly low when one considers all the publicity concerning driver education in the States. Even for the 7% the credit was often only $\frac{1}{2}$ or $\frac{1}{4}$ of a unit.

For academic subjects there is the following list.

Of all pupils:

> 91% had more than 3 credits in English.
> 83% had more than 2 credits in social studies.
> 42% had more than 3 credits in social studies.
> 72% had more than 1 credit in mathematics.
> 42% had more than 2 credits in mathematics.
> 20% had more than 3 credits in mathematics.
> 72% had more than 1 credit in science.
> 35% had more than 2 credits in science.
> 13% had more than 3 credits in science.
> 50% had some credit in a foreign language.

15% had more than 2 credits in a foreign language.
7% had more than 3 credits in a foreign language.

Table 19 of proportions of programme time per subject is a useful one:

TABLE 19.

	Pupils in the upper quartile %	Pupils in the lower quartile %	All pupils %
English	24	24	24
Social studies	17	19	18
Mathematics	15	10	13
Science	14	11	12
Foreign language	10	2	6
Business	7	12	10
Home economics industrial arts	5	10	7
Others	8	12	10
Total	100	100	100

These figures are averages and it must be remembered that many subjects in the curriculum are lost by this kind of treatment.

In the upper quartile the median pupil obtains between $17\frac{1}{2}$ and $18\frac{1}{4}$ units by graduation. This average of $4\frac{1}{2}$ to $4\frac{3}{4}$ credits per year is not a heavy programme load. Dr. Conant had recommendations aimed at altering this. This study also confirmed one of the caveats to his underwriting of the high school as a success story—the lack of interest in foreign languages by the able pupils as well as the less able. Evidence to a congress committee showed that over half the high schools in the U.S.A. offered no modern foreign language.

It is useful at this point to turn in detail to Conant's findings and recommendations. In his first report he investigated high schools in which more than half the pupils complete their education on graduation and where the graduating class was at least one hundred. Other schools he considered too small and he wanted increased efforts at consolidation. The closure and amalgamation of small high schools is a continuing process but the attainment of viable size by Conant's standards will be long delayed. His team worked out a check-list of points for consideration. In particular they were concerned with the adequacy of the general education (cf. the Harvard report); the availability and quality of the non-academic elective programmes, and the special arrangements for the academically talented looking carefully at the top 16% of the ability range and also at a more select group of high-fliers. His cautious commendation has already been quoted. In detail he called for a number of developments, but only the main ones can be considered here. In the required (obligatory) programme of English and social studies he asked for ability grouping with each individual's curriculum based on counselling. He decided a six-period day gave too much rigidity to programmes and asked for at least six periods in addition to one period for driver education and/or physical education and considered seven or eight periods of 45 minutes each might be preferable, giving the flexibility necessary for the most able 15–20% to take a series of more academically searching programmes giving 20 or more units of credit in 4 years without cutting them off from participation in programmes in music and the arts. He also emphasised the advantages of 4-year courses in *one* modern language and the provision of courses for varied abilities in science. Special attention to the very slow readers was another recommendation. In the twelfth grade he wanted free discussion, in heterogeneous groups, of current topics in a course broadly entitled American government—a plea in direct line with the historic role of the high school, the Americanisation and integration of a diversity of peoples.

When he came to consider large cities Conant argued against the establishment of selective academic high schools because he believed the comprehensive high school was doing an effective job. However, in *Slums and Suburbs* he appears to commend the "lighthouse" function of schools in college-oriented suburbs and presses for all high schools to establish advanced placement programmes in, at least, one subject. Also he wants a reappraisal of vocational content, asking in particular for industrial arts (cf. our woodwork and metalwork) to be restricted mainly to the junior high school.

All Conant's recommendations were a responsible call for progress to be made by building on what was already in existence. There were other voices calling for a more radical change—for a denial of the American heritage of comprehensive provision and the institution of *élitism* on a European model.* Admiral Rickover was one of these extremists. The period since the late fifties has seen very much more attention paid to academic education. Even before Conant's first report, the National Defense Education Act (1958)—its emotive title is significant—had made available, as already noted, federal funds on the basis of a dollar for each state dollar for a variety of programmes including:

> Instruction in mathematics, science and languages, including teacher re-training;
> Fellowships for advanced studies;
> Research in visual aids;
> Language development services, including language laboratories;
> Guidance and counselling;
> Area vocational services.

One result has been a large number of projects re-examining the content of the curriculum and suggesting new approaches for schools (cf. the establishment of the Curriculum Study Group by the Ministry here in 1962 and the subject reappraisal which have proceeded with funds from the Nuffield Foundation). First into the field were the science subjects which already had an administrative framework in the National Science Foundation of 1950. In 1958 the Biology Curriculum Study began, in 1960 the Physics Study, and in chemistry there was the Chemical Education

---

* See Rickover, H. G., *Swiss Schools and Ours*, Little, Brown & Co., Boston, 1962.

Materials Study and Chemical Bond approach. Project English began in 1961 and Project Social Studies in 1963. In mathematics there were a number of experimental projects and in many areas there were advanced placement programmes, successful completion of which meant a direct entry into sophomore year at college. By 1960–1 13,000 students in 600 schools were taking advantage of this provision which brings post-graduate work a year earlier. Everywhere there was an increased emphasis on academic content, a growing concern about creativity and the ability to think and an emphasis on individual differences.

As a sample of the changes taking place, the position of biology can be considered.* Before the reappraisal the biology taught was mainly descriptive. It was the summer of 1960 before the study was really under way. Seventy biologists at a summer school wrote preliminary texts which were tested in 100 schools during the 1960–1 session. That summer they were revised and tested in 500 schools, and in 1962 a further revision was followed by even wider testing and try-out. Final versions were then written and were ready for the start of the 1963 session. Three alternative approaches were available, viz:

1. Biological science: an inquiry into life. This was a balanced course with an emphasis on genetics and evolution.
2. High school biology. This course dealt especially with populations and communities.
3. Biological science: molecules to man. The emphasis here was on a molecular and cellular approach.

Each course had its supporting supplementary materials, manuals and laboratory aids and there were also 120 half-hour coloured films each with its explanatory manual. Whereas previous courses had emphasised content, these were invitations to inquiry with the student in the role of participant in discovery, instead of a mere recipient of knowledge. Students were led to be critical and the material dealt with was modern, up to date and exciting. A

* Roberts, M. B. V., A revolution in biology teaching, *Education*, 31 December 1965.

British teacher from a public school attempting to appraise the success of the scheme found it was eliciting a good response from some students though others confessed to confusion. Some of the approaches demanded too great a background of physics and chemistry for 16-year-olds and the most successful appeared to be the more traditional high school biology. However, good teachers were achieving good results with any approach and this really seemed to be the crux. Summing up Mr. Roberts thought the courses would be admirable for second- or third-year sixth-formers in England—a good indication of their academic level. With similar changes in other subject areas the charge of unacademic against American schools will have to be dropped.

A continual criticism of the high school and comprehensive education has been directed to its alleged tendency towards levelling down and catering for the average. The present emphasis on individual differences is an attempt to counter this. Sometimes this has taken the form of homogeneous grouping or curriculum tracking. The provision of three versions of the biology scheme allows for this. Often though attention to individual differences has meant enrichment courses leading to advanced placement rather than earlier admission. (It is interesting to remember that in the U.S.S.R. there is a provision of advanced courses in universities and institutes for capable pupils from the upper secondary schools designed to accelerate progress in mathematics and science.) Attention to individual differences has led also to more special attention for the slow learners. There was concern, too, over the "drop-outs" from school, a problem which varied from area to area, depending on socio-economic and ethnic factors. A survey in March 1963 revealed that of the 16–21 age group out of school or college 1 in 7 were also out of work. Reismann, well known for his study of the culturally deprived, had called for increased attention to styles of education which would fit in with working class culture and in the early sixties some headway was being made with work-and-school and school-and-community projects. In August 1963 President Kennedy inaugurated a campaign against "drop-outs" from the senior high school and many who were unemployed returned to school for further training. This concern was continued by the Elementary and Secondary Education Act of 1965 which made federal aid available for low income families with children between the ages of 5 and 17. Recognising the positive correlation between poverty and ignorance, it made aid available for families with annual incomes below $2000.

Thus since 1957 and the first Sputnik, schools, largely saddled with the blame, have responded quickly to the crash programmes in mathematics, science and languages and the accelerated programmes in the humanities so that a commentator could write:* "by the end of the decade (i.e. 1960) there was calculus in the senior high, foreign languages in the junior high, modern mathematics in the elementary school, and vocational education in the doghouse". This was his picturesque way of calling attention to the relative lack of attention being paid to vocational education in a time of academic advance. It was a relative lack only for the 1958 Education Act had included appropriations for area vocational education. Harris went on to develop the need for reappraisal of the vocational offerings, and the need for real attention to be paid to the service industries including distribution, repair and maintenance and a reduction of effort in machine shop provision and vocational agriculture which were becoming outmoded. These activities were the original vocational provision under the Morrill Act and the Smith–Hughes Act (1917) which had included aid for organised classes, at less than college level, in agriculture, home economics and industrial arts. Later the field of aid was widened to include commercial pursuits, and in 1946 nursing was also added. Thus vocational streams, which were federally aided, grew up in the high schools and in the larger urban communities there were separate vocational high schools. Over 400 separate vocational high schools were in operation in the early 1960's. Some were of very high quality as Conant points out in *Slums and Suburbs* where he considers this problem, but others were less worthy of regard. The notorious school described in *Blackboard Jungle* was one of these vocational high schools. The

* Harris, N. C., Redoubled efforts, in *Phi Delta Kappan*, April 1965.

TABLE 20. ENROLMENT IN VOCATIONAL CLASSES (000's)

Year	Total full and part time	Agriculture	Trades distributive	Home economics	Trades and industry	Practical nursing	Area vocational
1918	164	15	—	31	118	—	—
1940	2291	765	130	819	758	—	—
1960	3768	796	304	1588	939	40	101

figures in Table 20 show the enrolments in vocational classes near the beginning and end of our period, with the 1918 figures included to show the progress involved.

In 1960 about 20% of American youth were receiving full-time vocational education. There were also a number of technical high schools which included less shop work in their curriculum and taught generally at a more sophisticated academic level. A typical vocational high school programme was as shown in Table 21.

TABLE 21.

10th grade age 15+ years	Periods	11th grade	Periods	12th grade	Periods
Shop practice	20	Shop practice	20	Shop practice	20
English	4	English	4	English	4
Maths/ science	4	Mathematics	4	Mathematics	4
Drawing	4	Science	4	Applied drawing	2
History/ citizenship	4	History/ citizenship	4	Science	2
Health education and military science	4	Health education and military science	4	History/ citizenship	4
				Health education	4
	40		40		40

The forty periods per week are of 45 minutes' duration.

Conant, in *Slums and Suburbs*, came out categorically in favour of the educational experience of youth in an urbanised and industrialised community fitting their subsequent employment. However, he wanted vocational courses in grades 11 and 12 not to take more than half the available time and certainly not to replace the essential academic work. He was, nevertheless, convinced that practical courses were essential and wanted general high schools in cities where often practical courses were lacking, because of the parallel provision of vocational school, to institute auto-mechanics shops, and also electronics shops so that all adolescents should have practical opportunities relevant to the times.

National interest in vocational education was evinced by the Vocational Education Act of 1963. Just as there had been a call for separate academic schools so now those interested in vocational education began to call for more separate vocational schools, but balanced voices were not slow to point out the changing vocational structure, and the increasing employment opportunities in jobs requiring a more advanced educational level, so that soon over half the available jobs would have a cognitive content which made 2 years of education *beyond* high school desirable, if not imperative. Arguing like this, they contended that high school education would not be terminal but only preparatory and separate schools would mean a division at 15 years which was not soundly based but merely pre-destination (cf. our tripartite separation at 11 + and the arguments against it). Analysis of job opportunities showed that in the early 1960's in one community only 26 out of 207 industrial firms were willing to employ new high school graduates, i.e., 17- and 18-year-olds. The argument then goes on to develop the case for post-high-school occupational education in the junior community college, suggesting that all common learnings are not complete by the end of high school. So the junior college, which in 1922 began as a 2-year course of strictly collegiate grade to prepare students for transfer at a post-sophomore stage, and has since in some areas undertaken the major responsibility for technical and vocational education (currently Californian junior colleges have over one hundred occupational centred curricula) is now being regarded as potentially comprehensive in spirit and operation, making provision for academic and occupational education in a community setting. It is inexpensive to attend and allows a late decision on a career to be taken. Thus comprehensiveness beyond the upper secondary stage is coming into being. Is it really beyond the upper secondary stage? At the beginning of this chapter the bivalent attitude to the status of the junior college was noted. Sometimes the 2 years are labelled grades 13 and 14. However, the National Defense Education Act of 1958 deliberately excludes grades 13 and 14 from the definition of secondary school and emphasises that federal money is available for area vocational courses at "less than College level". This phrase, which is repeated from the historic Smith–Hughes Act (1917) dealing with vocational courses, is intended to keep the aided training at technician level rather than allow it to extend to professional level, because it is technicians who are in short supply. But in the rush to establish courses at a time of national need (after all Sputnik was up) the theoretical niceties of the wording were not strictly adhered to in practice. Some courses were set up to cover the senior high school proper and others as follow-on courses from high school in grades 13 and 14. By 1961 out of 120,000 in the new area vocational courses about 45,000 were in the junior colleges and another 3000 in the junior sections of 4-year colleges. So the demarcation becomes blurred.

The period since the war has seen many changes in the senior high school. Can they be summed up in a single paragraph? Aims concerning good citizenship held at the start of the period are now seen as life outcomes of education rather than as outcomes totally realisable in school. The mass media have taken over some of the roles formerly assigned to the school, and schools have begun to reconsider what their unique contribution can be. In this they have been helped by work on the clarification of educational objectives.* This has focused more attention on the individual and the need to get him to think for himself. Academic offerings have been re-oriented to this end and tracking at these upper levels has been accepted within the framework of the comprehensive principle which seems now to be extending beyond the traditional high school limits. If the school did lower its average levels to admit everybody however diverse their background, it has now begun the even more difficult process of raising standards for everyone.

---

* Bloom, B. S. (ed.), *Taxonomy of Educational Objectives*: (1) *Cognitive Domain*, Michigan, 1956; (2) *Affective Domain*, 1964.

CHAPTER 8

France—Restructuring

THE most exciting book on French education to appear in recent years is Louis Cros' *L'Explosion scolaire* translated as *The Explosion in the Schools*.* So apt is the title that the idea has also been used for the 1965 Year Book of Education entitled *The Education Explosion* which shows just how world wide is this phenomenon. However, it is not only the title, but the arresting diagrams and well-chosen tables of figures accompanying the commendably slim text, which all contribute a sense of the urgent need for a planned change. Cros' second chapter translated as "The Breaking Up of Structures" would make a good sub-title for this chapter on upper secondary education in France. M. Cros, in carrying his projections into the future and estimating what is likely, on the basis of the social, economic and demographic trends he has been analysing, to be happening in 1970 as compared with the beginning of the century, writes, ". . . sixteen times as many pupils in the *lycée* . . . means must also be adjusted to the ends . . . . Physical phenomena often change their nature when they change their scale; human phenomena do the same. A prolonged education spread out through an entire population has as its effect the breaking up of structures which were conceived in the past for entirely different needs and goals." As continued education becomes appropriate for the many, as it was once for the few, so the form of that education must be changed and expanded if it is to be appropriate in the new circumstances. This chapter aims to record and analyse the changes that have occurred in one sector in the 20 years from the end of the war, and since change in French education seems to be continuing—proposals vitally

* Cros, L., *The Explosion in the Schools*, Sevpen, Paris, 1963.

affecting the academic sections of the upper secondary school were announced in 1965—to finish with a forward look.

The structure of an educational system can be illustrated diagrammatically and Figs. 4 and 5, one depicting the state of affairs in the early years after the war and the other adapted from a 1965 publication* showing the current position, make plain the magnitude of the change which has taken place. A system which was

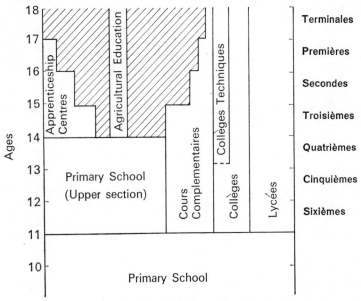

FIG. 4. France: the pre-reform structure.

characterised by longitudinal divisions by type has been largely altered to one with latitudinal division into more discrete groups according to age. The old system implied selection, which expressed differently may be seen as elimination. In the new structure the keyword is orientation, which is really direction-finding based on guidance, and the problem becomes one of the distribution of students to various courses. A warning needs to be given.

* Le Particular, *Guide Pratique de l'enseignement*, Paris, 1965.

Rectangular diagrams of this type suggest a simplicity which may be illusory and an equality of parts which is not a true picture. They need to be buttressed by explanation and statistics to give a reality to the pictorial representation.

Immediately after World War II the upper academic secondary school was only the last 3 years of a 7-year school which started at the age of 11 in the *sixièmes*. The course throughout the 3 years was a general one, carrying the subjects thought to be an essential

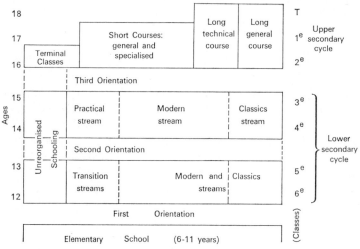

FIG. 5. France: the reformed pattern.

part of French culture through the first part of the *baccalauréat* at the age of 17 to the second part a year later. Although there was some specialisation leading to an examination in three parts, in essence the examination, which controlled the teaching, was a general one with specialisation a matter of emphasis and not a concentration on a few subjects. The options were:

(a) Latin and Greek;
(b) Latin and modern languages;
(c) Modern languages and science.

The examination was both written and oral, the written part being eliminatory. All three sections had written papers in French composition and mathematics, in addition to papers in the main subjects which gave the sections their distinguishing mark; and oral examinations in at least one modern language; history and geography; and physical science. So the classicists carried mathematics, physical science, a modern language and history and geography and the scientists carried on their own language, a modern language and history and geography. Although the content of the course was a heavy load, the emphasis in the written examination was on the presentation of the material and understanding. Following the first part of the *bachot* was the terminal year, once again of a general nature with a separation into two parts in either the philosophical stream or the mathematical stream. Primarily the year aimed at giving an overall view of the knowledge already gained but it also contained a considerable body of knowledge to be learned. The second part of the *baccalauréat*, like the first, led to both written and oral examinations in a wide range of subjects. The classicists who took the philosophical option had to prepare for a written test in physical and natural science as well as to write, in a 4-hour paper, a dissertation of a philosophical nature, and be examined orally in history and geography, a modern language, philosophy, and mathematics and cosmography. On the other hand the mathematical option required preparation for a philosophical dissertation, albeit less lengthy than in the *classe de philo* and also examinations in a modern language and history and geography.

It is obvious from the statement of what is entailed that this is a heavy and demanding course. Just how heavy and demanding it could be is emphasised in an interesting novel *Degrés* (translated *Degrees*) by Michel Butor, published in 1962. The main character, Pierre Vernier, a teacher of history and geography in a Paris *lycée*, decided to record faithfully and in detail, the complete life and actions of one of his pupils who is working in the second class (16–17 years). As part of his assignment he decides he ought to attempt to keep up with the work that this form is doing and know what his colleagues are teaching. The novel describes how he tries to do this and the effort it entails. It has been said that only in fiction is one able to tell the real truth. A few quotations from the book help to give the flavour of upper secondary academic work.

> "To complete this description of our class, I must begin a serious study of everything that can be learned by its members."

First he had to purchase the necessary text-books.

> "The next Wednesday I had in my brief case that Physics text-book for the second class, and its twin the Chemistry text-book as well as the Physics text-book for seniors, which I had also bought that morning. . . . I also had the Italian text-book that Monsieur Bonnini uses.
>
> I brought this entire harvest back to my apartment and put it on my big desk beside the pile of school books I had already bought to prepare these notes, the *Sixteenth Century French Authors* and its brothers, those of the seventeenth, eighteenth and nineteenth centuries, and the *Anthology of English Literature* Monsieur Bailley uses.
>
> I took my own class books *Medieval Europe* for the fifth class and the *New Course in Geography* for your class, with the photograph of a valley bordered with terraced rice paddies, *Contemporary Civilisation* for the classics seniors, and walked towards the *lycée*."

M. Butor introduces a number of vignettes of lessons into the novel and many of these are very revealing both in respect of method and content. Illustrating method the following is worth quoting:

> "Well, Abel will you read? I don't think I've heard the sound of your voice yet."
>
> "This done, he, with all his heart submitted his study to the discretion of Ponocrates. . . ."
>
> "Stop there for the moment, and let me see if you've understood what you have just read. Let's start at the beginning: analyse that first expression, that first little word: *this*: give me a grammatical analysis of that word, if you please."
>
> "It's a demonstrative adjective. . . ."
>
> "If it's an adjective there must be a word it modifies."
>
> "It modifies *done*."
>
> "And what is *done* then?"
>
> "A verb. . . ."
>
> "And what function does it have in a sentence, if you please? You're not going to tell me that *done* functions as a verb—what verb could it be? No, the verb goes with *he*, in the next expression. By the way, who is he?"
>
> "It must be Pantagruel."

"No, not Pantagruel, Gargantua! We're talking about Gargantua now. *This* is not an adjective; it's a pronoun and *done* is a past participle; it's as if Rabelais said: once this thing was done. Now what is the thing he did? . . ."

Turning to content:

On Monday morning, M. Bailley, having collected his classics senior's homework, a translation of De Quincey's chapter on Coleridge in his *Recollections of the Lake Poets* . . . (then) spent the whole hour telling them about Coleridge, and it was as if he were talking about an old friend, asking them to look for the next day at the first six stanzas of the *Rime of the Ancient Mariner*. . . . Notice the archaism of all the terms of this title. If we were to translate this as merely: the story of the old sailor (as you will find it in many French editions) you lose all the colour, all the unusual flavour of the words.

Two snatches from Pierre Vernier's own geography lessons are worth quoting too. In our system geography is only taken by specialists by the time the 15–16-year-old age group is reached and often it has been dropped since the fourth form. In France the best academics all carry it in the *seconde* and *première* classes and in the latest revision of the curriculum (see Tables 27 and 28) all but those proceeding to the technological *baccalauréat* carry it in the terminal class.

One of them is from his own recollection and the other as remembered by a pupil.

First, Pierre Vernier:

"On the floor above I was talking about the American Mid-West before moving on to the Rocky Mountain region, the old Far West, the Colorado desert, the various national parks, California, with Los Angeles and its Sunset Boulevard, with San Francisco and its Golden Gate, its marvellous bridges and its trolley cars climbing the hills, and finally Alaska describing its gold rush with reference to Chaplin's film;"

and second, a pupil:

"During the afternoon after having listened to you comment on the two maps of isotherms—January, July—in our text-book, showing us how these more or less parallel lines were curved by the continental masses, pointing out these two regions of extreme heat, in the Sahara and Central Asia in summer, and the region of extreme cold, in Siberia in winter bounded by the isotherm of January −40°C;

then, on the next page, these two juxtaposed photographs of landscapes of the same latitude, a Nova Scotian village buried in snow, the pines on the beach at Arcachon in the sunshine, adding parenthetically that for these pictures to be really informative it should have been stated at what time of the year they had been taken;
lastly, explaining the phenomena of inversions of temperature."

Pierre Vernier had problems with his work and eventually it was too much for him.

"I'm going slower and slower because of the effort demanded by the subjects my colleagues teach: few teachers, believe me, would be capable of going through the Second Class again."

This last sentence from M. Butor, is revealing, underlining the heavy load of work entailed in the upper secondary classes. This novel gives the spirit of the *lycée* in a way no educational treatise can, even though the method of its telling, and some of the content, makes it a less-than-easy novel to read. What is clear from both this novel and the curriculum previously described are the main principles behind the work of the *lycée*, principles which can be traced back at least 600 years.

Some understanding of these principles is essential background for an appreciation of changes that are taking place in French education. Principles that can be shown to have an identity extending over such a long period of time can hardly be expected to be jettisoned lightly and certainly the upper secondary programmes in 1966 owe much to history.

When, in the thirteenth century, the University of Paris was growing up with students in the age range 13–20 years, the arts faculty was a preliminary course for all students, with specialised courses in law, theology and medicine following a broad general course touching all the available knowledge of the time. The teaching method was a close study of the text followed by close argument, discussion and refutation. Thus at this early stage two principles could be distinguished:

1. the belief in the value of a broad general content for all students to a fairly advanced stage;
2. intellectual training based on a close study of authors.

Throughout French educational history these two strands can be identified. During the Renaissance the encyclopaedists claimed that the curriculum of the medieval schoolman was too narrow. Rabelais wanted his pupils to study everything. Knowledge was of supreme importance with no time to be wasted on dialectics. This was really underlining the importance of a broad general education. Concurrently the humanists were emphasising the importance of style, form and taste and the ability to discourse in a correct, elegant manner. With this background of Renaissance thought, the Jesuits were organising a system of schools which were consequently thorough-goingly classical with an emphasis, first, on content and second, on form and style.

As events worked out these emphases were repeated by Napoleon in the system of schools set up after the Revolution. The intellectuals preparing for revolution had so many reforming plans in education that when, in 1795, the opportunity for change came major changes were made too rapidly and muddle and inefficiency resulted, bringing a sense of disillusionment. A report, in 1799, condemned much of what had been done. At this time came Napoleon, and, in a climate of conservative reaction against the early excesses and failures, was set up the framework of the system of education which largely remains today.

The structure of secondary education was centralised and logically constructed. At the apex was the Imperial University under its Grand Master who has become the Minister of Public Instruction. The country was divided into a number of regions, called *académies*, each with its *recteur* and its inspectors. Schools (*lycées*) were founded through state machinery but later others (*collèges*) were founded by the local community though still subject to control by the state machinery.

The content of the course was prescribed by the central authority—to protect the right of the individual to participate in the national culture. In reaction against the modern curriculum of the central schools of the 1790's, the prescription was of good solid traditional subject matter for the first 5 years from the age of 10 followed by a choice in the sixth year between philosophy and mathematics. Later a seventh year, mainly devoted to philosophy, was added and some science was introduced at the upper end of the school.

Throughout the nineteenth and early twentieth centuries, there were differences of opinion and quarrels because of the gap between the mainly classical curriculum and modern knowledge and needs. But the quarrels were not really on fundamentals. Almost everyone believed in a broad general culture without much specialisation aiming at a body of knowledge coupled with the ability to reason and to express thoughts logically. The adjusters aimed to do this through modern studies and science, so any changes that were made were marginal rather than fundamental, and, in the main, the Napoleonic pattern survived.

Elementary education grew up in the nineteenth century after the state system of secondary education and so there was a carry-over of ideals and intentions from the one to the other, and elementary education found itself with the double aim of attempting to give a sum total of knowledge while at the same time cultivating exact thought, alert intelligence and good habits of mind. To try to realise this with a low leaving age was a formidable aim. (At present the leaving age is 14, though it should become 16 in 1967. However, there is a possibility that the date of implementation will be altered.) To offset this difficulty supplementary courses grew up in the elementary sector (*cours complementaires*) to give a longer 5-year course. From this sector some pupils went on to *écoles normales* to train for primary teaching. In these ways students in the elementary sector began to participate in upper secondary education.

Others leaving the elementary school continued their education in a vocational context and to this aspect it is now necessary to turn.

Vocational education has a much less venerable history than the academic side. There were early attempts in the eighteenth century and also in the ill-fated central schools of the revolution which were so soon superseded by the Napoleonic *lycées*. Later an international exhibition in Paris in 1878 revealed weaknesses in industry (as had the 1851 exhibition in London for the British) and more attention was paid to vocational education in the years which followed. However, the greatest progress came after the *Loi Astier* of 1919 under which young workers in certain industries were required to attend part-time schooling during working hours until they reached the age of 18. This schooling was financed by an apprenticeship tax on industry amounting to 0·4% of the wages bill. From this beginning apprenticeship centres grew up, and have proliferated, especially since World War II, to cater for workers in industry and trade. They are now called *collèges d'enseignement technique* (C.E.T.). The latest figures show 900 C.E.T.s with 347,000 full-time and 30,000 part-time students in September 1966. Although there is some part-time attendance, the majority of students attend full time for a course which has been described as being half way between a factory and a school. The course fills 40 hours of class time (see Table 22). General academic education accounts for about 10 hours per week and includes French, mathematics, history, geography, hygiene and some citizenship education. There is also 4 hours of physical education and the greater part of the remainder of the course (about five-eighths of the total time) is spent in the workshop, but there is a little vocational drawing and art, and some domestic science for the girls.

At the end of the 3-year course there is an examination, which passed successfully gives the award of the *certificat d'aptitude professionelle* (C.A.P.). The same award can be gained by students in works' schools and also by those actually working their apprenticeships with either a small firm or in a large industry. Some people contend that apprenticeship training on the job is advantageous because the youngsters are actually involved in production and learn methods which are economically sound. The methods are always up to date because in actual production change has to be introduced to keep the industry profitable. An alternative view insists the technical school is better because, where output is not the basic concern, training can give a really basic understanding of processes followed by specialisation in a skill. Such a training,

TABLE 22. CURRICULUM IN APPRENTICESHIP CENTRES
(now schools of technical education or *collèges d'enseignement technique*.)

	1st year		2nd year		3rd year	
	Boys	Girls	Boys	Girls	Boys	Girls
Academic education:						
Ethics and civics	1	1	—	—	1	1
French	3	3	3	2	2	2
History	1	1	1	1	1	1
Geography	1	1	1	1	1	1
Arithmetic, geometry	3	3	3	3	3	2
Hygiene	2	2	2	2	2	2
Total	11	11	10	9	10	9
Non-academic:						
Domestic science	—	3	—	3	—	3
Vocational drawing	2	3	2	2	3	3
Art	2	—	1	1	1	—
Technology and workshop	20	18	22	20	22	20
Physical education	4	4	4	4	4	4
Grand total	39	39	39	39	40	39

with proper attention to fundamentals in the early stages gives, it is claimed, more flexibility. In a technical school too, the practice and theory can be integrated to give a better balanced training. A works' school is sometimes claimed to combine the advantages of a C.E.T. (*collège d'enseignement technique*) and on-the-job training. Certainly it is likely to be up to date but it may become too commercial and specialised, and lack the opportunity of giving the more all-round training possible in a purpose-built centre.

In addition to this training at the apprenticeship level for crafts-men and trainees, a number of other institutions have grown up to provide vocational education for the next higher level, broadly the technician grade. Technical secondary schools and national vocational schools lead to the technician grade or higher, and have longer courses than the C.E.T.s, with more emphasis on theoretical work and less time occupied by workshop practice. Holding an intermediate position are the vocational sections of the *collèges d'enseignement général* (previously *cours complementaires* which followed the elementary school). They conduct courses mainly of a commercial type but also for some industrial jobs. Crowning this variety of provision in this upper secondary sector are the technical sections in the more academic schools which give a training which can lead to posts at the technological level.

The relative importance of the different branches in the voca-tional sector can be gauged by the following figures for enrolment. (Not all courses are of the same duration.)

TABLE 23. ENROLMENTS IN VOCATIONAL EDUCATION
1960–1
(Old names in 1961: renaming has occurred since)

Apprenticeship centres: full time	202,318
part time	21,719
Technical secondary schools ⎫	
National vocational schools ⎬	149,791
Trade schools ⎭	
Cours complementaires (vocational courses)	54,607
Technical sections in *lycées*	32,352
	460,787

So far the picture presented of the upper secondary sector shows a sharp division between the traditional academic course, on the one hand, and a variety of vocational courses, mainly growing out from the elementary sector, on the other, although a few voca-tional courses are connected with the more academic schooling. In the period since the war the progressive element in French education has been attempting to integrate the two divisions into a unified system. The demand for unification can be clearly seen in the programmes of Les Compagnons de l'Université Nouvelle after World War I and in the report of the Langevin–Wallon Commission of 1947. But not much progress was achieved until the advent of de Gaulle in 1958. During the Fifth Republic a greatly accelerated rate of change has been generated and proposals have been manifold. Present proposals aim to keep pupils working together until the age of 15 years in broadly undifferentiated courses with the possibility of interchange at various stages. After 15 years there will be a wide range of courses offering something for everyone—a demanding academic course, a demanding technical course as well as part-time vocational education with some general education.

The very latest proposals detailed in 1965 adumbrate even further reforms of the upper secondary academic course. The remainder of this chapter will describe the present outline which is gradually being implemented and mention the effect which these newest proposals will have on the 15–18 year age group in the *lycées*.

The reform of public education promulgated in 1959, and the ensuing arrangements made in 1962, 1963 and 1964 to ensure a proper organisation for it, all have the aim of making education available for all types of differing aptitudes and no longer making provision dependent upon the social criteria of family circumstance or father's profession or on regional differences due to place of birth.

To level up inequalities due to geography a new school map has been drawn—a national development plan for new school building throughout the republic. A recent key article by Monsieur J. Ferrez, Deputy Director at the French Ministry of Education, centres around a map showing on a "departmental" basis, the ratio of the 11–17 age group in secondary school. The differences mapped give point to the title of the article "Regional inequalities in educational opportunity."* M. Ferrez first draws attention to

* Halsey, A. H. (ed.), *Ability and Educational Opportunity*, O.E.C.D., 1961.

an outstanding line of demarcation which splits the country into a southern section showing generally higher ratios in the secondary school, and a northern section with, apart from Paris, generally lower ratios. He writes: "The reasons for this first difference are primarily historical; in early times Roman civilisation spread through Provence and Aquitaine leaving behind a strong cultural tradition whose effects are still evident." He is explaining present-day educational patterns in terms of the Roman Empire! The real reason is in the settlement pattern. In the south of France the basis of settlement is the small town as contrasted with more scattered settlement in the north. Secondary school attendance correlates with distance from school and parents are not eager for their offspring to travel very long distances to secondary school. This, and other regional inequalities, the New School Map is attempting to remedy so that all pupils whatever their social background or geographical location shall receive an appropriate education.

The teaching in the schools is organised in four stages:

A. Nursery or pre-school education catering for ages 2–6.
B. Elementary or primary education for ages 6–11.
C. The first or orientation cycle of secondary education catering for ages 11–15.
D. The second or determinative cycle of secondary education ages 15–18.

Although this latter section is the main concern of this chapter, in order to appreciate the possibilities at the age of 15 it is necessary to understand the options that are available in the lower secondary school, which is a 4-year course, split into two 2-year sections (see Fig. 5). All pupils go into the *sixièmes* which are also called observation classes. After 3 months of general teaching, some opt for the classical section and some for the modern course while the undecided or unready remain in transition classes where they have teaching suited to their ability. From the transition classes it is still possible to enter classical or modern sections (though some of these transfers will not be easy) or to go to the practical section. At the end of the first 2 years four sections are available for the second 2-year division of the lower secondary school. All the sections carry courses in general subjects with options as follows:

1. The classical section. Latin and one modern language are taken in class 4 and Greek or a second modern language is added in class 3.
2. The modern section (a). Here there is extra teaching in French and two modern languages, one of which is begun in class 3.
3. The modern section (b). A less academic course.
4. The practical section. This is a non-specialised pre-vocational education with quite a large allowance of time for practical subjects.

Throughout the 4 years of the lower secondary course pupils and their families are given guidance in the choices which are available at the next stage, so that at the end of the course they are in a position to choose a suitable course at the upper secondary level. The guidance is both educational and vocational: firstly aiming at a right decision concerning the length of course and its general nature, i.e. whether academic or technical; and secondly aiming at an informed choice among the professions and vocations catered for. The main choice is between the short courses and the long courses but within each course is a variety of options.

I. SHORT COURSES

(i) *General Education with an Occupational bias*

This option offers 2 years in a terminal course specially directed to employment in the equivalent of our trainee and craftsman grades. Successful completion of the course merits the award of a general educational certificate (*brevet d'enseignement général*) with the speciality listed.

(ii) *Vocational or Technical Education*

Pupils from any of the four sections of the lower secondary school can enter this course which consists of 2 years of practical and theoretical schooling. There are many internal choices which depend on the branch of industry or commerce which the student proposes to enter. Successful completion leads to the title of *agent technique* or to the *certificat d'aptitude professionelle* (C.A.P.) with an endorsement according to the speciality followed. This short course replaces (and extends) the course previously given in the apprenticeship centres. It is now an integral part of the second cycle and is known as a *collège d'enseignement technique*. (Reform in French education as in England and Wales has been accompanied by a good deal of name-changing.)

(iii) *Agricultural Education*

One of the strengths of France, and an important factor in her ability to make a quick recovery from the ravages of war, is the size and diversity of her agricultural resources. As agriculture becomes increasingly scientific and mechanised, so must the old type of peasant be replaced by an agricultural worker commanding a different, and wider, range of skills. Thus agricultural education is very important. Although it has remained under the control of the Ministry of Agriculture, agricultural education has been given the same kind of face lift as the other sectors of education. A law in 1960, followed by decrees in 1961, has harmonised the system by giving it a similar organisation and nomenclature. However, the specialisation tends to start after 2 years, rather than 4 years, of lower secondary education. Thus starting after the *cinquièmes* a 3-year course leads to the *brevet d'apprentissage agricole* (B.A.A.) with only the final year strictly at the upper secondary level. It can be followed by a further year in an agricultural college leading to the award of the *brevet d'agent technique agricole*. A longer course of 5 years (from the age again of 13 years) in a *lycée agricole* leads to the *brevet de technicien agricole* and this can lead on to further courses and qualifications at the level of higher education.

Communication between the general system of education and agricultural education is maintained by the presence of remove classes at various levels to enable transfers to be made in either direction. Thus transfer is possible to the general course from a *lycée agricole* at the end of the third class.

The target for 1970 (discussed later) shows an expectation of 15% of the age group (about 120,000) in agricultural training of the various types described above.

In this short section on agricultural education both the short and the long courses of education have been mentioned. Now the long courses in general education are considered.

II. LONG COURSES

(i) *General Education*

General education is given in *lycées classiques*, *lycées modernes* and *lycées techniques*. Three years of study lead to the *baccalauréat*, an examination which is in a state of change at present. The examination was in two parts up to and including 1964, but in 1965 the probatory part was discontinued and there are further plans for alteration in the near future. Here the arrangements for 1963–5 will be outlined and a later section will deal with the proposals for 1967–8. As ever, there must be a transition period when old arrangements work their way through the school (cf. the change from 11-year to 10-year school in the U.S.S.R. p.195). As long as the temporary nature of the arrangements described is realised, their consideration will form a useful pointer to the future.

In the first 2 years of this upper secondary school eight different sections are available.

Four sections which include classics are available for pupils leaving the classical section of the third class as follows:

A. This option has Latin, Greek, a modern language and carries a reduced load of mathematics and physical science. It is particularly useful for students who wish to become teachers of classics or follow careers as librarians or architects.

A[1]. This option has no Greek but has Latin, a modern language, mathematics and physical science. It requires exceptional aptitude in both science and letters and can lead equally to careers in either arts or science.

B. In this section the optional subjects are Latin, two modern languages and a reduced course (as compared with A[1]) in mathematics and physical science. It is a useful option for those who wish to teach arts, to enter administration or follow a career in literature.

C. Here there are curricula in Latin, mathematics and physical science. One modern language is obligatory and a second may be taken optionally. It is a useful section for any one who is later (in higher education) to go on to the science side and do research, scientific teaching or become an engineer or agricultural technologist. It is interesting to note how wide a curriculum is recommended for the future science specialist in France.

Two modern sections are available for those from the 3e—either classical or modern side:

M. This section carries two modern languages, mathematics and physical science. It is useful for students wishing to become higher grade technicians; industrial, commercial or agricultural engineers; or take up science teaching.

M[1].In this section students take mathematics, experimental physical and biological science and one obligatory modern language with a second modern language optional. This is a useful option for those entering the medical and associated professions or aiming to become teachers of natural science.

Two technical sections are available for students from technical courses:

T. This option contains one modern language, science and fundamental industrial techniques. It is a useful option for those who intend eventually to become engineers or higher technicians.

T^1. The curriculum includes two modern languages, mathematics and economics and is useful for students who will follow a career in commerce, administration or law, or teach economics or languages.

Of these options A^1 and C are regarded as the most difficult and attract the best pupils. M^1 is sometimes regarded as suitable for a late-developer from a *collège d'enseignement général* (see later) and M is a popular choice as it includes both science and modern languages. The technical options are looked upon as being difficult and as yet are not widely followed because the numbers coming forward from the technical *lycées* are small. Figures for those passing Part I of the *baccalauréat* in 1963 and 1964 are in Table 25.

TABLE 25. PASSES IN THE BACHOT (PART I)

		1963	1964
Classics	A	4,788	5,827
	A^1	1,671	2,133
	B	20,227	22,134
Modern	C	13,829	15,892
	M	26,948	32,582
	M^1	27,365	31,191
Technical	T	5,385	7,326
	T^1	799	1,452
Total		101,012	119,537

1964 figures represent a $17 \cdot 4\%$ increase over 1963. Since 1957 when the total was 54,100 the numbers have more than doubled. But now the first part of the *baccalauréat* has been abolished. Admission to the *terminale* in 1965 was decided for the first time by recommendation of a staff council. The government gave advice on how the staff council were to proceed and the importance to be given to the subjects in the different branches. In the case where a student receives an unfavourable recommendation but feels certain he ought to be able to go forward, a qualifying examination has to be taken.

In the terminal class the teaching gives an introduction to philosophy and prepares in the one year for an examination with five options:

(a) Mathematics. This option is suitable for students from A¹, C, M, M¹ and T in the first 2 years, and is suitable for those aiming for careers in science, medicine or technology, science teaching, architecture, higher posts in agriculture or commercial teaching.

(b) Experimental science. This is suitable for students from M¹ and is a useful option for intending primary teachers, teachers of natural science and para-medical careers.

(c) Philosophy. Students who have followed A and B and are looking for careers in literature, law and the arts or intend to teach arts find this their best option.

(d) Mathematics and technical subjects—students from T who are going to become engineers or proceed to higher technical careers are catered for by this option.

(e) Technical and economic subjects—students from T¹ interested in careers in administration, commerce or law and in teaching economics, history and geography and modern languages can use this option. As yet though it is not very popular as the figures in Table 26 show.

This is an increase of over 14% in one year. However, the increase is not as steep as in Part I. In 1957 the figure for success in Part II was about 49,000. The 1964 figure represents a pass rate of nearly 61%. In 1965 the first year with no probatory examination the pass rate rose to almost 63% but in 1966 fell sharply to 50%.

Although the long general academic courses have been described in terms of the options available, their common content must not be overlooked. The allocations (Table 24) in each of the three classes show exactly how much is common—history, geography, a modern language, mathematics, physical science. In the final

TABLE 26. PART II. BACCALAURÉAT

	1963	1964
Philosophy	31,942	38,351
Mathematics	19,113	23,531
Experimental science	19,632	20,075
Mathematics and technical subjects	4,354	3,645
Technical subjects and economics	433	566
Total	75,474	86,168

year in the philosophical, experimental science and elementary mathematical options everyone carries the same subjects with different weightings. It has always been assumed that the whole range of traditional subjects, taught in a certain kind of way, was necessary for the education of a really cultured person, and this has been the aim of the course in the *lycée*. However, the very latest proposals—the fourth change in this upper secondary academic sector during the life of the Fifth Republic—tend to veer away slightly from the previous very rigid adherence to a general curriculum, though by no means do they espouse the opposite viewpoint—subjectmindedness and the acceptance of the idea that culture is a product of the study of one subject or a related group of subjects.

In 1964 outline plans for a change in the *baccalauréat* and accompanying changes in upper secondary academic and higher education were announced and more detail concerning the proposals was forthcoming in May 1965. It is intended that the new examination will be introduced in 1968, with the intervening years forming a transitional period from what has already been described to the present proposals. From our point of view what is perhaps the most important change is that the new examination will be the crown of the 3-year course from 15 to 18, which will therefore become much more an entity than it has ever been in the past. It also means that it will be more difficult to change direction during the upper secondary course. French academic education has been noted for keeping all options open to a very late stage, in contrast to the usual English sixth form. The projected changes in France seem to lean towards the English position slightly.

At the age of 15 years, students entering academic education will have a choice of three options in their first year—literary, scientific or technical—though there will still be a considerable common content (see Table 27) which will make it possible, though not easy, to change from a literary to a scientific course at the end of the second class.

TABLE 27. LATEST CURRICULAR REFORM—WEEKLY ALLOCATIONS.
SECOND CYCLE—SECONDES

	Literary	Scientific	Technical
French	4	4	3
History, geography	4	4	2
First modern language	3	3	3
Latin or second modern language	3	3	
Greek or second or third modern language	3/4		
Mathematics	3	5	5
Physical sciences	3	5	5
Engineering drawing and workshop technology			12
	23/24	24	30

From the end of the first year there are five options for the last 2 years of the course. In each option the curriculum becomes more specialised in the terminal class, where the five options are (see Table 28).

Section A. A literary option without any science or mathematics in the final year. However, in the first class 6 hours of science and mathematics have been carried and mathematics can be taken as an optional subject in the final year. Modern languages courses instead of classics can also be followed in this section. Where there is sufficient demand, e.g. in large urban areas aesthetic subjects can be combined with this literary option (cf. Sweden's *gymnasium* reform, p. 171).

Section B. This section includes both literary and scientific subjects and carries 4 hours of economics and law in the last 2 years. The 5 hours of philosophy in the terminal class will be slanted in this option towards psychology and sociology. This bridge between the two cultures is favouring C. P. Snow's solution. In this context too the growing importance of economics as an A-level subject in the United Kingdom is worthy of note.

Section C. In the terminal class this carries 10 hours of literary subjects and 15 hours of scientific subjects but the weightings are nearly equal in the *première*. This option corresponds quite closely with the elementary mathematics option of 1965. Optional Latin or Greek can be carried in the terminal class.

Section D. This option corresponds to the 1965 experimental sciences section. To some extent it is weighted towards the biological sciences (3 hours in the *première*, 4 hours in the terminal class). The mathematics in this option will be directed towards statistics.

Section T. This is the technological option with 12 hours of mathematics and physics, 7 hours of literary subjects and 11 hours of engineering drawing and workshop technology so here, as elsewhere, general education has, by no means, been abandoned.

The aim in devising the course has been to give each group a separate identity and to make the course cohere by slanting the philosophical and mathematical content in the direction of the speciality. Certainly the necessity of keeping the scientist literate has not been overlooked for in each course there is a good literary content, but in the terminal class of Section A all the hours are on the arts side—mathematics is dropped at the end of the first class. Optional subjects can be taken to redress any imbalance but this is adding to what is already planned to be a demanding course.

The new arrangements are intended to cater for the wider range of entrants to the academic school and also to provide a

TABLE 28. WEEKLY ALLOCATIONS IN THE LAST TWO YEARS OF
THE ACADEMIC SCHOOL

	A		B		C		D		Tech.	
	P[a]	T[b]	P	T	P	T	P	T	P	T
French	4	3	3	2	3	2	3	2	3	2
Philosophy		8		5		3		3		3
History and geography	4	4	4	4	4	3	4	3	2	
First foreign language	3	3	3	3	3	2	3	2	3	2
Latin or second foreign language	3	3	3	3	3		3			
Greek or second foreign language, third foreign language or basic economics	3	3								
Total arts	17	24	13	17	13	10	13	10	8	7
Mathematics	2		$4\frac{1}{2}$	$4\frac{1}{2}$	7	8	5	6	6	7
Physical sciences	2		2		5	5	4	4	4	5
Natural sciences	2		2			2	3	4		
Economics			4	4						
Engineering drawing and workshop technology									12	11
Total science	6		$12\frac{1}{2}$	$8\frac{1}{2}$	12	15	12	14	22	23
Grand total	23	24	$25\frac{1}{2}$	$25\frac{1}{2}$	25	25	25	24	30	30

[a] P = *premières*.   [b] T = *terminales*.

better basis for work in higher education. Previously the possession
of the *baccalauréat* gave unrestricted access to any faculty at the
University. In future the options will lead to a restricted range of
possibilities and for those not passing the *baccalauréat* with a sufficiently high standard new institutes of higher technical training
(*instituts de formation technique supérieure*, known as I.F.T.S.) are
to be set up, utilising sandwich courses to train higher grade

technicians and executives. In this way those entering the upper academic school will not be cut off from technology.

(ii) *Vocational/Professional Education*

The long professional courses are given in *lycées techniques* or comparable institutions (and in the *lycées agricoles* already mentioned). The function of this type of education is to assure, on the basis of the general education given in the first cycle up to 15 years, that sufficient training is available for the technician grade. In general the course has led to the title *brevet de technicien* at approximately the same level as the *baccalauréat*. There has been much argument concerning its comparative position but in 1965 it was conceded that it was equivalent to the *bachot* in leading to admission to a faculty in the University. The new proposals for the *baccalauréat*, especially Section T, will help to regularise this. The *brevet de technicien* can also lead, after two further years of study, to a qualification as higher technician.

The education in the technical *lycée* or its equivalent has a worth-while cultural content and leads to a number of useful and essential careers. It is meant to attract all those with a practical, scientific bent who want a career in industry, commerce or agriculture. Five different courses are available from the end of the *troisièmes* as follows.

Section TI (Industrial Techniques). The course is made up of general education subjects and one technical speciality—mechanics, electronics, electricity, building construction, etc. In 3 years the course prepares for employment as a technician in one of the branches listed.

Section TE (Technical and Economics). This course leads to careers as secretary, book-keeper/accountant, and in commerce and distribution. It is a general course with specialisation in economics.

Section TH (Hotel Branch). A general course for students who will become either administrative or technical heads of hotels.

Section TSO (Social Work). This is a 2-year course preparing for the *brevet d'enseignement social* in two options:

(a) medical–social secretary;
(b) bursarship.

A third-year course in social work is being organised to lead to a higher qualification in the same branch.

Many technical *lycées* have additional 2-year courses which lead to qualifications at the higher technician level.

This section has now described the four main types of course available in the second cycle of secondary education. It all adds up to a very thorough plan with provision for a wide variety of specialisations in conjunction with a continuation of general education at the upper secondary level, the whole being founded on 4 years of general lower secondary schooling. Targets for 1970 have been set in order that priorities for new school building can be determined.

TABLE 29. TARGET DISTRIBUTION OF 14-YEAR-OLDS BY 1970

Long general course	170,000	22%
Long technical course	65,000	8%
Short general course	140,000	18%
Short technical course	235,000	30%
Agricultural training	120,000	15%
Industrial apprenticeship	60,000	7%
	790,000	100%

By presenting, side by side, a static description of secondary education in the late fifties and early sixties and a blueprint for a reformed system in the process of being implemented, the size of the projected change can be seen in its true perspective. Obviously a great deal of the rigour and detail of the old French *lycée* classical tradition is to remain in some of the options in the long general course. French education is not giving up its old traditions and excellencies, but is admitting new specialities by their side for, equally obviously, the new scheme is designed to prevent students choosing a course too early; to give a variety of talents a chance to mature before an irrevocable decision affecting the future is made;

to keep the way open for a freer choice at a later point in a scholastic career, particularly keeping the way open for a choice on the technical side. A decision on a choice of speciality at an early age is often proved wrong. Analysis of subject achievements in the *lycées* has demonstrated that abilities only begin to crystallise at a late stage: a more diversified upper secondary school is clearly the intention of the reform. Will the reform be carried through in its spirit as well as in its letter or will the attitudes engendered by a long, and often brilliant, history prevail and bring only small gains as in the recent past? In 1956 the Billières proposals, which suggested merely 2 years of common education for all before differentiation into separate courses, were wrecked by the cross-currents of French educational ideas. In the first 2-year period of observation, which was intended to postpone selection, some pupils were allowed to start biased courses at the end of the first term. This was largely due to the influence of the devotees of Latin in whose eyes the study of Latin could not be put off for more than 3 months. They even succeeded in getting permission to introduce some of the elementary principles of Latin into the curriculum of the first term for children who had started on a "classical" curriculum!* Neither must the fate of the *classes nouvelles* be forgotten. The historical tradition and continuity of French education will not be lightly cast aside.

But working with the striving for reform, and inextricably intermingled with these educational changes because they are in part the cause of them, are the socio-economic and demographic changes which have posed such problems for the schools. Parents are no longer content with a low level of education for their children. No longer can the long school course be the almost exclusive preserve of the professional classes, though the working class seem to still distrust the *lycées* and prefer the *collège d'enseignement général*. The rising social demand, however, means the long courses must open their doors more widely and the national need for more trained manpower reinforces this feeling as one appropriate

* *World Year Book of Education*, 1965: *The Education Explosion*, Merlier, A. Expansion and crisis in secondary education in France, p. 279.

to the requirements of the times. The French birth rate has soared from a low of 520,000 in the early 1940's to a peak of 869,000 in 1950 and has since settled down more steadily at the level of about 800,000. Working together these factors have brought millions (over 3 million in the 10 years 1954–64) more pupils into the schools and secondary school enrolments have more than doubled. New building has been necessary, and, latterly, in accordance with the national school plan, this new provision is increasingly in the form of *collèges d'enseignement secondaire* (C.E.S.). These C.E.S.s are polyvalent or multilateral schools, providing all the necessary courses for the 11–15 age group—secondary education of the first degree. Then at the age of 15 pupils transfer to the nearest *lycée*, if they are taking a long course. A curriculum laid down from the centre eases this type of transfer. Twenty-three C.E.S.s opened in 1963 and by September 1964 about 200 were operating. This momentum has increased and in September 1966 733 C.E.S.s were open. Already the technical *lycées* are recruiting at 15 and catering for students from the second class upwards. Increasingly it seems other types of *lycées* will be doing the same and there will in effect be a growing number of sixth-form colleges drawing pupils from the *collège d'enseignement général* (C.E.G.) or the newer C.E.S.

Figures* for enrolments in September 1966 show the new institutions are making their mark and reorganisation is becoming a reality: a blueprint is being turned into a structure.

	Number of pupils
C.E.S.s	365,000
C.E.G.s	941,000
Lycées	1,628,000

At the same time numbers in the *écoles primaires elementaires* are falling slightly (despite larger age cohorts) because more pass at 11 into the various sections of the first cycle.

* *L'éducation Nationale*, 22 September 1966.

This chapter began by referring to the "breaking up of structures" and in the last paragraph have been cited some concrete examples of the process in action. Since 1959 a great movement for reform has been at work and many ideas and ideals from the Langevin–Wallon report of 1947, once looked upon as an excessively idealistic and impracticable document, are on their way to realisation. In the introduction to that report we read:

> The structure of education must in fact be adapted to the social structure . . . (which) . . . has undergone a rapid evolution and fundamental transformations. Mechanisation, the utilisation of new sources of power, the development of means of transport and communications, the concentration of industry, the increase in production, the massive entry of women into economic life, the spread of elementary education—these have profoundly modified living conditions and social organisation. The speed and extent of economic progress now poses the problem of recruiting an ever-increasing number of people as *cadres* and technicians. The bourgeoisie, hereditarily called upon to occupy the managerial posts and posts of responsibility, can no longer be sufficient for this by themselves. The new needs of the modern economy impose the necessity for a recasting of our educational system which, in its present structure, is no longer adapted to social and economic conditions.

The years since 1959 have seen great steps towards the changes in structure argued above: changes which should reorganise the education of French youth to fit the pattern of the country today.

CHAPTER 9

Sweden—Successful Progress in Integration

"Too few representatives from the working class reach the upper secondary school."

"Choices made too early concentrate the best brains in the academic school to the detriment of other occupations."

Findings of this type from early investigations confirmed the Swedes in their intention to go ahead with a reappraisal of the educational system. They found too that changes at the upper secondary level could only be made after fundamental changes at younger ages. Starting, at first then, from ideals of social unity and later buttressed by the conviction that in this direction lay progress, Sweden has, during the years since World War II, taken careful stock of her educational system and, methodically and without undue haste, transformed a differential *élitist* system with secondary and elementary strands running parallel in a traditional pattern, to a unitary or comprehensive system catering for all pupils in 9 years of schooling leading, in a planned fashion, to a variety of opportunities at the upper secondary level. To write "have transformed" is almost strictly true for though the change will not be entirely completed until 1972, by 1966 authorities representing 95% of pupils had accepted the new pattern of schooling for their area. This evolution of the school has been backed by a massive programme of sociological, psychological and educational research which has uncovered much that is relevant for education elsewhere, and pilot schemes have shown what can be achieved by the new pattern, as well as the things to be avoided, when it becomes country-wide. The forces which have brought these changes in education have also been working else-where in the country and to be fully understood must be seen against the socio-economic background.

Sweden is a large country with a relatively small population. Some areas are quite well endowed naturally but in areas further north a good livelihood is more difficult to achieve, and a country-wide organisation for mutual support and solidarity is necessary. In forestry, in transport and in the provision of hydro-electric power much state organisation is entailed and the widespread co-operative enterprises, as elsewhere in Scandinavia, need a spirit of cohesion if they are to be successful. The forces that have brought political democracy, social security and the Welfare State have also brought about the school reform. Thus has arisen the feeling that the structure of the school system and the schooling itself should foster social solidarity and unity. It is with this idea in mind that Dixon* in *Society, Schools and Progress in Scandinavia* describes the school which is elsewhere spoken of as the compre-hensive or unitary school as the unity school. Similarly,† Orring writes, "One of the aims of the present reform of the Swedish edu-cational system is to adapt schools to the development of society, besides giving the school such an organisation and content that it will encourage continued social development in a desired direc-tion". Following from this, although private schools are not for-bidden, and parents are able to choose a private education for their children, "the community must demand that private schools shall not be established, organised and run so that they counteract or make difficult the realisation of the aims on which the current reform of public education is based. It must therefore be deman-ded that a private school shall, as regards type and extent and the general trend of tuition, as well as the actual competence of the teachers, be equivalent in all essentials to the comprehensive school". This leaves little doubt that one of the aims of the school reform is social cohesion.

* Dixon, L. J., Pergamon Press, 1965.
† Orring, J., *Comprehensive Schools and Continuation Schools in Sweden*, Stockholm, 1962.

Another aim is that the school shall help in the plan for general economic development. Thus, for instance, every child should be educated to the maximum of his ability. Early selection for academic courses as under the old system confirms the social stratifications in the community and eventually limits the choice of vocation. A general education for all to a later stage gives a better basis for later vocational training and perhaps re-training. The whole question of the dichotomy between a liberal and a vocational education, and the age at which differentiation should start has been carefully considered by the Swedes especially in a conference at Sigtuna which produced the report *Differentiation and Guidance in the Comprehensive School* (Upsala, 1959). This problem is of general importance for the upper secondary school in all countries, and this is probably the best place to review the total evidence using the Sigtuna conference as a guide. (France seems to be working to the same ends—keeping choice fluid so that the best brains shall not choose the classical side and so impoverish technical education.)

An interesting book by Gaston Viaud (translated from the French) called *Intelligence, its Evolution and Forms** suggests that the intelligence of adult man has developed along two distinct lines:

1. action—the practical intelligence of *homo faber* characterised by the production of tools; and
2. thought—the conceptual intelligence of *homo sapiens* with its mental tools of abstract thought and logical methods.

Usually these two aspects complement each other but "it is a fact, however, that all men are not equally capable of developing these two forms of intelligence".

Viaud refers to the work of Louis Weber who, in *Le Rhythme du progrès* suggests a cyclic alternation in the history of human thought of the technical and the speculative type of intelligence. Although the exact phases of the periodic swing are difficult to determine he suggests that broad trends are discernible, e.g.

* Viaud, G., Hutchinson, London, 1960.

Ancient Egypt — technical inventions,
Greece — the flowering of speculation,
Middle Ages — rebirth of the practical,
Renaissance — speculative,

perhaps now giving way to the technical in our highly scientific civilisation. It is a pretty theory which, says Viaud, is true in essence if not in detail. The two tendencies do exist and can be observed in the differences between the everyday outlook and behaviour of the practical man and the theoretician.

It was thinking broadly along these lines which led to the idea of the secondary technical school in Britain. Pamphlet 9 *New Secondary Education* (1947) said "it should be possible for the brightest and ablest pupils to go to whichever type of secondary school would best agree with their interests, their special abilities and the kind of career they have in view". A tremendous amount of experimental work was carried out on selection for technical education using spatial tests, performance tests as well as ordinary intelligence tests. Many suggestions as to the best method were made but none was found to be effective. Sir Cyril Burt summing up said that at the age of 11 there were wide differences in innate general intelligence but the presence of special aptitudes at that age was questionable—the non-psychological reasons for placement, e.g. community needs, parental wishes were far more important. Rodger, working in Navy schools, showed allocation on special abilities was difficult at 15. Work in France by Bonnardel carried out in the *lycées* showed a broad distinction at *baccalauréat* level between literary and scientific abilities and, other workers, during the fifties, investigating, by means of factor analysis, pupils from the *sixièmes* to the *secondes* showed that ability was governed by a single factor in the 6e and 5e, that a discrepancy between scientific and literary began to show in the 4e and the discrepancy became more marked in the 2e than in the 3e. Thus evidence suggests it is much better to keep pupils together at 11 and provide different courses later. Some evidence also showed that specialised education tends to structure or crystallise the aptitudes that are brought into play. If they are true aptitudes this may be good but if they are pseudo, or wrongly diagnosed it could be dangerous. In Britain with no good evidence for allocation to secondary technical schools at 11, they generally tended to become a second choice after the grammar school, and the schools themselves seem to have grown together and worked for the same ends so that they are not clearly distinguishable. This has been helped as technology receives greater status and there is, therefore, an incentive for more attention to practical subjects in the grammar school. Hence schools have been renamed grammar–technical or amalgamated and their numbers have decreased. Sweden saw the connection between technical ability and economic progress and decided to design a system which would delay definitive choices as long as possible.

Reform based on the desire for social cohesion and the fostering of technical ability at the proper time was helped by the force of circumstance. Some change became a necessity. In the *Year Book of Education** for 1965, Torsten Husen writes, "It may be contended on good grounds that the educational explosion has anticipated the realisation of a basic school common to all young people". Increasing numbers going to the lower academic school (*realskola*) have "blown it up from the inside", because the larger percentage not only caused a pressure on the physical space available but caused changes in the curriculum which in its pre-expansion form could only cater for the needs of a minority of the age group. In 1929 9% of the age group continued in the *realskola*; by the end of the fifties it exceeded 40%. Enrolment at the lower secondary stage almost doubled from 1944–5 (85,000) to 1957–8 (162,000) while at the upper secondary level in the academic *gymnasia* the numbers increased from 17,000 in 1945 to 63,000 in 1962. Looked at as enrolment ratios against the age cohort the percentages shown in Table 30 can be quoted.

Changes of this magnitude make reappraisal essential. To understand the changes a description of the pattern of education just after the war is necessary. The traditional "dual" system,

* Husen, T., *The Educational Explosion in Sweden,* chap. 8.

TABLE 30. ENROLMENT RATIOS (%)

	1932	1953	1960
Lower secondary	10	38	over 50
Upper secondary	4	*c.* 16	20

	1945	1961	
Graduating from:			
Lower secondary at 16+	16	40	
Studentexamen	5	13	

	1950	1960	1965
Enrolled full time:			
16–18 years	16	34	46
19–24 years	8	16	18

which is now largely being replaced by the 9-year unitary school, consisted of the academic school with its liberal arts curriculum running parallel to the elementary school, with the first few years basic and common for all. The biggest debating point was the age of transfer. Some wanted an early transfer to the academic school, while others wanted 6 years of basic school for everyone. As a compromise a double transfer system existed so there were two possibilities:

(a) 4 grades elementary plus 5 years secondary, or
(b) 6 grades elementary plus 4 years secondary.

The lower secondary school (*realskola*) and the girls secondary school (*flikskola*) led on to the upper secondary stage (*gymnasium*). However, most upper secondary establishments were combined with the lower secondary stage to form a state secondary school. The upper secondary school courses were of 3 or 4 years' duration. Three-year school was for those who had passed the examination at the end of the *realskola—the realexamen*—while 4-year school was for those who came from the penultimate class of this school.

The upper secondary school is divided into three streams according to the nature of the studies—classical, natural science and general. If sufficient students are enrolled, in the last 2 years of the course, each stream may be subdivided: the classical stream has the full classical branch (with Greek) and the semi-classical branch; in the natural science stream is a biology and a mathematics branch: the general stream has a modern languages section and a social studies branch. There are arrangements for modern languages and social studies when the general branch is omitted. Philosophy is included in the curriculum and handicrafts are absent. The course is completed by the higher certificate examination (*studentexamen*) which has both written and oral sections.

Something of the rigour of the course in the *gymnasium* can be realised by a study of the subjects followed in the classical and semi-classical branches.

The very great stress on languages which are studied for over half the time is noteworthy. Later, in Table 35, the new proposals

TABLE 31. THREE-YEAR ALLOCATIONS

	Classical line	Semi-classical line
Religion	5	5
Swedish	12	12
Latin	22	22
Greek	12	—
English	8	9
German	4	7
French	8	13
History with civics	10	10
Geography	$1\frac{1}{2}$	$1\frac{1}{2}$
Philosophy	3	3
Biology and health	2	2
Physics	$\frac{1}{2}$	$\frac{1}{2}$
Chemistry	$\frac{1}{2}$	$\frac{1}{2}$
Drawing	1	2
Music	2	3
Physical education	10	12
Three-year total	$101\frac{1}{2}$	$102\frac{1}{2}$

for the various options will be listed and a comparison will indicate the reduction in the allocation of time to languages and the diversification of subjects which is being introduced.

There is also a varied provision of vocational and technical schools once again forming a mainly parallel system:

(a) Technical secondary schools: to gain entrance to these schools requires the completion of the lower secondary course (*realskola*) and at least 2 months' practical experience in industry. Other periods of practical work are also required during the 3-year course. Some technical schools are more specialised dealing solely with subjects such as mining, textiles and industrial arts.

Parallel with these technical schools are commercial secondary schools, usually municipal establishments, giving theoretical and practical training for clerks and book-keepers.

These types of school are broadly on a par with the *gymnasium*.

(b) A second system, mainly run by the Board of Vocational Training, consists of schools with courses which recruit mainly from the elementary sector. They are both full time and part time. The most common is a 2-year full-time course which includes practical as well as theoretical training. Often these vocational schools are combined with industry in such a way that the practical training takes place in the industrial undertaking (about 34 hours per week) while the theoretical training (8 hours per week) is given in the municipal vocational school. As an alternative method there are some firms with schools which carry out the complete training. A few specialised industries, such as watch-making, have schools of their own. As might be expected in a sparsely populated country, some of the vocational training centres are residential.

At this level there is also some provision for office training and commercial work though this is one place where the otherwise parallel streams come together for although it is usually only the completion of compulsory schooling which is necessary for entrance, in some cases the standard of the *realexam* is required. There are also schools for household management and nursing.

To sum up the pre-reform system briefly we can say the system bifurcates at the age of 10 or 12, and at the upper secondary level there are many quite separate courses in a number of different institutions. The pattern is shown visually in Fig. 6.

Having sketched out the school system as it was before 1950, and as it remains still where the reform is not yet operative, and discussed the arguments for reform, it now remains to describe the

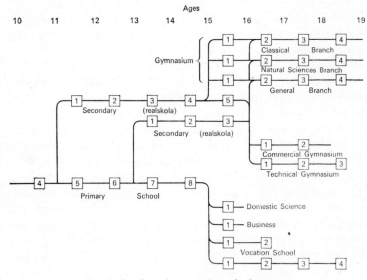

Fig. 6. Sweden: the pre-reform dual pattern.

steps which have been taken to bring about the reform. A blueprint for a new system has been drawn up and is gradually being implemented. There can never be a complete change from one system to another; at some stage they must exist side by side though the speed of operation can vary. It took the U.S.S.R. 2 years to change from 11 years of school to 10. In England the Crowther report spoke of all-age schools as vestigial remains when, in 1958, over 30 years after the Hadow report which advocated separate schools for seniors, they still housed 10% of the secondary pupils below compulsory age. And in 1967 some all-age schools still remain! Sweden expects to complete her reform by 1972.

In this account emphasis is laid on the arrangements at the upper secondary level but the underlying basis cannot be completely omitted.

In 1946 a school commission was set up with the task of considering the way in which the educational system was organised. It reported in 1948 and suggested the lengthening of the compulsory course to 9 years with a leaving age of 16. Also it proposed that all types of school parallel to the basic school should be integrated in one system called the unitary or comprehensive school (*enhetskola*). The government decided to start experimental work on this basis in a number of school districts keeping careful records. The 9-year school was organised in 3-year stages; the first two stages replacing the basic or elementary school and the third stage replacing the *realskola*. It was in this third stage that the main debating points arose. In general most people were satisfied with no streaming or homogeneous grouping in the first six grades with form teachers being responsible for most of the teaching but from grade 7 onwards there was a difference of opinion. The argument was mainly on the old lines though now at a slightly higher age group. The radical reformers wanted a common course for all to grade 9, the last compulsory grade, while the more traditionally minded looked longingly at the alternative, a division into different tracks from grade 7 onwards. A compromise was agreed and tried out in the pilot scheme. Grades 7 and 8 were characterised by a free choice of optional subjects with three alternatives:

(a) German as a second foreign language
   (usually English was the first);
(b) an additional course in Swedish;
(c) a practical subject.

Then in grade 9 a more definite division into sides was made; one preparing for the *gymnasium*; one with a vocational bias and the third a course of general education for those leaving at 16.

In 1957 another School Commission was appointed to prepare a report on the basis of the results of earlier commissions and the pilot experiments with the 9-year school. This commission made further suggestions and in 1962 the Swedish parliament decreed the 9-year school should become country-wide between 1962 and 1968. However, since changes start in the first five grades, it will be 1972 before all new schools have reached the ninth grade. The continuation school will be organised while the change over is taking place.

With these broad outlines in mind it is now time to turn in detail to the upper secondary level, though because of the careful transition phases that have been built into the system the division line between lower and upper secondary is not easy to draw. Compulsory school goes on to 16 years and the Commission has been insistent that the final grade of the unitary school shall not be joined to the next stage in any part because this would make the already complicated ninth grade less viable especially where numbers are small. However, there is no doubt that grade 9 is a preparatory stage looking forward to the next cycle of education and an approach to lines of specialisation is being started at lower levels. Thus any discussion of provision at the true upper secondary level must take cognisance of what has gone before, and especially of grade 9 which with 15–16-year-olds is part of our assignment.

The design of the upper department gives grades 7, 8 and 9 each 35 periods per week. Some are common periods and others are optional on the following pattern:

Grade 7	30 common and	5 optional
Grade 8	28	7
Grade 9 either	28	7
or	13	22

In grade 7 there are five optional groups which allow a start to be made on a second foreign language, or on a practical course or towards a commercial course. All these can be followed up in various ways in the nine optional patterns possible in grade 8. But it must be emphasised that the major part of the course in these grades is a common offering taught in undifferentiated groups. Only in English and mathematics is regrouping allowed. In these subjects two separate courses are offered and pupils may choose which they will follow. An important part of the work of the school is the vocational orientation of pupils towards a choice of occupation. This takes place in classroom lessons but also in a practical

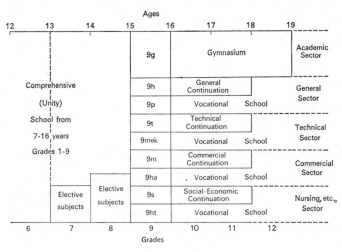

FIG. 7. The new Swedish system.

way. For 3 weeks during grade 8 pupils have experience outside school in industrial undertakings, sampling two or three different types during the time available. While half the 14–15-year-olds are out of school on this activity, the other half are taught in half classes.

All this preparation leads on to a choice of streams in grade 9 where five sections are available, viz. theoretical, general, technical–mechanical, commercial and domestic (see Fig. 7). As each of the last four sections is available in two alternative forms, one broadly practical and the other with a more theoretical approach, it gives a choice of nine streams in all. A number of these streams have a common nucleus of subjects so the wide choice does not mean each stream will be an independent unit. There will be joint lessons in common subjects, and for the options the teaching will be in smaller groups. As groups as small as five will be permissible in options, it follows that most schools will be able to make available all the specialities which are:

1. 9 g   preparation for the *gymnasium*
2. 9 h   humanities
   9 p   general–practical
3. 9 t   technical
   9 mek   mechanics
4. 9 m   mercantile
   9 ha   commercial
5. 9 s   social–economic
   9 ht   domestic science

TABLE 32. THE WEEKLY ALLOCATIONS OF TIME IN GRADE 9

	9 g, h, t, m, s (theoretical)	9 mek, ha, ht, p (practical)
Compulsory:		
Swedish	5	3
Mathematics	4	—
English	—	—
Religion	1	—
Civics	2	2
History	2	—
Geography	2	2
Biology	2	2
Chemistry	2	—
Physics	2	—
Music/art/domestic science	4	2
Physical education	2	2
Optional	7	22
Total	35	35

In the theoretical streams English occurs in the optional courses. The practical courses have a special schedule of vocational subjects according to Table 33.

In grade 9 it is the intention to provide for students who wish to specialise in music and the arts—an aesthetic stream—if there is sufficient demand.

TABLE 33.* VOCATIONAL SUBJECTS IN STREAMS 9 mek, ha, ht, p

Stream	Subject	Periods per week	Total weekly
Mechanics 9 mek	Vocational work, bench work, machine work, hot machining, practical training	17	
	Vocational theory: tools, techniques (e.g. cutting, welding), accounting, workshop hygiene, etc.	5	22
Commercial 9 ha	Swedish, practical course	2	
	Commercial mathematics	4	
	Commercial theory	2	
	Book-keeping	3	
	General material theory	2	
	Typewriting	3	
	Shop or office work	6	22
Domestic science 9 ht	Home and furnishing	4	
	Economy and work organisation	2	
	Food and cooking	7	
	Textiles and needlework	5	
	Child and family care	4	22
General–practical 9 p	Vocational work: store work, goods office work, bench work, machine work, hot machining, maintenance, care of motors, care of home and clothes, cooking	18	
	Vocational theory: tools, reading plans, accounting, vocational hygiene, practical vocational guidance	4	22

* Source Tables 32 and 33, Orring, J., *op. cit.*

An analysis of choices in the pilot schools operating in 1959–60 showed that 20% of students followed the option leading to the *gymnasium*; 50% chose preparatory vocational training, and the remaining 30% followed the general course.

The comprehensive school is for everyone up to the age of 16 years. On this the Commission have been quite adamant. Schools after the age of 16 are organised for smaller more specialised groups. These must adapt their teaching to follow the unitary school and not the reverse. As already noted, suggestions to amalgamate grade 9 option g with the *gymnasium* to make a 4-year school have been condemned as have parallel attempts for the establishment of 4-year agricultural vocational schools. Possibilities for change and re-orientation are to be preserved to 16 years in an uncompromising way. The 1957 Commission were strengthened in this decision by information from the pilot schools on vocational maturation and the development of interests. With an increasing age it is easier to find an increasing trend of interest in an individual even though aptitudes have not been shown to change with age. Yet even at the beginning of the ninth grade, any indications can only be regarded as tendencies and those who follow a general course will keep open longer the choice of career they will eventually make. Because of this, the rather strict specialisation in sides tried in the pilot schools has been abandoned in favour of less specialisation which allows freedom for manoeuvre. In particular for those who have not and cannot make up their mind there is grade 9 option p—the general–practical course which will provide suitable preparation for a large sector of the labour market. In the pilot schools 30% chose a general course.

During the final years of the compulsory comprehensive school pupils are made aware of the choices that are available, and, in choosing which of the alternatives they will follow in grade 9, many have already made some progress towards their eventual choice of occupation. But because many pupils are not ready at that stage to make a decision the Commission decided that there ought to be available some provision for continued education which would form a middle way between the academic school (*gymnasium*) and the vocational schools proper. As living standards rise, so a wider and longer education for greater numbers of children comes to be the expected norm, and so the proposal is to establish a 2-year continuation school based on, and continuing, the work started in the comprehensive school. Although the tuition in these schools will be forward-looking towards a choice of vocation, it will not be tightly tied to one specific branch since the demand appears to be for a less specialised education to extend to a progressively later stage. This new type of upper secondary provision will be made available in four branches: general, engineering, commercial and social–economic. It will operate alongside the academic school.

In the description of the options Fig. 7 showing the structure of the continuation school and the way in which it articulates with the final comprehensive year will be found useful.

The general option. This section will take pupils from 9 g and 9 h in the ninth grade and widen and deepen the education given in the unitary school and allow for some specialisation in either science or languages. Further specialisation will be given by allowing a free choice of options which will reinforce primarily the basic subjects. In this section too there will be provision for aesthetically inclined and talented pupils, whether on the science or the languages side, to take classes in art or design and other forms of creative work. This general section will not be given any obvious vocational orientation.

The engineering option. This will be a general engineering course based on option t of grade 9 of the comprehensive school but not definitely restricted to it. It will, however, require a good level of knowledge and ability in mathematics and science. The course will largely replace and take over from the municipal vocational–technical schools which have previously had a $2\frac{1}{2}$-year course and have found their recruits from the elementary school. A reduction to a 2-year course, which is naturally administratively more convenient, will not be difficult, as the commencing standard will be higher and uniform. This engineering section will offer three possibilities for specialisation: machine-technical, electro-technical and building-technical are Orring's terms for the courses but it is easy here to recognise the familiar approaches through the mechanical, electrical and civil sides of engineering.

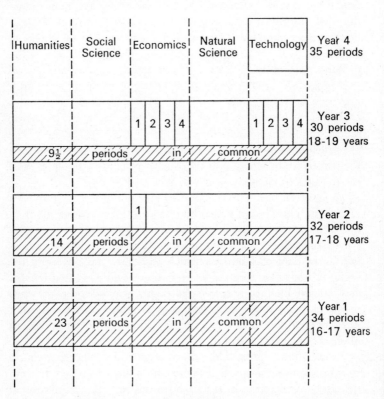

Fig. 8. The five options in the academic upper secondary school in Sweden.

Key to specialities

Economics Branch	*Technological*
1. Economics-languages	1. Machine
2. Finance	2. Building
3. Distributive	3. Electro-technical
4. Administration	4. Industrial chemistry

The commercial option. As more machinery and more complex systems come into use in offices, so a much higher standard of general education is required before specialisation begins. The commercial stream in the continuation school will give more practical training than the commercial *gymnasium* (see p. 159) but will, nevertheless, be more theoretical than the commercial institutes. Specialisation will be possible inside the general option and will consist of grouping for certain sections of the course to give:

1. a distribution speciality;
2. a financial bias;
3. an administrative speciality.

This last line of specialisation will provide a good training in languages as well as in general office work so that students will be able to use languages efficiently in correspondence. The section with a financial bias is intended for administrative personnel and will teach business economics, while the distribution speciality will train students for the buying and selling sides.

The social–economic option. This side of the school will help those whose work it is to provide others with information, help and advice. An increasing number of state and municipal agencies need workers who come mainly in this category and require a good general knowledge, an interest in, and sympathy with, other people and the ability to co-operate and organise. Such people are also required increasingly in the tourist industry.

Although entrance to the 2-year continuation school will normally be directly from the last grade of the comprehensive school, a period of work experience may be useful especially for the engineering option, and there will be nothing to prevent students entering the continuation school after a period at work. An examination at the end of the course is not thought to be appropriate and so students will be continuously assessed on the work done during the course.

The full system of continuation schools will take some time to establish but it is expected that by 1970 such schools will be catering for 20–25% of the age group while the reorganised *gymnasium* (described below) will be taking 30% leaving something less than half the age group for the vocational schools and apprenticeship training. It is useful to keep these percentages in mind when looking at Fig. 7 which is drawn to make the structure clear but does not show to scale the numbers expected to be found in any of the branches.

Simultaneously with the planning of the continuation schools a study and replanning of the academic side of the upper secondary school has gone forward and a report—*The New Gymnasium*—was presented to the Minister in 1963. The intention was that it should be implemented from the beginning of the academic year 1965, but the changes will take time to work through the school. As explained earlier the *gymnasium* is organised in three sides for academic work and there is some provision for technical and commercial work in separate institutions.

The strength of each of the branches is shown by the enrolments for 1962.

TABLE 34. SPECIALITY IN GYMNASIUM

	No. of schools	No. of students	%
Academic	132	69,388	82
of which classical		17,344	
modern		36,667	
general		15,377	
Technical	28	9,531	11
Commercial	31	5,078	6

The academic school is much the most important and some Swedish educationists think too many students are following the academic courses and there has been some persuasion (albeit unsuccessful) for students to choose other courses. In just the same way our own sixth-formers go on preferring the humanities. Now the Swedes are attempting to induce different choices by a diversification. The new recommendation is that all the courses shall be united in a single 3-year *gymnasium* which will offer five specialities: the humanities, social studies, science, engineering

*TABLE 35. THREE-YEAR ALLOCATIONS OF TIME IN REFORMED GYMNASIA

	Humanities	Social science	Economics — Language speciality	Economics — Others	Natural science	Technology	(4th year)
Swedish	10	10	9	9	9	8	—
Modern languages	30	25	30	21	18	12	—
General linguistics	3	8	4	4	—	—	—
History	8	2	2	2	6	4	—
History of music and art	2	3	—	—	2	2	—
Religion	3	2	2	2	2	—	—
Philosophy	2	2	—	—	2	—	—
Psychology	2	2	—	—	1	—	2
Social studies	10½	10½	8½	8½	5	5	—
Legal knowledge	—	—	2	2	—	—	—
Business economics	—	—	10	13	—	—	3
Other economics	—	—	5	7	—	—	—
Mathematics	5	11	—	11	15	15	—
Physics	—	—	3	—	10½	10½	—
Chemistry	—	—	—	—	7	6½	—
Biology	7	9	—	3	5	—	—
Nature knowledge	—	—	—	—	—	—	—
Technology	—	—	—	—	—	11	—
Other technology	—	—	—	3	—	11½	30
Typing	—	—	4	—	—	—	—
Shorthand	—	—	6	—	—	—	—
Music or Art	2	2	—	—	2	—	—
Physical education	8	8	7	7	8	7	—
Free studies	3½	3½	3½	3½	3½	3½	—
Totals	96	96	96	96	96	96	35

* Source: Dahlloff, U., Recent reforms of secondary education in Sweden, *Comparative Education*, vol. 2, no. 2, March, 1966.

and commerce. The first three branches are the descendants of the traditional academic school. Engineering and commerce, from the vocational side, will join them under the new plan. It is hoped the percentage of students in the three academic branches will fall to about 60% of the total in the *gymnasium*, with engineering and commerce taking 20% each. This fall in percentage for the three academic sides does not necessarily involve a fall in actual numbers as more pupils are expected (and this seems to be the trend) to take the new *gymnasium* course which is a unitary school at this level, attempting to minimise the differences between liberal and vocational studies.

Figure 8 shows the amount of common learnings decreases during the 3 years and by the last year there is a very considerable degree of specialisation. In some instances offerings which appear common are not strictly so because subjects, e.g. mathematics, which appear in all lines are taught at varying depths.

The Swedes realise that skill in modern languages is necessary for all and, as Table 35 shows, there is a good allocation of time for languages even for technologists and scientists. English is kept up, French or German improved and sometimes a third language is started at an elementary level. For the classicist time for Latin (and Greek for some) comes from the 30 hours of language in the humanities section, where all have some general linguistics too. Students gifted in the arts who follow the humanities line may take an aesthetic option from the time allocation for languages.

Everyone takes history and religion, and some psychology is compulsory for all. Social science has been widened to include consideration of international problems and problems in planning in general. Geography has been split between social science and a new "subject" listed as nature knowledge which is to be the orientation to the sciences for those not taking natural sciences or technology.

The number of periods per week has been reduced and a little free time given. More independent methods of work are to be pursued conscientiously through long essays and assignments. The examination at the end of the course has been reorganised.

Centrally constructed standardised achievement tests are to be set and moderators are to visit schools regularly and fairly frequently to help to equate standards between schools. Each *gymnasium* will begin to offer all five courses, so technology and economics previously only offered on a restricted basis (see Table 34) will now be available at 130 locations. However, the fourth engineering year consisting largely of technological expertise will still, for reasons of economy in costly equipment and staffing, be available in about thirty centres.

In Sweden all curricula are centralised and the new arrangements were published a year before their introduction in school. For those teachers whose programmes are greatly changed, a series of refresher courses have been organised. The whole reform has been undertaken in a very thorough manner.

Rearrangements at the level of higher education are also being made and offerings parallel with, and equivalent to, the University will help to consolidate diversification at secondary level, but such considerations lie outside the scope of this work.

In 20 years the framework of a new pattern has been carefully erected. From any point of view it is a formidable undertaking but the Swedish policy-makers believe the pace of change is such that waiting for something to evolve is no longer possible: what is required is a national system geared to buttress economic growth. A national system helps also in the re-deployment of labour by diminishing the concern of parents when movement of home is necessary. But a plan is only a skeleton which needs to be clothed with flesh and blood. As Torsten Husen* writes: "educational changes . . . seem to occur according to some inherent rank order. The organisational structure is revised and changed by Parliamentary initiative and decision. New course prescriptions are issued by Government agencies. Finally teacher training starts to be changed and slowly affects the 'inner work' of the school." Sweden seems now to be entering the last of these stages. There are sure to be some other problems to be met before the new really comes to be the accepted.

* Husen, T., Educational change in Sweden, *Comparative Education*, June 1965.

CHAPTER 10

Japan—Adoption and Adaptation

THE school system is based on a 6–3–3 pattern with 6 years of elementary education starting at 6 years of age, followed by 3 years of lower secondary education in comprehensive institutions giving nine compulsory years in all, with a further 3 years of upper secondary education in co-educational schools offering general and vocational courses. At this upper level are many elective subjects, and both these and the required subjects, if followed satisfactorily for a specified number of class hours (a class hour is defined as an instructional period of 50 minutes' duration) give a unit of credit towards the total required for graduation.

Thus might begin a potted description of the United States system of schooling, though actually it is the Japanese system that is being described here. Writing of the position a few years ago, a sentence or two on the decentralised system and the position of social studies in the curriculum would have highlighted other items in common between the two systems. The chapter has been started in this way to underline the borrowings that have occurred. These "borrowings" from the United States and the ways in which they have and are being adapted in a different culture make a fascinating study for the student of comparative education. At present adaptation is the keynote. Dr. King writes:

> Increasingly, despite the obvious American externals of the 6–3–3 school system followed by 4 years of college, and despite all the genuine talk about democracy or equality of the sexes, or dedication to peaceful pursuits, the school system's adaptation to the future of Japan is also being made in Japan. Wholesale copying has gone for good, as it has from industry. One does not copy an article when one thinks an improvement has been made upon it.*

* King, E. J., Educational progress and social problems in Japan, *Comparative Education*, vol. 1, no. 2, 1965.

To appreciate the present position of the upper secondary school it is necessary to know something of this background of borrowing and adaptation. First, though, it is useful to look at a few statistics which give some idea of the magnitude and importance of the upper secondary sector. Comparisons with U.S.A. are easiest because of the parallelism of the two systems. In 1960 the enrolment ratio for the 15–19-year-olds was 65% in U.S.A. and 39%

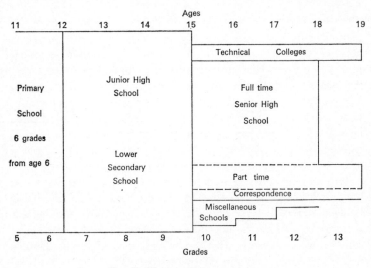

Fig. 9. The new Japanese system.

in Japan, but by 1963, out of a total population in this age range of 9,240,000 in Japan, there were 4,930,000 enrolled in educational courses giving a ratio of 53%. Figures for the school year 1964 show over 70% as entering the senior high school. Locally much higher percentages are recorded. In the Tokyo prefecture in 1964 97% went on to the upper secondary sector: in Osaka 95%. The U.S.A. will not be showing this rate of increase, for the great acceleration there occurred much earlier, so there is no doubt Japan is catching up, at any rate, numerically. In 1958 the U.S.S.R. had an enrolment ratio of 49% and the United Kingdom

17%. The Japanese figures include part-time as well as full-time students (see Fig. 9) but the latter are in a great predominance, e.g. 1964–5: total enrolment in upper secondary schools 4,634,406 of which full-time 4,152,249, part-time 482,157.

In the same year 70·6% of graduates from the lower secondary school went on to the upper secondary sector with boys and girls in almost equal proportions. In part-time courses males (67%) predominate over females (33%), but in full-time schools the proportions are almost equal. Schools for part-time students are much smaller than those for full-time students. This difference in size, shown by the following figures for 1964, is connected with the geographical distribution of schools—full time in cities and urban areas and part time in the more remote districts.

	Schools	Teachers	Pupils
Full time	3934	181,151	4,152,249
Part time	2304	27,104	482,157

This gives an average size of just over 1000 students in a full-time institution while part-time schools average about 200 in enrolment. All-in-all the figures quoted demonstrate that few countries surpass Japan in provision at this level, and for this reason her system is worthy of close consideration. A little background is useful here.

In modern times Japanese educational development can be divided into three periods:

1. The initial modernisation, 1872–1937.
2. The war-time era, 1937–45.
3. The democratisation, 1945 to the present.

It is, of course, this last period which is of especial interest. It falls into two parts: the first under the occupation (1945–52) when the borrowings occurred; and the second since 1952 during which responsibility has passed back to Japan and adaptation has occurred to make the system fit more closely the true Japanese culture. During these 10–15 years one of the principles of comprehensive education can be seen at work. Ushinsky, the great Russian comparative educationist wrote, in 1847: "But in every public phenomenon there are two sides, historical national tradition which cannot be transferred, and the rational (general humanitarian), the negation of which because some other nation applied it first would be extremely illogical."* The first period saw the attempt to transfer everything (almost lock, stock and barrel) from the U.S.A. to Japan. The second period has shown what is historical national tradition and non-transferable, and what has been assimilable and helpful, and therefore reasonable to copy.

In its twofold division this period since World War II featuring the growth of democratic forms in Japan reflects a similar duality in the initial modernisation era. The first few years after the opening up of Japan to the West (1872) saw a wholesale borrowing of ideas in many fields: in education a centralised system on the French "academy" lines was set up but many of the approaches were culled from American experience and practice. The Japanese were warned that straight borrowing was difficult and that it was important that the educational system should reflect national culture. Asked for an opinion, an American professor wrote: "There are traditional customs which it would be unwise to undertake to subvert. Every successful school system must be a natural outgrowth from the wants of a nation."† However, borrowings continued, but from 1886 onwards Japan began to revise the system to conform more closely to her own values.

Thus twice in less than 100 years the attempt to transplant an alien system to Japan has been tried. On the first occasion the Japanese, eager for progress, were the instigators. After 1945 the second attempt was made with the occupying power, the U.S.A.,

---

* Quoted in Hans, N., *The Russian Tradition in Education,* Routledge & Kegan Paul, London, 1963.

† *Education in Japan,* New York, 1873, quoted in Anderson, R. S., *Japan: Three Epochs of Modern Education,* U.S. Govt., Washington, 1959.

playing a major role, but with the Japanese very willing to fall into line and demonstrate their conversion to democratic forms. Even before the occupation got under way the Japanese Ministry of Education tried to conform to what it imagined the Allies would wish and began to institute democratic reforms and forbid militaristic organisations and teaching in schools. The first acts of the occupation confirmed this democratic trend and also prohibited the dissemination of Shinto (militaristic and ultra-nationalistic) doctrine. More specifically it suspended the courses in morals, Japanese history and geography. The geography course had new texts prepared and restarted after 6 months; the Japanese history course took 3 months longer, but the morals course was not re-introduced until much later (1958) and then only after a long debate, which because of its importance will be discussed in detail later. In January 1946 a United States Education Commission visited Japan and issued a report which became the official policy guide. It contained ten main suggestions and most of them were adopted and implemented by the Japanese Education Reform Committee which had worked closely with the U.S. Commission. The suggestions were:

(a) the introduction of freedom and democratic participation in education;
(b) decentralisation of control;
(c) the substitution of social studies for morals;
(d) a 6–3–3 ladder;
(e) greater emphasis on physical education and vocational education at all levels;
(f) the independence of private schools;
(g) changes in methods of guidance;
(h) the development of adult education;
(i) an increase in the number of universities;
(j) the broadening of teacher training.

The report provided a blueprint for the changes which were made. Its provenance in American practice is easy to see and one wonders how far the distinguished American comparative educationists on the Commission expected these ideas to succeed unchanged. They were largely implemented by the Fundamental Law of Education which provided a new set of aims and the School Education Law which altered the structure. Both were passed in March 1947.

A single-track system replaced the multi-track system which had operated on a 6–5–3 basis previously. Secondary education was now divided into two parts of equal duration: the first three lower secondary years became part of the compulsory 9-year period of free education (see Fig. 9). Before the reform both general and vocational education had been conducted in different types of middle school. Now the lower secondary school became of a single type with some subjects compulsory and some elective. The upper secondary school began to offer various courses in one school and what had previously been specialised schools with distinct curricula were now merged in the common system. Existing school buildings and school staff were used and many schools were upgraded. Some institutions offered only the general secondary course; others had both the general course and various vocational courses and some still offered vocational courses only, but of several types. However, the vocational courses all carry a considerable element of general work. Most commonly schools began to organise a diversified curriculum, based on a Ministry of Education prescription, with a number of optional courses so that both academic and vocational students could be accommodated. Already by 1949 43% of upper secondary schools were of this comprehensive type and only 20% were still of single type vocational—with agriculture, industry, commerce, fishing and home-making occurring in decreasing order of frequency. This represented good progress in a short time. To some extent this progress was helped by the difficulty of catering for diverse vocations so there was a tendency to concentrate on general education in the early days of the reform. Now, however, the vocational or technical courses cover a wide range—agriculture (including general agriculture, forestry, sericulture, gardening, stock-raising, horticulture, agricultural civil engineering), commerce, domestic arts, fishery, science, technology (including mechanical, electrical and civil engineering, communication, shipbuilding, chemical industry, construction, metallurgy, mining, textiles, ceramics). Some can be very specialised though they still contain a large general element as explained later.

In an attempt to remove the idea of a hierarchy of schools and to equalise quality, and also to help social integration and give continuity between lower and upper secondary schools, catchment areas were defined so that schools would serve one district or neighbourhood. There were, however, more entrants than places in upper secondary schools and so entrance examinations had to be introduced and "districting" of schools was relaxed in some cases. Nevertheless, in one area the achievement examinations designed for entrance had all to be set on one day and this prevented the growth of a hierarchy that was too rigid.

The upper secondary course is organised by awarding credits for the work in school. Thirty-five school hours per year are required for one unit of credit and the school year consists of, at least, 35 weeks of 6 days. For graduation from upper secondary school the minimum number of credits to be collected during the course is 85. The number of credits obtainable differs from subject to subject and also varies within a subject area, and hence the curriculum becomes very complicated and can best be illustrated by examples of general courses and vocational courses. The 85 credits required for graduation must include at least 38 units of general education including Japanese language, some courses in social studies, some science and mathematics, and 9 units of health and physical education.

The courses of study in upper secondary schools are prescribed by the central authority, and curricula in individual schools have to be compiled to comply with these central standards. All students, no matter what course they are taking, have to take subjects in the areas as stated. The subjects (see p. 181) are required for students taking either the general course or a vocational course.

For the general course there is a longer list of specific

TABLE 36. COURSES PROVIDED IN EACH UPPER SECONDARY SCHOOL

Area	Subjects	Standard no. of credits
Japanese language	Modern Japanese	7
	Classics A	2
	Classics B. I	5
	Classics B. II	3
Social studies	Ethics–civics	2
	Political science–economics	2
	Japanese history	3
	World history A	3
	World history B	4
	Geography A	3
	Geography B	4
Mathematics	Mathematics I	5
	Mathematics II. A	4
	Mathematics II. B	5
	Mathematics III	5
	Applied mathematics	6
Science	Physics A	3
	Physics B	5
	Chemistry A	3
	Chemistry B	4
	Geology	2
Health and P.E.	Health	9(B) 7(G)
	Physical education	2
Fine arts	Music I	2
	Music II	4
	Fine arts I	2
	Fine arts II	4
	Handicrafts I	2
	Handicrafts II	4
	Calligraphy I	2
	Calligraphy II	4
Foreign languages	English $\begin{smallmatrix}A\\B\end{smallmatrix}$	9(3)
	German	15
	French	15
	Other foreign languages	15
Domestic arts	General home-making	4(G)
	Other subjects	
Other vocational subjects		Electives

TABLE 37.

	(1) General all-round course				(2) Academic course			
	Year 1	Year 2	Year 3	Total credits	Year 1	Year 2	Year 3	Total credits
Modern Japanese	3	2	2		3	2	2	
Classics A / I				12	2	3		15
Classics II / B	2	3					3	
Ethics–civics		2				2		
Political science–economics			2				2	
Japanese history							3	
World history A		3		13				15
World history B			3			2	2	
Geography A	3				4			
Geography B					5			
Mathematics I								
Mathematics II A	5							
Mathematics II B		2	2	9		5		15
Mathematics III							5	
Applied mathematics								
Physics A			3			3		
Physics B							3	
Chemistry A		3		12		2	2	16
Chemistry B								
Biology	4				4			
Geology	2				2			
Health	4(B) 2(G)	3	2	11(B) 9(G)	3	4(B) 2(G)	2	11(B) 9(G)
Physical education		1	1		1		1	
Music I / II			2					
Fine arts I / II	2				2			
Handicrafts I / II		2		6		2		4
Calligraphy I / II								
English A / B	3	3	3					
German				9				15
French					5	5	5	
Other foreign language								
General homemaking	2(G)	2(G)		4(G)		4(G)		4(G)
Electives		6(B) 4(G)	9	15(B) 13(G)				
Special curr. activities	1	1	1	3	1	1	1	3
Total	29	31	30	90	32	31(B) 33(G)	31	94(B) 96(G)

B Boys   G Girls

COURSES TO BE TAKEN BY ALL STUDENTS

Area	Subject
1. Japanese language	Modern Japanese and either Classics A or Classics B-1
2. Social studies	"Ethics–civics" and "political science–economics" and two other subjects
3. Mathematics	Mathematics I
4. Science	Two subjects
5. Health and physical education	Health and physical education
6. Foreign language	One language

requirements and another list for the vocational course. Some of the vocational courses, while carrying this required basis of general education, do become very detailed in their elective subjects. An example of this is an agricultural course in horticulture with emphasis on vegetable culture, which can then be further specialised in the pomology of floriculture.* In this course 53 units of credit would be gained from general subjects and 55 from the agriculture—the specialised—side of the course. One home-room period is required in each year giving a further 3 units. Hence the 3-year course gives a total of 111 units (85 units is the minimum for graduation). Table 36 shows the courses and the credits they earn. Choices within these offerings can give a whole gamut of courses. Illustrated in Table 37 are:

(a) a general all-round course with some elected vocational subjects; and

(b) a more specifically academic course taking a wide range of academic subjects and omitting electives.

Now examples of two vocational courses are given (Table 38). Here the academic subjects are listed by areas only and the vocational courses are given in greater detail. The subdivision into specific courses during the 3 years is given, but the division of the courses between the years is not included. In both these courses,

* Ministry of Education—Japan, *Education in Japan*, 1964.

TABLE 38. TWO VOCATIONAL COURSES. THREE-YEAR ALLOCATIONS OF
WEEKLY TIME (class-hours)

Machine technology		Clerical	
Japanese language	9	Japanese language	12
Social studies	9	Social studies	9
Mathematics	11	Mathematics	9
Science	8	Science	6
Health and P.E.	9	Health and P.E.	9
Fine arts	1	Fine arts	4
Foreign language	9	Foreign language	9
Total general	56	Total general	58
Machine shop practice	14	General home-making	4
Machine shop theory	6	General business	4
Materials	2	Marketing	3
Mechanical drawing	10	Business law	2
Machine drawing	4	Merchandising	2
Applied dynamics	4	Commercial book-keeping	5
Prime mover	4	Other book-keeping	2
Industrial measurement	3	Business mathematics	6
General electricity	2	Business correspondence	4
Industrial management	2	Business practice	4
Outline of Industry	1	Typewriting (Japanese)	2
		Typewriting (English)	3
Total vocational	52	Total vocational	41
Home room	3	Home room	3
Grand total	111	Grand total	102

which differ widely in type, it will be noted that over half the time
is spent in general education covering a wide range of subject-
matter.

Opportunities in the upper secondary sector were increased by
the provision of part-time schools with a 4-year span ideally, but
sometimes lengthened beyond this. The courses followed are the
same as those in the full-time schools but they are provided at a
time convenient for the taker—in the evenings, in vacations or in
a slack farming period. The credits obtainable are equivalent to
those in the full-time course. In a similar way correspondence

schools were set up. In these students receive specially prepared texts, study guides and questions and have their corrected work returned monthly. Often full-time schools are found only in the towns and cities, but they have branch establishments operating part time in outlying small towns and villages. It is possible for youngsters to combine correspondence, part-time and full-time education to build up a complete course. In 1952 22·6% were following the part-time route: by 1964 the percentage had fallen to 11·6%.

Before the reform, except in a few vocational schools, education was given on a single-sex basis. The reform made co-education the rule up to the end of compulsory school at the age of 15, but while co-education was encouraged at the upper secondary level it was left optional. However, by 1949 over half the upper secondary schools were co-educational.

Since the end of the occupation in 1952 progress has continued, some changes have been instituted and other changes have been discussed and resisted. Thus, for instance, in 1957 the principals of upper secondary schools wanted to set up a separate track for university-bound students and make it a 6-year school by combining lower and upper secondary schools and giving a 6–6 pattern for these students while leaving a 6–3–3 pattern for vocational courses. This proposal is reminiscent of the outlook of those connected with the brighter academic elsewhere—the insistent demand for the classics course low down in the orientation period in the French *lycée*; the downward extension of the *gymnasium* to include the ninth grade in Sweden; the objection to splitting the 7-year school in Britain. In Japan the suggestion was debated widely but not implemented.

As already noted, over two-thirds from the lower secondary school go on to the upper school and most take a general academic course preparing for university entrance. However, only 30% of those who take the course continue to university, leaving 70% who go to work at 18 without taking a vocational course and there-fore, it is argued, without an appropriate vocational education. Because of this state of affairs some employers' associations have called for a 6-year vocational school, though how this would help is not clear. Anyway this suggestion for early specialisation has also been rejected.

Although decreasing in the post-occupation era, part-time and correspondence courses are still important, and it is now possible to graduate from upper secondary school by correspondence course only. In the early days only part credit could be obtained in this way. A number of the students in part-time education are those who have failed to get the necessary credits in full-time school and are attempting to complete the requirements. There are also some special schools which help repeaters or coach others to gain entrance to favoured universities. In 1957, the Dean of Tokyo University said that the 6–3–3–4 system should really be the 6–3–x–3–x–4 system, with x standing for an unknown number of years spent in cramming outside the ordinary school system to get entrance to famous schools or universities.

In Tokyo no one appears to be in any doubt which are the top institutions. An article in one of the top newspapers,* highlighting the problems brought by the educational explosion, names Hibiya Senior High School, Sundai Preparatory School (one of the cramming institutions) and the University of Tokyo. Of the 3000 freshers at the University of Tokyo in any year only about half are direct from school (colloquially these are nicknamed the *gen-eki* or soldiers on active duty) and about a half are *ronin* (whose nickname signifies unemployed *samurai* or noblemen-soldiers) rejected the previous year and obtaining entrance after a cramming course. In 1966 there were 130,000 *ronin* looking for places: in 1967 with the post-war bulge leaving school, the number is expected to be 210,000. Hibiya Senior High School heads the entrance stakes for the University of Tokyo, gaining about 6% of the places, but Sundai Preparatory School, which specialises in obtaining entrance by concentrated cramming and the setting of weekly mock examinations, supplied 38% of University of Tokyo freshers in 1964 and 31% in 1965. Sundai School also gains many

* "Japan's educational rat-race", *Mainichi Daily News*, Monthly International Edition, 1 March 1966.

places at other top level universities and institutes. Private senior high schools (32% of all senior high schools were private in 1965) also cram for entrance.

Despite the "districting" already referred to, there are many "border-jumpers" whose parents "rent" apartments to get an address inside the coveted zone though they never intend to live there. This tactic extends to junior high and even primary levels in the struggle to get to Hibiya Senior High School. Under these conditions real education suffers.

With the demand for education so intense, resulting so often in an unsuitable education being given, there has been a growing feeling that there ought to be some kind of post-compulsory education for everyone beyond the age of 15. To this end in 1963 the Ministry asked the Central Council for Education to provide advice on the expansion and improvement of education at the upper secondary stage. This inquiry—the counterpart of our Crowther investigation—was split into two parts, one dealing with the purposes of education and the other concentrating on organisation.

In January 1965 an interim report from the purposes section sketched out "The ideal image of a Japanese."* First it pointed out some of the problems of Japanese society in the post-war period, emphasising the dehumanising effect of industrialisation and the difficulty of the void caused by the conscious striving to turn away from a past which had led to the excesses of the war era. While not asking for a return to a narrow and extreme patriotism, it underlined the need for the growth of a national consciousness and sketched out a model of the ideal Japanese. It lists the attributes required by the citizen as an individual, a family man, a member of society and a citizen. Inevitably a model of this kind, when viewed from the standpoint of reality, appears to be wildly overdrawn, asking for such attitudes as a respect for work, a mastery of machines, a respect for the social order, an appreciation of beauty, a love of Japan and the urge in a spiritual and moral sense, to be a strong Japanese.

Many critics found the image, and especially its nationalistic

* *Times Educational Supplement*, No. 2602, 4 February 1965, p. 1012.

slant, disturbing, and asked if it was possible for one image to fit a whole people: if strength was not to be found in diversity, and if in a true democracy an opposition viewpoint is not essential. Some saw it as an echo of earlier strivings which had led to an ultra-nationalistic feeling and pointed to an average committee age of 68 which meant a completion of formal education before World War I. This is an interim report and it appears that arguments about it will continue.

On the organisational side the committee reported in 1966, prefacing its suggestions by recommending that opportunities for all 15–18-year-olds should be available according to aptitude and ability (cf. our 1944 Act, though in the higher age range it is likely that aptitudes will be more amenable to ascertainment). Six definite suggestions were made.

1. It would be desirable to differentiate courses in high schools to clarify such trends as arts or science or girls' courses.
2. For part-time courses day release on a one-day-per-week basis should be granted.
3. Short course high schools with 2-year and 18-month courses should be instituted.
4. Secondary courses at schools offering only such subjects as cookery, beauty-care, art, dressmaking and typewriting should be integrated into the unit structure with units gained qualifying as formal credit towards the graduating total.
5. Youth-worker schools should be established with a course of 300 hours per year part time and including general cultural subjects as well as vocational training. Units gained here should help towards a formal qualification.
6. In larger cities the Government should build or establish youth centres for the age range 15–25.

Since the war the emphasis in high school has been on a common core with specialisation added. These suggestions seem to represent the introduction of a more narrow specialisation and lead away from the idea of common courses for all. In fact, if the institutions suggested by the committee are considered along with those already available there is a striking parallelism between what is recommended for Japan and the analysis made by T. R. Weaver (discussed in Chapter 5) asking for attention to plodders, pedestrians, hurdlers and fliers. Both advocate wide and diverse provision.

To complete the picture of upper secondary provision a brief reference to the miscellaneous schools shown in Fig. 9 is necessary. For some years they were of two main types: schools which specialise in music and art for the educationally gifted but also teach general subjects; and some schools, more nakedly vocational than any described so far, with a shorter course teaching professional skills. It is this second category which the commission recommends should be integrated into the credit-awarding system. Since 1962 a further institution—a hybrid of school and college—has been inaugurated. Taking students from the lower secondary school these 5-year special high schools combine senior high and junior college to provide an integrated education primarily for technological training. As yet numbers are small, but the rate of growth is rapid.

NUMBER OF 5-YEAR SPECIAL HIGH SCHOOLS, 1964–5.

	Institutions	Teachers	Students
Number	46	1418	15,398
Increase over 1963–4	35%	73%	80%

SOCIAL STUDIES AND MORAL EDUCATION

The curriculum is centrally controlled and can and does change from time to time, but on the whole modifications have not been unduly great except in the area covered by the broad term "social studies". The attitude towards social studies is important and worth a detailed survey, because the whole problem of moral studies is intimately connected with it.

The U.S. Education Commission recommended, in 1946, the substitution of social studies for morals, and this was quickly implemented, but by 1958–9 moral education was re-introduced into all grades of elementary and lower secondary school. In this context moral education was stated to be designed to develop in the child an awareness of basic moral principles, and an appreciation of those qualities which are recognised as being essential for good character and habitual right conduct. In the upper secondary school, from 1957, all students have been required to take four courses under the broad heading of social studies. Two of these must be courses in "ethics–civics" and "political science–economics", while the other two must be chosen from a series of courses in geography and history. These choices replace courses in general social studies and current problems. So, in little over 10 years after the institution of courses of social studies in place of morals, the change has been reversed and moral training below the age of 15 and "ethics–civics" above, have become compulsory and there are separate courses in history and geography though they are still presented under the general heading of social studies.

Actually this is the second re-introduction of moral education in Japan. In the initial modernisation era the teaching of morals was dropped temporarily, only to be introduced again after a short intermission. Thus is shown the persistence of national traits and aims in a country's educational system. This *volte-face* is worth studying in detail because it shows clearly the difficulties of culture borrowing and, at the present time, may have lessons for practice in the United Kingdom where the Schools Council in its Working Paper No. 2, entitled *Raising the School Leaving Age*, is making a case for an amalgam of subjects, an even wider field than the words "social studies" connote.

> There is traditionally a large area of the curriculum which has to do with understanding man and his place in this earth. Sometimes this area is comprised under the term "the literary subjects"—history, geography, English and religious education. Here, however, the term "humanities" is used because it is more descriptive of the purposes the Council has in mind.
> Within this area of the curriculum the teacher has a great deal of room for manoeuvre. It is also quite evident that the modern world cannot be

understood without impinging on the field of economics, and that sociology, psychology and anthropology have a contribution to make to a teacher's armoury, even though these descriptions are unlikely to appear on the pupil's timetable.

The task is . . . one of showing that humanity is engaged in a long, exciting and strenuous venture; that those who are willing to shoulder some responsibility for the quality of life are helping: that if you cannot explain everything that puzzles you, your actions are still your own responsibility. It is a matter of indicating the range of judgements any ordinary person is liable to face, the chanciness of life in both big and little things, the tenuousness of the threads by which civilisation is held together, the inevitability of conflicts of interest.*

These long quotations indicate the wide field which the Schools Council hope can be taught together: broader even than morals, geography and history in the Japanese setting but certainly including them. One can visualise many problems and the Schools Council write:

We are not alone in facing this problem; In the U.S.A. the whole matter of social studies is under review once more. And in Sweden . . . social studies topics are among the least popular subjects among Swedish students.†

Certainly the experience from Japan should not be neglected.

Before 1872, when Japan was opened up to Western influences, she had been imbued for centuries with Confucian doctrines teaching respect for the past, obedience to authority and loyalty to superiors. Confucianism was treated not as a philosophy but as an ethical system having to do with the affairs of government and social relations. In particular the acceptance of the authority of tradition and loyalty to parents became an integral part of Japanese culture.

After 1872 the aim of the school became a practical one—to enable students to master a great body of information in a brief time. Japan wanted to be able to meet other countries on equal terms, and knowledge became of first importance. However, it did not take long for reaction to begin. Leaders in the Government

* Schools Council, Working Paper No. 2, *Raising the School Leaving Age*, H.M.S.O., London, 1965, pp. 14–17.
† *Ibid.*, p. 15.

became alarmed at the independence of students and conserva-
tively-minded people began to campaign for a return to Confucian-
ethical doctrines, and in 1880 a morals course become compulsory.
The education department began to compile books giving guidance on the principles of loyalty and filial piety. Then, in 1886, a
uniform standardised educational system under central control
was instituted, and it was stated "what is done (in the schools) is
not for the sake of the pupils, but for the sake of the country".
Included in the programme were the teaching of morals, military
training and nationalism. 1890 saw the publication of the Imperial Rescript on Education which tied together religion, patriotism and the family system. It became a catechism memorised and
recited by the people and it periodically became the centre of a
religious ritual in school assemblies. Until 1946 it remained the
central philosophy of the curriculum and, although primarily
taught in the morals course, it also affected history, geography
and other subjects. The Rescript was continually re-interpreted
in line with rising nationalism and became of immense importance.
With the defeat came, even before occupation, the suspension of
the course in morals, history and geography and then, at the
beginning of the occupation, the introduction of social studies,
due to encouragement from United States' influences. The change
in orientation was aided by the provision of a new set of aims set
forth in the Fundamental Law of Education which became a substitute for the Imperial Rescript on Education. The latter was
eventually officially withdrawn in 1948. Where the Rescript had
stressed duties, the new law emphasised rights—of equal opportunity according to ability; of academic freedom; of freedom from
discrimination on account of race, creed, sex and family origin.
Education was now to promote full development of personality
and esteem pupils as individuals. On the basis of this new philosophy the social studies course was erected. However, even as
early as 1950, the social studies curriculum became a target for
attack on a variety of grounds. First, there was the general dissatisfaction with the nature of the course and a demand for the
re-institution of separate subjects especially in geography and

history. The parents and public wanted subjects which could be taught factually rather than only by the discussion of problems. It was suggested that the materials used in the course were often inadequate and the subject badly taught. The new methods were, in fact, not understood because there was a lack of tradition of integrated subjects. Parents, and adults in Japan generally, as elsewhere, were concerned with the moral development of the youngsters and feared that some of the questioning attitudes fostered by problem-solving methods encouraged rebellion and rejection of the traditional. Japan, they pointed out, had no Sunday schools to teach morals as happens in U.S.A. Hence, they argued, morals should be taught in the day school. Public opinion polls on this question conducted in 1955 and again in 1957 showed support for more moral training. In 1955 72% thought that better manners and stricter discipline were necessary in the compulsory school ages; 66% thought teaching should include respect for parents (filial piety had been a corner stone of the Rescript).

Younger people and those with a longer period of education were less decided in favour of "morals teaching" than the older and less well-educated.

In 1957 70% of those over the age of 20 wanted something like "morals teaching" restored in a certain degree and 62% said lack of moral standards made such teaching a necessity.

However, when asked if special time should be set aside for such teaching, 42% said "No" and 38% said "Yes". 30% would be willing to approve a special text-book on morals.

The 1955 poll showed 46% wanting history taught as a special subject but also 33% as being against the compartmentalisation of the course.

In 1953 the Ministry of Education had wanted straight teaching of history and geography in order to awaken national self-consciousness. They condemned social studies as unmethodical and wanted systematic teaching to ensure real learning. Social studies, with its problem solving, they categorised as an American import based on American experience. It ought, they contended, to be replaced by education characteristic of Japan. Some educators resisted the reverse trend but revision went ahead and reorganisation of social studies took place on a voluntary basis in 1956–7. In particular, the scope of morals teaching was expanded, and history and geography were to be taught systematically. In the lower secondary school the former social studies course was broken up into separate fields—geography in the seventh grade, history in the eighth grade and politics, economics and sociology in the ninth grade with moral education conducted simultaneously but without a separate course.

After 1954 specialised history and geography text-books and books based on a unit of work and problem-solving could not find a publisher.

At the upper secondary level, in 1956–7, general social studies and current problems were abolished and civics became a required course along with two courses from Japanese history, world history and cultural geography. Nearer to the present came the changes already listed—morals in the compulsory school, and at the upper secondary level only a general subject area called social studies with clearly defined subjects inside it. An "ethics–civics" course became compulsory.

This experience suggests that amalgams of subjects are hard to establish. No one, of course, would suggest on this evidence that because integration was not successful in Japan it will not work elsewhere. The exercise can suggest, though, where problems may be encountered. It also reflects the Japanese approach to the curriculum which has tended to stress what can be tested rather than more general life-outcomes which are less susceptible to examination. The annual nationwide scholastic achievement tests which have been conducted since 1956 are a testimony to this approach to education. Each year a test has been given in two selected subjects to a random sample, designed to give a true cross-section of the country, of 5% of elementary and lower secondary schools and 10% of upper secondary schools. In 1961 a complete survey of second- and third-year secondary pupils was carried out in Japanese, social studies, mathematics and science—

the whole of the compulsory core. Thus upper secondary schools know precisely the foundations on which they have to build. A major objective of the achievement testing is to provide data which will help the central authority to improve school curricula and also help each school to evaluate its efficiency as compared with national averages. However, not only overall national scores are published: there is a breakdown showing the averages obtained in a wide variety of areas—industrial urban, commercial urban, rural, mountain villages, fishing villages and remote areas to list a few of the classifications. The test is given simultaneously all over the country with identical questions in a 50-minute test prepared by a Ministry of Education committee.

This chapter began by emphasising the American appearance of the Japanese system. The pattern remains but internal adaptations have gone on to satisfy Japanese ends, so although it may outwardly reflect an alien pattern, inwardly it becomes more and more Japanese. As King puts it:

> The obvious attractions of many features in the American school system have been tried in a totally different context over a period of twenty years. It is possible to discern how much of what Americans attribute to the educational system in *their* country is not due to the schools at all, but to the surrounding matrix of American institutions and practices. It is also easy to see what the same school pattern will do in Japan, and what it will *not* do—at least just now.*

Like much else in modern Japan, what the educational system does show is that a great deal can be accomplished in two decades of real endeavour.

* King, E. J., Educational progress and social problems in Japan, *Comparative Education*, vol. 1, no. 2, 1965.

CHAPTER 11

U.S.S.R.—Links with Life

MOST commentators on the Russian scene agree that educational growth since the 1917 revolution is one of the success stories of the Bolshevik regime. During this period of almost half a century the system has evolved quickly through the stages outlined by Laska (see Chapter 1). Before the Revolution Russia was in Stage I, but, after the initial chaos following 1917, it went rapidly through Stage II, despite some difficulty in realising a primary completion ratio of near 100%, and before 1940 it had entered Stage III. De Witt* lists the following comparative figures for U.S.A. and U.S.S.R. in the mid 1950's.

U.S.A.		U.S.S.R.
23	Entering higher education	10
57	Graduating from complete upper secondary	30
85	Entering upper secondary school (age 15)	55
99	Completing elementary school	98
100	Base	100

This is a very considerable achievement which certainly outstrips the performance in England and Wales which the Crowther Committee were analysing for more or less the same period. In reviewing progress in the U.S.S.R. it is usual to pinpoint 1957

* De Witt, N., *Education and Professional Employment in the U.S.S.R.*, Washington, 1961.

194

with the successful launching of Sputnik as a highlight. As already noted in Chapter 7, this event accelerated a reappraisal of education in the United States. Stocktaking in one form or another became the order of the day from the production of *What Ivan knows but Johnny Doesn't* at the primary level to the strictures of Admiral Rickover on the high school. Khrushchev's reform of American education it has been half-jokingly called.

Reappraisal was also the keynote in the Soviet Union in the same decade. Growing confidence of their ability to produce the necessary high level leaders in science and technology led to a continuous questioning from 1952 onwards of the educational system that had been built up during the years of Stalin's rule. These questionings were concerned with the social stratifications which education was tending to build up, and with the lack of the right attitude to physical work by the academically trained products of the school system. Success in 1957 may have been the final event which made possible the Khrushchev theses of 1958, reforming the educational system and aiming to strengthen the ties between education and life.

But less than 6 years later this reform has been unscrambled, though without the formality of a new law. The change is, indeed, called an amendment.

> The experience gained . . . has made it possible to appraise all the aspects of the reconstruction work and to introduce some amendments. In August 1964 the Soviet Government resolved to cut secondary education by rationalising labour training but without detracting from general educational standards. Reorganisation of the general educational secondary school into the ten-year school has been going on in the 1964/5 academic year, with the curricula for general education subjects previously established being preserved. The instructional material, however, is somewhat differently distributed over the academic years.*

A cut of 1 year from 11-year school to 10-year school is a considerable amendment especially when it follows so quickly after the extension. The implementation of the 1958 reform was to be completed over a period of 5 years and it was stated to be

* Ministry of Education R.S.F.S.R., *Public Education in the Soviet Union*, Moscow, 1965.

complete by 1963. A retrenchment after only 1 year seems to suggest a hurried attempt to retrieve a wrong development. The 1964 amendment will take 2 years to become fully operative and so the beginning of the 1966 school year will see the new school pattern of 4–4–2 working fully.

In recent years then the pattern of Soviet education has changed as follows:

(a) Pre-1958. 4 years primary; 6 years secondary.
(b) Khrushchev's reform; 4 years primary; 4 years incomplete secondary (to compulsory school age); 3 years upper secondary.
(c) 1964 amendment. 4 years primary; 4 years incomplete secondary; 2 years upper secondary.

It can be seen that under the latest revision the upper secondary school remains as an entity after the end of compulsory schooling at the age of 15. The period since the end of the Great Patriotic War, as the Russians like to call World War II, has also seen the provision of several alternative modes of educational provision for the post-15 age group. The opportunities available are outlined in Article 121 of the Constitution of the U.S.S.R. as amended by the law of 1958. It reads:

> Citizens of the U.S.S.R. have the right to education. This right is ensured by universal compulsory eight-year education; by extensive development of secondary general polytechnical education, vocational–technical education, secondary specialised education and higher education, based on the principle of the tie between education and life and production; by extensive development of evening and extension-correspondence education; by free education in all schools; by a system of state grants; by instruction in schools being conducted in the native language; and by the organisation in the factories, state farms, machine and tractor stations and collective farms of free vocational, technical and agronomic training for the working people.

At the upper secondary level this indicates three strands, though if on-the-job training in factories and farms is included it can be looked upon as a quadripartite system (see Fig. 10). This latter strand is not confined to the upper secondary level but includes

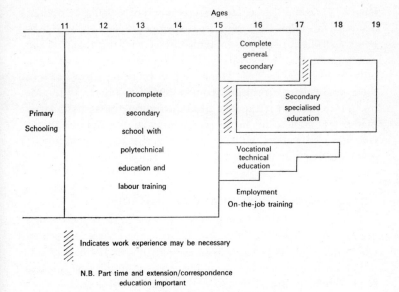

FIG. 10. The new arrangements in the U.S.S.R. (post-1964).

the training and retraining which goes on throughout life. In 1964–5 the total student body was 69 million giving a fraction of about one-third of the entire population (minus pre-school children) in different establishments of an educational nature. The figures for students completing courses in 1964 are given as follows:

Leaving the 8-year school	4,000,000
Completing	
General education secondary school:	
full time	1,040,000
part time	700,000
Vocational–technical school	943,000
Secondary specialised education	550,000

These figures, already rounded when they arrive from Soviet sources, give some idea of the relative present importance of the different strands, but, as will be detailed later, the courses vary in length, so useful percentage figures are not calculable. When dealing with figures for those leaving upper secondary establishments in 1964 it must also be remembered that the valley on the demographic curve for the U.S.S.R. reached the end of compulsory schooling in 1960. Hence upper secondary institutions in these years were recruiting from a reduced cohort. With this taken into account it appears, from the figures given, that a large majority of adolescents in the U.S.S.R. have some kind of upper secondary education, built on a basis of 8 years of compulsory schooling starting at the age of 7.

UPPER GENERAL SECONDARY EDUCATION

This type of education may be given in separate schools which are now of 2 years' duration, or in the senior classes of a school which takes pupils through from the age of 7 (a 10-year school) or in a complete secondary school which takes pupils from the age of 11. Whatever the pattern of school organisation the curriculum is uniform throughout the Union. Except in foreign language there is no choice of academic subjects. In the case of foreign language each school normally concentrates on one which is begun at the age of 11 though experiments are being tried with commencement at an earlier age. In theory, at any rate, parents can choose which language their children will learn by opting for the English school, the German school, the French school and so on, the school being one which specialises in the language stated. The idea is to give a mastery of one language rather than a smattering of several. In 1964 school number 20 in Moscow was an English school achieving high standards and in the upper secondary section some pupils were learning Japanese in their productive labour time. Other complications arise where the native language is not Russian as in a number of republics. In Riga schools in 1964, the productive labour requirement was 6 hours weekly against 12 hours in the Russian Soviet Federal Socialist Republic, thus allowing extra time for Russian language as well as Latvian and a foreign language.

The curriculum is broad, unspecialised and laid down centrally. Mathematics and science form a good proportion of the work, but everyone continues with Russian language and literature and history. This latter subject includes much instruction in civics and current affairs, slanted, of course, to the Communist Party and the tenets of Marxism–Leninism. Carrying a whole range of subjects means a lower standard is reached age for age than in English schools. For instance in mathematics, calculus is not normally started in school though recently there have been opportunities for the better pupils to take special courses at institutions of higher education and so accelerate their progress. These arrangements are very similar to the advanced placement programmes in the United States. Also in the U.S.S.R. there are growing up a few very specialised schools like the one at Academogorodok near Novosibirsk in Siberia which will be mentioned again later. Thus, although it is possible to be fairly dogmatic about the curriculum in the schools there are some exceptions which must be allowed for. The most recent change cutting the upper secondary school by 1 year has meant little alteration in the actual curriculum but merely a redistribution over the years. A few rearrangements have affected the years below the upper secondary grades, but it is mainly the reduction in the productive labour requirement that has made the redeployment possible. Table 39 is the curricular scheme for the upper school before and after the amendment.

Worthy of note is the allocation of one period per week to astronomy. This can only give the briefest of introductions to a vast subject. Contrary to what might be expected the introduction of astronomy owes nothing to Sputnik. It has long been in the time-table and even appeared in pre-revolutionary curricula.

Of prime importance is the time given to productive labour training and socially useful work. Much of the debate on education in the last 15 years has centred on this requirement. To understand the position properly it is necessary to look at it in its historical perspective. The full title of secondary education is "general secondary education with polytechnical and labour-training". The education given in the first 4 years from 11 to 15 is

TABLE 39. WEEKLY ALLOCATIONS IN UPPER SECONDARY SCHOOLS

	1958–64				1964–present		
	IX	X	XI	Total	IX	X	Total
Language and literature	3	3	3	9	5/4	4/3	9/7
Mathematics	4	4/5	4	12/13	6	6	12
History	2	3	6	11	3/4	3/4	6/8
Social science	—	—	—	—	—	2	2
Geography	—	2	2	4	—	2	2
Physics	4	4	2	10	5	5	10
Astronomy	—	1	—	1	—	1	1
Chemistry	2	3	2	7	4	3	7
Biology	3	—	—	3	2	—	2
Foreign languages	2	2	3	7	2	2	4
P.E.	2	2	2	6	2	2	4
Drawing	2	—	—	2	1	—	1
	24	24/25	24		30	30	
Productive labour	12	12	12		6	6	

styled incomplete. It becomes complete with the addition of the two (previously three) upper secondary years. The keyword is polytechnical which is of such fundamental importance that sometimes education in the U.S.S.R. is merely described as being polytechnical. The obvious derivation of the word suggests "many-sided applied science" but as used by the theorists of Soviet education it has a much wider meaning. In attempting to put the theorists' ideas to work the practitioners in education have interpreted the meaning in varied ways to meet the exigencies of the period, and the changes taking place in 1965 are another example of the way theory is being worked out in practice. To achieve an understanding it is necessary to look at the problem from the theoretical viewpoint first.

Marxian analysis of capitalism showed how it led to the degradation of workers and craftsmen, relegating them to the position of cogs in a system of hyper-specialism. Marxists have a hatred of over-specialisation, believing education should play a unifying role by removing the distinction between mental and physical labour. By combining productive labour with theoretical learning they believe an all-sided education can be effected. This, for them, is polytechnical education.

As assessed by present theoreticians it includes learning about the major branches of the economy and also work in industry so as to acquire definite industrial skills. It is certainly not merely vocational education but is meant to be the basis of a truly liberal education. Certain principles are to be taught as a part of poly-technical education. Shapovalenko has spelled it out in great detail in his book.*

A brief summary will be attempted here.

Two important facets are:

1. Teaching should pay attention to organisational problems showing the implications of the changeover from more simple to more complex processes; and of the advent of automation and cybernetics. This should inculcate a pro-gressive attitude towards change.
2. Teaching should pay attention to the economic and social principles of production in a socialist regime. Planned de-velopment for increased productivity and the attitudes re-quired to work in a society where the means of production are publicly owned are included here.

These two facets indicate that quite as important as the factual content of the teaching are the attitudes which are to be en-gendered. From such subjects as physics, chemistry, mathematics, geography, natural sciences and technical drawing will be ac-quired the solid foundation of basic knowledge needed in each field of industry and agriculture. Work in school workshops and laboratories and training in factory workshops and in the fields of collective and State farms will enable the theory to be applied practically. From this will come the most general values so that

* Shapovalenko, S. G. (ed.), *Polytechnical Education in the U.S.S.R.*, UNESCO, 1963.

eventually each individual will combine "love and respect for work; knowledge and skills necessary for work in mechanised and automated production so as to guarantee high-quality, low-cost products; (and) interest in scientific and technological developments". Other values from education will combine with polytechnical values to give an "all-round intellectual, physical, technical, aesthetic and manual development; high cultural and moral standards based upon an understanding of obligations to society; a communist outlook and a devotion to country". This is Shapovalenko's recipe for the all-round Soviet man.

Polytechnical education, it thus appears, can be analysed into three strands:

(a) a knowledge of science and technology to give a good understanding of modern processes of production;
(b) a knowledge and ability in some of the skills necessary in modern industrial life;
(c) the right moral attitude towards industrial and manual work.

These are no mean tasks for education and educators to achieve, and no one is likely to be amazed that there has been some faltering on the way to the goal. With the lofty aims from the theorists in perspective, it is now time to look at the practical attempts to put them into effect. Before assessing current changes in detail, it is helpful to take a brief backward glance to see how the present position developed.

Though Russia proper has a long tradition of education and certain commentators, e.g. N. Hans in *The Russian Tradition in Education*,* have stressed the continuity between past and present, there were exceedingly grave areas of backwardness in Russia proper before the Revolution, and in some areas now part of the Soviet Union, there was an almost complete educational gap. The chaos, famine, civil war and foreign intervention which followed 1917, and lasted until 1921, caused some falling away from even

* Hans, N., Routledge, London, 1963.

the low standards that had previously been achieved. At this time Soviet leaders believed in "the algebra of Marxism"—communism would come with international revolution and the present was merely a holding operation. This was a justification for the new economic policy (N.E.P.)—a tactical flirtation with capitalism to help surmount immediate difficulties. In education similar compromises were accepted, and progressive practices in education, especially those based on Dewey's precepts which rejected the dichotomies between pure and applied knowledge, between culture and vocation, were tried out in schools. In essence, at any rate, they are not too dissimilar to the principles of polytechnical education, and in this early experimental period were regarded as sufficiently fulfilling these principles.

Change came with the consolidation of Stalin's ideas at the end of the 1920's. His theory was that if Russian communism was not for ever to be held at the N.E.P. stage, it must work for communism in one country without waiting for world revolution. The U.S.S.R. was an enormous country, rich in resources, and, provided capitalist intervention was not renewed, the Russian proletariat, drawing on Russian wealth, and protected by the vast spaces of Russian geography, could accomplish the task. This became the aim, and educational objectives were changed to make this achievement as quick and sure as possible. A retreat from polytechnicism to a traditional academic education began. From one point of view this change can be construed as a new interpretation of the meaning of polytechnic, which now took on the sense of a firm acquisition of applied knowledge and learning in physics, chemistry, mathematics and the natural sciences. This was still the character of the education given at the end of the war, at the point from which changes are here being reviewed.

The guiding directive of 1931, which remained extant until the reforms of 1958, said: "the combination of learning and productive labour is to be based on the principle that the entire social and productive labour of the pupil is completely subordinate to the process of learning and upbringing, which is the major task of the school." To put this in the kindest theoretical light, it can be pointed out that this interpretation is stressing the first of the three strands into which the polytechnical principle has been analysed. It seems to neglect entirely the other two strands. In schools this meant a return to the time-tested methods of the continental European school, with an emphasis on discipline and obedience, on learning and grading; on a mastery of basic academic knowledge. The social and political aspects of education moved into the extra-curricular field. Inside the school the authority of the teacher became paramount. Polytechnical education now ceased to be actively discussed, and many educators who had been in the vanguard in the experimental period were lost in the "pedology" purge of 1936. Academic standards were now of first importance, and, despite the preparations for war, and the war itself, when it came, the Soviet educational system went on developing through Stage II and on into Stage III. Set-backs suffered during the war were overcome during the early "iron curtain" years, and, as the necessary mastery of the sciences was achieved, and the requisite number of properly-trained personnel began to become available —one might almost write "began to roll off the production line"— so the idea of polytechnical education began to be discussed once more. One of Stalin's last pronouncements in 1952 spoke of the need for a many-sided education to give full mental and physical development so that people had a free choice of occupation and were not chained to one. Malenkov reiterated the same thought in the same year, and polytechnical instruction was incorporated into the fifth 5-year plan (1951–5). At first it was a moderate adjustment of the curriculum to supplement theory and to stimulate interest in technical fields.

During 1954–5 an experiment was undertaken in twenty-six schools in the Ukraine. Special study groups in 10-year schools worked for their graduation certificates and for a work qualification at the same time. The experiment was declared a success, and a large number of schools in other republics began to work along the same lines. Simultaneously, at educational conferences, lack of ideological keenness was being blamed on the schools, and a useful labour requirement was suggested as a remedy. In 1956, at the twentieth Party Congress, Mr. Khrushchev also indicted the schools for failing to give sufficient preparation for practical activity and there followed a revision of school programmes stepping up manual training by about 1000 hours during the 10-year course. The following year it was announced that fifty experimental schools had been set up with 11- and 12-year programmes. The upper grades in these schools spent 3 days in classes and 3 days in actual work outside the school.

This period in the middle fifties was thus one of debate and of innovations. The academic schooling, introduced in the thirties, was now producing all the necessary academically inclined adolescents willing to proceed to advanced work at university level. What was required now was a reorientation to some kind of specialised training which would develop lower and middle work skills to give a correct balance. Technologists must be supported by the correct ratio of technicians who also need their own supporting grades (our own pamphlet, *Technical Education*, which came out in 1956 was making the same point; see Chapter 5). All the attempts so far had been small innovations and relatively slight rearrangements. Others were wanting more drastic changes. Some educationists and some Communist Party leaders were in favour of shortening the 10-year school to 7 or 8 years of straight schooling, followed by a further period of 2 or 3 years organised on parallel tracks and including vocational education—a kind of tripartite system at the upper secondary level, and, in fact, the current practice is really very much in accord with this idea. The suggested cut in the length of schooling from 10 to 8 years was attacked by some teachers as a retrograde step, but some of the opponents were prepared to accept diversified schooling at this level. Thus by 1958 there was much discussion concerning change and a trend in school towards the development of labour skills. In April of that year the thirteenth conference of the Communist Youth League (Komsomol) accused schools of separating themselves from life and production and inculcating a wrong attitude of contempt for productive work. Labour training was stressed and the vocational aspect of polytechnical education was singled out for approbation; in fact it was almost redefined as work training in a single branch of production. The Komsomol conference was followed by more discussion and the publication of the Khrushchev memorandum "On the strengthening of the relationship of school with life and the further development of public education in the country". Again were expressed the criticisms of the school—that it suffered from abstraction and verbalism; it was too bookish; it promoted social snobbishness; it was separated from life and failed to foster the true Communist morality in its students. It was really an attack on the attitudes being engendered to physical and manual work. Once more discussion followed and there were even some dissentient voices but in December 1958 the new law was adopted. It was to come into force as soon as possible but it was to be fully implemented, at the latest, by 1963. The essence of the new law seems to be the stress on the school and life link—the moral angle—and the work experiences which are introduced are intended to put this right. Polytechnical education, in the context of the new law, had a connotation of vocational training, even a narrow introduction to one variety of work. The law set out the task of the school as follows. "The Soviet school is called upon to prepare well rounded educated individuals who have mastered the foundations of knowledge, and, who, at the same time, are capable of systematic physical labour; to instil into the young the desire to be useful to society; and to take an active part in producing the values society needs." The law also lays down afresh the organisation by which the educational system will achieve these ends. This is article 121 which has already been quoted. It incorporated a number of changes from the pre-1958 period, and as the 1964 changes have really only affected the general secondary school it is opportune at this point to consider the other provisions at the upper secondary level which still continue unchanged. After this description an analysis of the working of the productive labour requirement will lead to the current reappraisal.

After eight-year school pupils who do not proceed directly to the general secondary school or to employment have two other alternatives mentioned clearly in article 121—the vocational–technical school and the secondary specialised school. Entrance to the latter, which is a kind of hybrid institution—a combination of upper secondary and higher education—requires an intervening period of employment before entry. These two institutions have no close parallels elsewhere and their function is perhaps best explained by a comparison with our terminology. The pyramid of technologist, technician, craftsman, operative and trainee is a familiar simplifying concept, though in reality there is a good deal of overlap between the categories. Applying these terms to the U.S.S.R. trainees and operatives are mainly trained on the job by brigades or teams. A list of 10,000 different job categories has been drawn up and all crafts requiring less than 1000 hours of training can be taught on the job itself in 6 months. There are 4500 job categories susceptible to this treatment. The vocational–technical school is for craftsmen at higher levels of sophistication; the secondary specialised institutions train the technician while the future technologist is at the general secondary school. But not all who complete the general secondary school become technologists who will need higher education. Increasingly they proceed to shortened specialised courses at technician level.

VOCATIONAL–TECHNICAL SCHOOLS

The system of schools for craftsmen and technicians was instituted to supply the large numbers of skilled workers required by the industrialisation programme. Between 1928 and 1958 the number of workers in non-agricultural employment increased from 10 million to 50 million. Forty million added to the industrial labour force in 30 years, as well as replacements, has meant a huge programme of recruitment and training. In the late 1930's when the progress of industrialisation was exceedingly rapid, there was a shortfall in the numbers coming forward and in 1940 the State Labour Reserve Administration was set up and over half a million youths aged 14–17 years were directed to various types of course, of a duration between 6 months and 2 years. Right up to

1958 a similar average recruitment figure was maintained. Originally all courses were oriented towards industry, but from early in the 1950's agricultural courses were added. Recruitment was mainly from those who had completed seven grades of school and were not able to continue academic education, but boys from rural districts who had left school early were also admitted. In this way youths were transferred from a rural environment to urban jobs. The schools took mainly boys: only about one-fifth of the entrants were girls. Later some youths who had completed ten grades of education were taken. There were a variety of schools: mining, trade, railway, factory, and mechanisation of agriculture were some of the titles. All operated a similar broad allocation of time as follows:

> 80% to applied skills and trade subjects;
> 20% to general education, political teaching and physical education.

With the educational reform to include productive work the State Labour Reserve was reorganised in 1959 as the State Committee on Vocational–Technical Education, which offered courses of varying length, from 6 months to 3 years, in vocational–technical schools and also overlooked the production training in the general secondary schools.

On the basis of a fresh analysis of the skills required the new vocational–technical schools were organised on three levels:

(a) Courses lasting from 6 to 12 months, training operatives for one speciality only, e.g. bulldozer driver or lathe operator. These courses are based on 1600 instruction hours per year, of which only 200 hours are of a general nature.

(b) Two-year courses entailing 3000 hours instruction and training aimed at craftsmen for more general work such as welding, automatic machine-tool operating and electrical work.

(c) Three-year courses with 5000 hours of instruction, training craftsmen needing a higher degree of skill e.g. toolmakers, die makers.

The trades in the first two of these groups could also be followed in the production training section of the upper section of the 11-year general secondary school.

The function of the whole range of vocational–technical schools is to provide for a steady flow of trained operatives and craftsmen for industry. Because of the nature of the course these schools have not been affected by the 1964 amendment to the 1958 law though, of course, it is just this kind of training in the general secondary schools which has been eliminated.

SECONDARY SPECIALISED EDUCATION

The secondary specialised schools function at a higher level to produce the personnel required for intermediate levels of responsibility, and overlap to some extent in function with the institutions of higher education. These secondary specialised schools are known as *technikums* which is hardly sufficiently explanatory of their purpose because, in addition to such specialities as electronic technicians, technical draftsmen, machine-shop foremen and so on, they also train medical aides (who often function as G.P.s in rural areas), nurses, primary school teachers, veterinary aides and dentists. The specialities for which they train each have a curriculum carefully worked out and are divisible into five broad groups, the relative importance of which has changed over the period under survey.

TABLE 40. GROUPINGS AND PERCENTAGE OUTPUT OF SECONDARY SPECIALISED EDUCATION

Group	No. of specialities	Percentages of graduates	
		1940	1955
Engineering	289	25	51
Agriculture	12	12	17
Socio-economic	29	4	7
Educational–cultural	34	38	14
Health	9	21	11

However, during this same period enrolments have doubled from almost 1 million in 1940 to almost 2 million in 1955 ($3 \cdot 3$ million in 1964–5) so a lower percentage, as for instance in health specialities, does not mean a reduction in actual numbers though, of course, a doubled percentage, as for engineering, does indicate a fourfold increase of yield.

Previously the administration of these institutions was under the control of the individual ministries in charge of the different branches of the economy but now it is co-ordinated under the Ministry of Higher and Secondary Specialised Education. This emphasises the overlap with higher education and underlines the important point that many of those enrolled are now outside the 15–18 age group though this was originally not so marked as at present. Thus until 1950 the usual recruitment was to a 4-year course from those who had completed 7 years of school, but since that date, 2-year courses for those who have completed the 10-year school have been instituted. In 1954 some specialisms, e.g. law, dentistry, pedagogy began to accept only those from 10-year school, and by 1956 about two-thirds of entrants to secondary specialised education had completed 10 years of schooling. However, even under the 1958 law there is still a recruitment from the 8-year school. Entry is by competition with an examination in Russian composition (or native language) and mathematics, and for some specialities also in a history of the peoples of the U.S.S.R. Students get financial aid, the actual amount depending on the course taken and the degree of seniority reached.

The main object of the 1958 reform as far as these institutions was concerned was to unite the study of the speciality with practical experience and socially useful labour. This lengthened the course for now, in addition to a semi-professional qualification, mastery of a skilled trade was also required. The longer course became of $4\frac{1}{2}$ years' duration and the shorter course $2\frac{1}{3}$ years though a part of each course became part time—something like a sandwich course—though evening attendance was required at the college after a working day in industry. However, this was not an innovation, for alongside the full-time method of qualification there had always been part-time study, either in the evenings or by extension–correspondence course. The figures of Table 41 for 1959 indicate the importance of the alternative methods in secondary specialised education.

TABLE 41. ALTERNATIVE METHODS OF STUDY (SECONDARY SPECIALISED SCHOOLS, 1959)

Method	Numbers enrolled	%
Full-time day	1,067,000	56
Part-time evening	318,000	16·7
Extension–correspondence	523,000	27·3

Thus 44% were following a secondary specialised course while still carrying on with a job. For these the practical experience added by the 1958 law was unnecessary: these students were already at work. Figures for students completing the course in 1964 show a total of 550,000, and, of these 245,000 achieved success by the part-time method—about the same percentage as in 1959 but still a lower percentage than in higher education where about 50% take the course part time. Students following the extension–correspondence method visit their tutors at regular intervals, and for all part-timers there are statutory arrangements concerning study-time free from work before examinations. The general secondary school has a part-time alternative in what are called alternating-shift schools. This may be evening provision for day-shift workers or day provision for those working in the afternoon. As shifts alternate so classes are available. Part-time methods lead to the same examinations as the full-time course and so admittance to higher education is always possible even for those who leave school at 15 but have the necessary perseverance.

The curriculum of the secondary specialised schools requires about 40 hours of work each week on the full-time course, and 15 hours on the part-time evening course after 40–45 hours at a full-time job. There are three basic divisions to the curriculum:

(a) The general (academic) education subjects including Russian, history, a foreign language, physics, chemistry, political economy and physical education. This takes up one quarter of the time or slightly more.

(b) The technical subjects which can be further subdivided into two parts:

   (i) non-specialised technical subjects common to a number of specialisms;

   (ii) more narrow specialist subjects geared to one specialism only. Each of these two subdivisions demands almost one quarter of the time allocation.

(c) This leaves one quarter or slightly more for applied workshop instruction and industrial practice which is the third element in the course.

The 1964 amendments reducing production practice have been felt mainly in this third section of the course. In some courses it is hoped to reduce the course by as much as 12 months though obviously in some of these specialities a good deal of applied workshop instruction is essential.

The actual number of hours involved in a course can best be realised by a tabulation of time for a course in radio-engineering.

TABLE 42. TOTAL HOURS IN A 4-YEAR COURSE
IN RADIO-ENGINEERING

	Hours
(a) General subjects	
Humanities and P.E. 868	
Maths and pure science 702	
	1570
(b) (i) General engineering including	
theory and technical drawing	1108
(ii) Specialised engineering	1116
(c) Applied instruction	1440
Total	5234

This course was being taught from 1956 to 1958 before the Khrushchev reform.

In interpreting these figures it should be remembered that a British sixth-former is at school for 25–30 hours per week for 40 weeks in a year—a total of 1000–1200 hours. Not all this is face-to-face time, though sixth-formers nowadays have fuller time-tables and fewer free periods than 10 or 15 years ago. In addition, the sixth-former has a considerable load of homework—but his Russian counterpart has this too. There is a good deal of discussion of "overburdening" in the Soviet system. The large amount of memory work in the general secondary curriculum is realised. New approaches are being investigated as in the United States and the United Kingdom but it seems to be accepted that the mastery of a good deal of content will always be inevitable. Steps are taken to make sure the learning load is not too heavy. An article in *Pravda* in December 1964 by the Minister of Public Education in the R.S.F.S.R. was headed significantly "Senior classes—better conditions for teaching and recreation". It spoke of the curriculum and programme changes necessary because of the change from 11 to 10 years of school and pointed out that no lowering of standards was envisaged. The rearrangements would make it certain that education in the basic sciences was not below that of the 11-year school. It reiterated that class hours should not exceed six per day and it warned specifically against the construction of a massive out-of-class hours arrangement of lessons. The article also contained strictures against excessive amounts of homework.

Not all who start on a course of upper secondary education, complete it; some drop out on the way. Of those following regular programmes it appears about 70% complete the course successfully, but for those on the more arduous extension–correspondence course, despite arrangements for examination preparation leave, a figure of 40% is quoted. In Moscow in 1964 a 3-year general secondary school had seven classes in the ninth grade but only five in each of the tenth and eleventh grades. Even when allowance is made for a few pupils being required to repeat a year, it still indicates a considerable wastage though to quote a percentage and argue from a specific case would be invalid. In England and Wales the percentage enrolment in school decreases considerably with age (see Table 7, p. 28).

PRODUCTIVE LABOUR AND THE 1964 AMENDMENT

The two important reorientations which the 1958 reform introduced were:

(a) the integration of school and life, and
(b) the productive labour requirement.

The latter was intended to give point to the former and produce a right attitude but the evidence is that this has not materialised and the productive labour programme has been heavily criticised. Integration of school and life has been pursued consciously in all subjects. Any list of articles in pedagogical journals will indicate the thought that has gone into the problem of strengthening the ties between learning and life. In mathematics, for example, schools have collected industrial examples to exemplify their teaching. Changes in teacher training have been introduced to make entrants to the profession better qualified to introduce the new attitude into their teaching.

However, the requirement of 2 days' work in factories during the three upper secondary years has been a main point of contention. Very early the main difficulties became apparent. They can be considered under three headings.

1. *Staffing*

The training in work skills is to be carried out in productive enterprises. Ordinary production workers are not necessarily good teachers and may in fact be the reverse. The collection and training of a body of good teachers will be a lengthy process. Highly skilled workers may not wish to transfer to posts as instructors, and factory managers are often not keen to allow such people to move from production to training.

2. *Physical facilities*

In many cases factories lack the necessary training facilities and it is a lengthy, costly process to provide what is required. When provision is made it will mean that training will be separate from the real work of the factory and may not be effective in producing the required attitudes. Moreover, factory managers do not seem to want adolescent trainees on a part-time basis in the factory where they may so easily interfere with the attainment of production norms.

3. *Academic standards*

The reformed system gave pupils a dual aim and the problem of the maintenance of academic standards under this pressure has been much discussed. The sheer amount of knowledge increases rapidly and every country faces the difficulty of syllabuses loaded too heavily with material. Though the 3 years of schooling give 2 years for general academic work, spread over a period of increasing maturity, many fear a falling off in attainment.

Since 1958 the debate has continued with increased volume while "the workers in public education have considerably cemented the ties of school with the life and work of the entire people" as the Soviet pamphlet *Public Education in the Soviet Union 1964–5* cautiously expresses it. Reorganisation begun in 1964 will be complete by 1966. An article in *Pravda*, 6 January 1965, on production training by school children explains from an actual example the reasons for the change. Significantly it is entitled "Not by calling, but for duty".*

> NOT BY CALLING, BUT FOR DUTY.—On Production Training of School children. (By Staff Correspondent N. Antonov and N. Alexandrov. Pravda, Jan. 6, 1965.) In Kaluga recently, we interviewed people connected in one way or another with production training for secondary-school students. This city possesses substantial possibilities for teaching workers' occupations to upper-grade students. Eighteen instructional shops and sections have

---

* Slavic Studies, *The Current Digest of the Soviet Press*, vol. 17, no. 1, 27 January 1965.

been created at its enterprises. Experienced, knowledgeable foremen have been selected to instruct the students. Many schools have established close ties with the production collectives and with Communist Labor collectives and brigades, a connection that is having a positive effect on the upbringing of boys and girls.

The first interview took place in the instructional shop of the Kaluga Instrument Plant. Eleventh-graders from School No. 9 were at work in the mechanics department of the shop.

"Did you choose this specialty yourselves?" we asked the youngsters.

"There was almost no choice: either mechanic or lathe operator," Vladimir Alkhimov answered for all. "We preferred the mechanic's trade: from what our elders had told us, it seemed the more creative field. But I, for one, would have been delighted to study radiotechnology."

"Who among you intends to stay at this plant after graduation and to work in his specialty?"

"Almost no one," Tanya Lebedeva admitted.

"Why?"

"Some are thinking of entering an institute, and others of finding somewhat more interesting work," the youngsters answered.

We visited a group of lathe operators, tenth-graders from School No. 11. We learned that some of them liked this occupation. But here too, many would have preferred other specialties. Some wanted to be truck-drivers, others were interested in electronics and still others were thinking of studying radio. However, the enterprise at which the school-children were working can teach them only two occupations—lathe operator and mechanic.

The city's pedagogical community has no complaints about the plant. The lathe and mechanics' departments are housed in spacious, well-lighted premises and are well equipped, having modern machine tools and other implements. There are 11 experienced production workers giving instruction to the youngsters. The enterprise is carrying out its duty to the school conscientiously. But R. Ya. Krylov, the plant's director, says:

"Judge for yourself, it costs the state more than 20,000 rubles a year to maintain the instructional shop. And what is the return? Out of 60 school graduates who underwent instruction with us, only ten youngsters have stayed at the plant to work. Hence, the training of each young worker has cost us roughly 2000 rubles. And an expenditure of 45 rubles is sufficient to teach an occupation to any literate individual who comes in from outside."

It is scarcely worthwhile to recount in detail our other meetings with students and with the people who bear the responsibility for their production training. The picture is approximately the same everywhere. The only difference is in the fact that the upperclassmen of some of the city's schools do not like the occupations they are acquiring. And the result is that youngsters are attending the production lessons without the slightest interest, only because it is their duty.

Students, teachers, parents and enterprise managers are discontented with production training in its present form. Where is the way out?

We decided to hear those to whom this matter is primarily entrusted. In the Kaluga City Department of Public Education, a large group of experienced school directors and their assistants in charge of production training gathered at our request. Honored Teacher P. G. Bukatin, director of School No. 9, was first to take the floor.

"Aren't we confusing polytechnical instruction with vocational training?" he asked. "The very term 'polytechnization' has disappeared from our vocabulary in recent times. We live in a day of electricity and cybernetics. Today children are constantly dealing in their daily lives with complicated instruments: television sets, radios, refrigerators and so forth. Meanwhile, our pupil frequently finds himself unable to repair an electric iron. Narrow professionalization is to blame here. Granted, the vocation of lathe operator is fine and necessary. Whoever is attracted to it will master it without compulsion. But if the student does not like a specialty, the lessons will scarcely help to inculcate a respect and fondness for labor in him."

In P. Bukatin's opinion, vocational training also takes up too much of the youngsters' time, so that they do not have time to study their general-education subjects in depth.

"If you ask me, it is necessary to make the school polytechnical in the broad sense," the director concluded. "Then it will be able to prepare its charges to make a bold choice of their paths in life."

"And it would be better to replenish the working class through organizational means, chiefly with the aid of special educational institutions," the foreman M. G. Dementyev added. "I think it would be more correct to expand the network of technical academies and not try to replace them with general-education schools."

"There is no need to endeavor to have all graduates mandatorily acquire some kind of worker's vocation," the school directors M. K. Kayukov and M. V. Yudin declared. "The main thing is to give the students diversified polytechnical knowledge and serious work habits in the school production shops. Most of the boys and girls are not hopeful that the vocation acquired in school will suit them. Therefore, many quit secondary school beginning in the ninth grade. They transfer to technicums or vocational–technical schools or get jobs, completing their education later in evening school."

V. M. Markov, a province public education department inspector who is much concerned with the organization of production training, supported his colleagues. He emphasized that whereas the secondary schools in Kaluga are relatively well provided with instructional production facilities, matters are far worse in the other cities and workers' settlements of the province. Upperclassmen in many schools are compelled to master vocations at small local-industry enterprises with obsolete equipment and technology.

There were also some kind words spoken for production training. Ye. M. Khanin, assistant director of School No. 17, told of the fascination with which boys and girls were studying in the laboratory assistant and office worker sections at the synthetic aromatic substances combine. These lessons have helped many to find their calling: they have entered chemical technology institutes. The only trouble is that the graduates who fail to be admitted to higher schools find it somewhat difficult to obtain jobs in their specialty. The combine has hired only one of its alumni.

Our interviews came to an end. Almost all of those we talked with expressed themselves against narrow professionalization and for the broad polytechnization of the Soviet school.

Of course, the positive experience accumulated through the joint efforts of the pedagogical and production collectives, along with Soviet society, cannot be denied. The school's ties with life must be strengthened still further. All the best aspects, including the material facilities created in recent years, must be used to carry on a well thought-out, broad and scientifically-grounded program for the further polytechnization of the school.

The pedagogues' thoughts and concerns should long ago have met with a response from the Russian Republic Ministry of Education and Academy of Pedagogy. The return to the ten-year schooling period should, in our view, be used primarily in order to extricate the school from narrow professionalization. However, this has not as yet been done. Moreover, what is being curtailed in the revision of the upper-class curriculums for the transitional period is, for example, the section on electronic technology—the basis of modern production.

The groundless restructurings and reorganizations that have been carried out in recent years in various branches of our country's national economy have impinged on our schools as well. It goes without saying that the mistakes must be corrected without haste, without premature solutions, in a thoughtful way and with a careful analysis and consideration of what experience and practice have shown. It seems to us that thought should be given in this same spirit to the considerations expressed by the Kaluga pedagogues, enterprise managers and commanders of production.

This long article is worth quoting in full because it rehearses all the arguments and in places is very outspoken even taking the Ministry and Academy to task. Kaluga is a town about 80 miles south-south-west of Moscow with good conditions in its production shops, and knowledgeable foremen but the choice of trade is very limited and the training cost is high. Even so the training is vocational and not polytechnical education. The polytechnical spirit could be better given in school workshops. If this happens in good conditions how much worse it must be where conditions are poor. True some successes have been achieved, but on the whole the training has been too narrow; the substance has been attained but not the spirit. Links with life must continue and right attitudes must be inculcated. It is in this spirit that the amendment has been made. Everyone has still one day on practical work.

The change is not then a *volte face* but an amendment to reduce an excess. Now at the upper secondary level following a comprehensive system to the age of 15 years which only gives an "incomplete" course, is a broad provision of courses varying from mainly general education with some productive training in the "complete" school, through the specialised institutions with less general education and more professional productive training to the vocational schools with a small general educational element but training mainly for a trade. (In 1964 the director—a lady— of the polygraphic specialised school emphasised first the general education aspect—the library, the orchestra, the summer camp and had a history lesson demonstrated before taking our party to see the pupils printing a higher mathematical text-book ready for sale when it left the school and preparing a coloured poster, requiring eight printings, showing the summer amenities of the Moscow River port.) Even when the British system of further education is included in the reckoning, the U.S.S.R. is making more provision and enrolling a greater percentage of the age group. In this they are helped by their co-ordinated provision of part-time education directed towards qualifications identical with those obtained full time.

Not in the main stream of the school organisation are the schools for gifted children. In Russia, even from pre-revolutionary times, there is a long tradition of separate schooling for the aesthetically gifted and recently other very specialised schools have been organised for outstanding mathematicians and physicists.

For the musically talented there are twenty-five schools in various parts of the Soviet Union. Children are accepted from the age of 7. The normal school curriculum is also followed, though spread over an extended period, to give time for special musical tuition and individual practice on an instrument, in addition to the piano. There are also music schools where after-school tuition is available.

Each of the main ballet theatres has a ballet school taking pupils from the age of 8 or 9 and there are also special art schools for talented pupils. Again the normal curriculum is followed, not only because this is looked upon as a part of the birthright, but so that if talent does not develop as expected, the students can easily transfer to the mainstream of the ordinary school.

A much publicised special institution is the Physics and Mathematical School at Academogorodok near Novosibirsk. This town built since 1957 is a high-powered scientific centre with many scientific institutes and a developing university. Even one of its clubs is called "At the sign of the integer". Here in 1963 was opened a boarding school for young "high fliers" selected by special olympiad. (Sports competitions are *spartakiads*.) They have special tuition in mathematics and science, but in order not to burn them out they have only 5 hours of school work daily instead of the usual 6, and teachers have a difficult job preventing them from reading "shop" in their spare time. From some schools advanced senior pupils attend special classes at universities in order to get an accelerated programme. In 1964 at least one Moscow school for 16–18-year-olds had cybernetics as a part of its productive training programme. All these schemes are deviations from a true comprehensive system though the existence of the common curriculum for all is a comprehensive basis.

There is also a provision of boarding education but again these schools run parallel with the normal day school and have the same curriculum. Provision is first for children without parents or with homes broken in some way, but others are admitted, though fees are charged. Often they are weekly boarding institutions with pupils going home at weekends from Saturday afternoon to Monday morning. The numbers are increasing and in 1964 enrolments had reached about 3 million, an increase of 600,000 in one year. With this must be compared the figure of 46 million in general secondary education as a whole.

Towards the end of 1966 changes in the productive labour requirement already adumbrated earlier in this chapter were taken a stage further. A party-government resolution on the general secondary school published on 19 November 1966 details a number of measures to be implemented by the end of the decade.

First it stresses that the Soviet school must continue to develop as a general education, a labour and a polytechnical school with the chief tasks of giving a firm knowledge of the principles of science, moulding a high Communist consciousness and preparing for life and vocation. It is still emphasising the threefold nature of the school's task as imparting knowledge, giving the right moral attitude and inculcating skills. However, "the diversion of school children in school-time to agriculture and other work not directly connected with the educational process, widespread in recent times will not be permitted".* This seems to end productive labour for its own sake. Nevertheless, all agencies are to assist the school to improve polytechnical instruction and the preparation for socially useful labour.

The Minister of Education for the Russian Republic returns to this again in an explanatory article where he points out that the idea that polytechnical training is inseparable from vocational training has recently been intensely pressed, but practice has shown that it is not justified. Schools have neither the time, the conditions nor the personnel. If favourable conditions exist good can result and one-third of secondary schools in the Russian Republic have continued production training voluntarily although it is no longer a requirement. Figures for places available for work training for 1965–6 are given as follows:

| In industrial enterprises | 68,734 |
| In schools | 482,517 |

About half-a-million places on a 1-day per week basis could cater for 3 million students. Numbers in the upper secondary grades are well in excess of this figure.

One of the aims of productive labour was to give the correct attitude to work. With the change in emphasis in the nature of work experiences in school moral aspects of education are to be catered for in a new way. All secondary schools are to get a deputy headmaster to organise the extra-curricular and extra-mural upbringing work and so inculcate conscious discipline and standards of conduct. Sensible programmes of summer labour camps, practice work, student chores and practical hobby clubs are to be continued.

* *Current Digest of the Soviet Press*, vol. 18, no. 46, 1966.

It now seems definite that a wrong turning taken in 1958 has been rectified.

Other aims to be implemented by 1970 are also made explicit.

The introduction of complete secondary education for everyone is stated as an important task. In 1965 58% of pupils went on to grade 9. By 1967 67% should be continuing in grade 9 and 15% going to technicums full time. For 1970 the target is 100%, i.e. education to the age of 17 years for all Soviet youth.

At the upper secondary level 30 hours per week is the standard maximum but from grade 7 onwards optional lessons can be arranged to deepen knowledge and develop diversified interests. In grades 9 and 10 a certain number of secondary schools can offer more profound theoretical and practical study in the following fields:

> mathematics and computer technology
> physics and radio-electronics
> chemistry and chemical technology
> biology and agro-biology
> the humanities

Both these measures seem to introduce more specialisation than has hitherto been allowed. At the same time modernised courses are being introduced as new basic text-books and study-aids for pupils and methods-literature for teachers become available.

In the Reith lectures for 1966 Professor J. K. Galbraith said: "All industrial societies must plan . . . and, in consequence, there are strongly convergent tendencies as between industrial societies. This is despite their very different billing as capitalist or socialist or communist."* Professor Galbraith did not extend his thesis directly to education, but it is fairly straightforward to see convergence between these latest proposals involving specialisation and the advanced placement programme in the U.S.A. In a more general sense trends at the upper secondary level in the U.S.S.R., the U.S.A., France and Britain all tend towards a common pattern though to categorise the four systems as "strongly convergent" would be, as yet, an overstatement.

* *The Listener*, vol. 76, no. 1964, 17 November 1966.

CHAPTER 12

West Germany—
Academic and Vocational

UPPER secondary educational provision in the Federal Republic of Germany is a most complex affair. From one point of view the system is very advanced for compulsory education covers the years from 6 to 18, though for the last 3 years, i.e. those with which this book is concerned, it may be (and often is) part time in nature. The requirement of education for everyone, either full time or part time, to the age of 18 was accepted as long ago as 1919 (cf. our Fisher Education Act, 1918), and it has been fully applied since 1945. The complexity arises from two sources.

Firstly, the basic law of the Federal Republic of Germany dated 8 and 24 May 1949 has one main sentence dealing with education. It states: "The whole school system is under the supervision of the State (*Länd*)." As there are eleven member states (eight *Länder*, two city states—Hamburg and Bremen—and West Berlin), each of which is responsible for its own system of education, there is a good deal of variety, despite the existence of a co-ordinating body—the Permanent Commission of Ministers of Education—which meets at stated intervals in Bonn to discuss problems of a general nature and to adopt resolutions. It has no legal powers to enforce its decisions so has to be cautious in its approach if it is not to be disregarded and become entirely ineffectual. However, it has brought some uniformity and some items (granted not particularly startling) were incorporated in a treaty signed in February 1955 to run for 10 years. This specified that school grades should be numbered consecutively from 1 to 13. Therefore, since school starting age is 6, this study is mainly concerned with grades 9 onwards. Schools taking pupils as far as the tenth grade were to be known as intermediate schools and all schools running up to grade 13 were to be called *Gymnasien*.

This attempt at a system of nomenclature is noteworthy for the second cause of complexity is one of terminology. The use of the term "secondary education" to denote all forms of education at this level is not universally accepted, and there are over forty different types of school all told. Even plans for the future do not envisage a true integration. The German committee for the educational system, an advisory body of twenty-three distinguished persons, appointed in 1953, to make an overall study of German education, published, in its third bulletin in 1959, a study of the basic principles for the general reorganisation of German education. This *Rahmenplan* (skeleton or outline plan) makes no attempt to integrate general and vocational education. In fact the plan excludes the vocational aspects from its title which is "The Skeleton Plan for the Reorganisation and Standardisation of the Academic School System". In essence this plan for the future is a tripartite structure on traditional lines. The first 4 years of elementary education from the age of 6 are uniform for all pupils in the *Grundschule* (basic school). After 4 years a few are to be chosen for a 9-year school, the *Studienschule* (school of studies) which is really a new name for the present humanistic *Gymnasium* or classical languages grammar school. All those not selected for this 9-year course will have a further 2 years in the basic school extending their knowledge but still using activity methods. After the 2 years of this *Förderstufe* (furthering step) the pupils are separated into three streams in different kinds of upper school.

For most pupils it will be an education in the *Hauptschule* (principal school). Principal is an apt name for it will take over half the pupils, for a 2-year course in some states, and a 3-year course in others, though the hope is that it will eventually be 3 years in all with a common leaving age of 15 years. Pupils from this school will pass into vocational education. Another stream will be in the *Realschule* (practical school) which will offer a 5-year course leading to a certificate of middle maturity. The upper part of this school will be in the upper secondary sector.

The brightest pupils will go to the *Gymnasium*—the 7-year grammar school parallel with the 9-year school. The base of this 7-year school will be 4 years of common work followed by specialisation in modern languages or natural science and mathematics in the last 3 years. Pupils who leave after 4 years will be able to take the certificate of middle maturity and there will be possibilities of transfer for those who do well in the *Realschule* to this upper secondary portion.

Compared with plans in other countries, and what is actually happening in some, e.g. Sweden, the *Rahmenplan* is old-fashioned and unadventurous with its thinking appearing to belong to the pre-war or Spens epoch. It certainly depends on an early decision on transfer from the primary (basic) school for the bright pupils. Some *Gymnasium* teachers have opposed the idea of 7-year grammar school side by side with the 9-year school. They dislike the idea of the furthering step which puts off transfer to 12+, saying that early selection and a long course are necessary to maintain high standards. Others welcome it, and in Hamburg and West Berlin there has been a good deal of experimentation with methods of transfer. Standardised tests play little part in selection: attainment is more important. Experiments with lengthy assessment procedures under school conditions and the use of primary school recommendations have been carried out. One suburb in Hamburg has tried out a kind of orientation period of 2 years from 10+ to 12+ with a system not widely different from the *classes nouvelles* of the early fifties in France. But in the main, determination of the most suitable type of education is by selection from above rather than by self-selection, though this is not unknown. For instance, in West Berlin parents are recommended by the primary school as to the most suitable type of secondary education for their children but a free choice is allowed and 10% do send their children to schools other than the one suggested.

Selection is not only early: it is also very strict. In 1962–4 only about 16% were entering the grammar school and as over half who enter do not complete the course, there is evidently a built-in system of continuous selection during the course.

All this early selection, continuous selection throughout the course, and inequality in the sizes of groups entering different schools, means that rectangular diagrams purporting to explain the system must be treated with great reserve and full weight given to all the implications of Fig. 11 annexed from the *UNESCO World Survey of Education*, vol. 1, p. 302. This gives actual figures for a year in the early fifties and shows the drop-out from the *Realschule* and the *Gymnasium*. It also underlines the great importance of the vocational sector where the rate of drop-out is also seen to be slight.

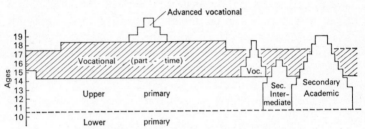

Fig. 11. Educational pattern: Federal Republic of Germany

Hauptschule	Upper primary
Realschule	Secondary intermediate
Gymnasium	Secondary academic
Berufschule	Part-time vocational
Berufsfachschule	Full-time vocational

There is then in West Germany a basic differentiation at an early age between those who will have a general academic education and those whose education will be vocational. This differentiation originated in history, for vocational education came into existence much later than the *Gymnasium* which is an institution hallowed by tradition. Plans for the future retain this bifurcation, although it is sometimes claimed that the distinction is becoming less clear and there is a second way (*der zweite Weg*) to higher education. However, Federal Office of Statistics publications show that in 1961 of all students entering universities and technical high schools, 97% of boys and 98% of girls had completed the grammar school course, leaving very small percentages of both sexes who had gained entry with other qualifications.

To sum up, there are three types of schools to be distinguished at the lower secondary level:

(a) the popular or senior primary school;
(b) the intermediate practical school; and
(c) the very academic grammar school.

Since education is compulsory from 6 to 18 years, the course, though very different in all other aspects, has almost the same length in each of the vertical divisions and so at the upper secondary level it is really only necessary to distinguish two types:

(a) the academic in the *Gymnasien*: this has a clearcut, straightforward structure;
(b) the vocational: this has many variations because, while it is mainly part time, it has also a number of full-time possibilities.

ACADEMIC EDUCATION

The secondary school *par excellence* is the *Gymnasium* which aims to transmit, using a scholarly approach, the cultural heritage to a highly selected group of students who are preparing to go to university. Some are selected very early for a 9-year course which runs from 10 to 19 years, but there is also a shorter course of 7 years or even 6 years starting at 12 or 13 and there are even shorter courses in "promotion" schools or classes which, end-on to the *Realschule*, cater for a few late developers to go on to the examination at the end of the *Gymnasium* course—*Abitur*. At the upper secondary level it is the last 4 years which are important.

The 9-year course is of three types:

(a) classical;
(b) modern;
(c) mathematical and scientific;

and they may be found in separate schools, or as parts of a single school. Each course is very wide ranging and carries many subjects to the end of the course though there are a variety of different weightings as a study of Table 43 will show. Distinctions between

TABLE 43. ALLOCATION OF WEEKLY PERIODS FOR GYMNASIEN. YEARS OF SCHOOLING

	Modern				Maths and science			Classical			
	10	11	12	13	11	12	13	10	11	12	13
Religious instruction	2	2	2	2	2	2	2	2	2	2	2
Philosophy	—	—	—	2	—	—	2	—	—	—	2
German	4	4	4	4	4	4	4	4	4	4	4
History	2	2	2	2	2	2	2	2	2	2	2
Civics	2	2	2	2	2	2	2	2	1	2	2
Geography	2	1	2	—	1	2	—	1	1	2	—
1st foreign language	3	3	3	3	3	3	—	4	5	5	4
2nd foreign language	3	3	3	3	3	3	3	4	5	4	4
3rd foreign language	4	4	4	4	—	—	—	3	2	2	2
Mathematics	4	3	3	—	4	4	4	4	3	3	—
Physics	1	—	3	3	6	6	6	1	—	—	—
Chemistry	3	3	—	—	1	2	1	2	3	3	3
Biology	—	—	—	—	—	—	—	2	—	—	—
Handicrafts and art	1	1	1	1	—	—	—	1	1	2	1
Music	2	2	2	1	2	1	1	1	2	1	1
Gymnastics	2	2	2	2	2	2	2	2	2	2	2
Domestic science (for girls)	+1	—	—	—	—	—	—	—	—	—	—
Total	35	32	33	29	32	33	29	35	33	34	29
Free hour	1	1	1	1	1	1	1	1	1	1	1

one course and another are mainly in the languages which are included and the relative amounts of time allotted to them in the final years.

Thus the classical course requires 9 years of Latin, 6 years of Greek and 7 years of English or French, but it also includes mathematics and science. The natural science course gives greater weight to mathematics and science but also requires two languages—English and Latin or French.

The 7-year and 6-year courses only provide for the modern and the natural science branches. These two branches have a common course until the last 3 years when they vary somewhat but still carry in common a list of general subjects and some practical subjects too.

The allocations given in Table 43 show the compulsory subjects and periods in Hessen but the variations from *Länd* to *Länd* are small so this can well be taken as typical of all. At the end of the course the examination is both written and oral and because of the heavy load entailed in keeping a large number of subjects going there have been changes which split the examination between the final and penultimate years and where this is happening fewer subjects are carried in the final year. Previously, a load of thirteen subjects was not uncommon. The course is a strenuous one. As in Britain, there is discussion on such topics as overpressure in the sixth form, specialisation and modernisation of the curriculum. The aim of the teaching is again familiar: not to give merely a mastery of factual material or so much specialist knowledge, but to give training in the handling of ideas and in conceptual thinking. The form of the examination for *Abitur*, which is very individual and unstandardised, emphasises this aim.* To our way of thinking it has some unusual features, i.e. 5 hours is allowed for an answer to one question.

A great deal of attenuation occurs on the way, e.g. in 1957 there were about 150,000 15-year-olds in the *Gymnasien*, 91,000 in the 17-year-old age group and only 60,000 at the age of 18 despite a larger age cohort on which to draw. Enrolment ratios best

* Thomas, B. S., The *Abitur* examination in Germany, in *Trends in Education*, H.M.S.O., April 1966.

TABLE 44. PERCENTAGE OF AGE GROUP IN GYMNASIUM

	1960	1963
15-year-olds	13·9 (78,000)	13·3 (101,000)
17-year-olds	11·1 (87,000)	9·8 (65,000)
19-year-olds	5·2 (50,000)	6·3 (50,000)

illustrate this fall out, and Table 44 gives figures at three ages for 1960 and 1963.

The course finishes at the age of 19 so some at this age will have finished the course anyway. Therefore not too much should be read into the last line of figures, especially as no one is allowed to enter the final year unless their previous performance is satisfactory. Because of this the failure rate is very low, something between 2% and 4% (cf. the 1966 figure of 50% for the *baccalauréat* in France). In 1964 7·2% of the age group were successful. However, the attenuation of ratio between 15 and 17 is clear.

There are a few special types of *Gymnasium* of which the secondary general school with an economics bias is the most noteworthy. It comprises the last three grades of school and its curriculum includes two modern languages and the usual common subjects along with a bias in economics and sociology. It is endeavouring to gain recognition as a fourth type of *Gymnasium* course.

A small amount of upper secondary work is found at the top of the *Realschule* for some pupils who stay on after the end of the normal course which terminates at 16 years. Besides the "promotion" course already mentioned, which gives a further chance to prepare for *Abitur*, there is quite a diverse programme including some practical subjects giving a course combining general education with the elements of a vocational course.

VOCATIONAL COURSES

Vocational courses proper are very well developed. In 1938 part-time vocational schooling (accepted in 1919) was made compulsory between the ages of 14 and 18 and the requirement has been continued since the war. Generally 8 hours of school attendance is the requirement but some skilled jobs require 12 hours. There is, unfortunately, a shortage of schools and, in some cases, what can be given falls below the requirements.

Compulsory school attendance on this part-time basis is closely connected with apprenticeship training. Immediately after World War II, when a tremendous re-building and re-habilitation programme was necessary, there was a detailed inquiry into the actual jobs done by the workers in industry and trade, and by 1948, for each skilled or semi-skilled occupation an inventory (*Berufsbild*) was drawn up giving a kind of vocational picture of the work skills and knowledge involved. As jobs change in character there is machinery for revising the *Berufsbild*. Recently there were 500 skilled and 160 semi-skilled trades listed for commerce and manufacturing alone. Apprenticeship begins immediately after the end of full-time compulsory school and from the detail in the *Berufsbild* both apprentice and employee know exactly what they are undertaking. Responsibility for the practical training lies with the firm, but the apprentice keeps a work book in which he has to describe week by week what he has been learning. This forms a record which can be inspected. Theoretical training is given at the part-time vocational school (*Berufsschule*).

The training given at the school has three objectives:

(a) to impart the theoretical knowledge necessary for the trade or skill being learnt, and the knowledge necessary for good citizenship;
(b) to develop as far as possible the intellectual faculties;
(c) to lay a sound moral foundation.

Obviously these are lofty aims for attainment during a short part-time programme and, as always, with aims of this nature they can only be relatively successful. A few examples of weekly time schedules give an idea of the curriculum which is followed. (See Table 45.)

At the end of the course there is an examination which is

TABLE 45. WEEKLY ALLOCATIONS IN DIFFERENT COURSES
(BERUFSSCHULE)

	Hours per week		
	Year 1	Year 2	Year 3
Commercial course:			
Religious instruction	1	1	1
German	1	1	1
Arithmetic	1	1	1
Book-keeping	1	2	2
Management	1	1	2
Social studies	1	1	1
Stenography	2	2	1
Total	8	9	9

Agricultural course:	Hours per week
Religious instruction	1
Agriculture: machinery and peasant crafts	3
German	1
Arithmetic	1
Social studies	1
Total	7

Trade school:	
Religious instruction	1
Trade: theory and practice	3
Mechanical drawing	2
German	1
Arithmetic	1
Social studies	1
Total	9

Home economics:	
Religious instruction	1
Cookery and needlework	3
Health, nursing, child care	1
German	1
Arithmetic	1
Social studies	1
Total	8

practical, written and oral and is held twice a year. Ninety per cent pass the examination and gain a certificate. Those who fail the examination can resit after 6 months. (Further education, sometimes at a full-time vocational institution, can lead to a higher qualification for the foreman grade.)

The examination is a check on both the teaching and the practical course and helps to maintain standards. Because the practical training is followed at the place of work it is responsive to change as it occurs on the job. Practical training in institutions away from the job with instructors permanently employed can soon become "fossilised" unless it is of very general application. An advantage is the fact that the course begins immediately after school with no wasted period of intermission, though the course is sufficiently flexible to allow for a later entry. The time at the *Berufsschule* is additional to a 5-day week and this makes a heavy load. The training is specific and for some semi-skilled occupations the inventory is pretentious but it is a serious attempt to provide training for all—something which is in the future as far as the United Kingdom is concerned. Because it is compulsory and all-embracing the numbers involved at any one time in the 3-year course are impressive, e.g. in 1959 there were over 2 million undergoing the part-time training though with smaller age groups numbers have fallen since, so that in 1963 there were nearly 400,000 17-year-olds in vocational–technical education—nearly 59% of the age group.

There are also some full-time vocational schools of which many prepare for vocations in the field of commerce or domestic science. The courses usually last for 2 years. The numbers involved are much less than in the part-time training, e.g. in 1959 about 150,000 enrolled.

Many countries have detailed plans for integrating academic and vocational–education and some are actually implementing their blueprints. All considered here have plans for continuing common schooling to a later age. Only the Federal Republic of West Germany, in the plan already described, intends to keep differentiation at an early age. Because of this, reports suggest that education may be in for a difficult time and there is talk of a "break-down" by 1970.* Even drastic change could have little effect in the short period before that date, so problems seem inevitable.

There is, as has been shown, much that is very commendable in the German system but each advantage can be quickly neutralised by the drawback which goes with it. Everyone is involved in education to 18 years, but most of these (about 84%) at the upper secondary stage have only a short part-time course. The standards in the *Gymnasium* are high and the teaching is exceedingly thorough but this is only achieved at the expense of high selectivity and a heavy drop-out rate. It is estimated that only 6·8% of the age group will pass *Abitur* in 1970. Comparative figures for countries with similar types of examination based on wide-ranging courses carrying many subjects to a late stage show much better success, e.g. Norway and Sweden which are, perhaps, most nearly comparable, 22%, and France, where the *bachot* is taken normally a year earlier, 19%. There is, of course, the second way to the university but few appear to use it. *Die Deutsche Bildungskatastrophe*, already cited, points out some of the pressing problems. *Abitur* is compulsory for all intending teachers (except for a few special cases) but the numbers going forward to the examination and passing are so small, they will only be sufficient to supply the teaching profession in 1970 if no *Abituren* go elsewhere. Obviously what is required is a massive educational programme with other schools beside the *Gymnasien* leading to the final examination so there is a quick end to rigorous selection and far more participation in *élite* education by the lower socio-economic classes who have so far, it appears, not been too worried about this discrimination, because they have been able to command a satisfactory living without academic education.

The *Rahmenplan*, even though it only plans minimal reforms, has not been widely welcomed. Public interest in the plan has been small while the professional educationists have been divided. Generally, while the primary and elementary teachers have been

* Picht, G., *Die Deutsche Bildungskatastrophe*, reviewed in *Comparative Education*, vol. 1, no. 2, 1965.

more progressive, the grammar school teachers have shown a conservative attitude. This reflects the pattern in other countries. The Catholic Church has been mainly interested in preserving its influence which is well-served by the present pattern, and the federal structure of the Republic has not encouraged reform.

However, an article* by Ursula K. Springer early in 1965 suggests there is a change of heart and that action is now to be substituted for an hitherto insubstantial ideal. This has come about because a survey of school needs to 1970 has shown many shortcomings, some of which have already been discussed. Combined with this survey, research into the economics of education has shown the lack of provision available for certain social classes. A system that will tap the reserves of talent both geographically (by placing schools more expeditiously, cf. the French school "map", and by consolidating present facilities by the closing of what are picturesquely called dwarf-schools), and sociologically, is needed. In its present lack of definite plans for widening opportunities at the upper secondary level Germany is the odd-man out in this survey as it was in the *UNESCO World Survey* where, despite

TABLE 46. ENROLMENT OF 17-YEAR-OLDS IN 1963.
(TOTAL AGE GROUP 669,400)

	Enrolment	%
Realschule (intermediate school)	17,528	2·6
Gymnasium	65,643	9·8
Total general education	83,171	12·4
Part-time vocational school	366,285	54·7
Full-time vocational school	17,324	2·6
Technical school	8,621	1·3
Total vocational–technical	392,230	58·6
Total in secondary education	475,401	71·0

* Springer, U. K., West Germany's turn to *Bildungspolitik, Comparative Education Review,* February 1965.

its high secondary enrolment ratio, it was the only European country to show a decrease in ratio in the 1950's, e.g. average 1950–4, 83%; 1955–7, 79%.

To be quite fair it must be pointed out that once a high enrolment ratio has been established an improvement is difficult to sustain.

Probably the best summary of the position is given by recent figures for 17-year-old pupils (see Table 46).

In the same year in England and Wales 13·2% of 17-year-olds are still in school, so the Federal Republic's percentage is not much smaller. On the other hand, the percentage in vocational–technical education in Germany is much larger (in England and Wales boys' part time is 38·8%, girls' 24·0%) so it is plain to see where the present strength of the German system lies. Whether it can evolve to provide an efficient system for the future is a point of conjecture even for the West Germans themselves.

CHAPTER 13

Spain—A Project in Planning*

EACH chapter, dealing with upper secondary provision in separate countries, has been analysing and describing either systems actually in operation, as in Germany or the U.S.S.R., or plans, as in France and Sweden, which are already largely implemented. This chapter is different in that it describes a long-term plan for change in a country with educational provision so small as to inhibit the required rate of economic growth. What is of paramount interest is the way in which the plan, based on careful economic planning, recommends changes in the educational pattern in line with what has been observed to be taking place elsewhere—in particular the prolongation of undifferentiated education to a later age and a wide provision of opportunities when differentiation eventually occurs.

The Mediterranean Regional Project, for which detailed information became available in 1965, is a series of plans aiming to increase educational facilities and, thereby, achieve a higher rate of economic growth, in a number of countries bordering the Mediterranean Sea. The importance of the upper secondary sector is well illustrated by a consideration of the current position in Spain alongside the plan for the future. It is brought out most clearly by two sets of figures showing enrolment ratios in educational institutions by age groups. As explained in Chapter 1, below compulsory school-leaving age ratios should be high, approaching near 100%. Upper secondary ratios are naturally less than this. For instance in 1958 the U.S.S.R., for the 15–19

---

* This chapter relies greatly on: O.E.C.D., *An Experiment in Planning in Six Countries*, Paris, 1965; O.E.C.D., *The Mediterranean Project. Spain*, Paris, 1965.

age group registered about 50% and the U.S.A. 65%. With these high figures in mind it is possible to interpret more usefully the following figures for Spain—actual in 1960 and projections for 1975:

Enrolment ratios	Age groups			
	6–11	12–14	15–19	20–24
Actual, 1960	85	45	10	3
Projected, 1975	95	80	35	6
Increase expected	12%	78%	250%	100%

While the plan anticipates considerable progress at all levels, the great importance of advance in the upper secondary age group is immediately apparent. To achieve this advance the plan shows that altering the pattern of lower schooling so as to avoid premature structuring, is as important as providing more opportunities in the later stages. The chapter looks at the plan from this point of view, but in order to do this meaningfully a certain amount of background is necessary.

The Mediterranean Regional Project (from now called M.R.P.) is an attempt by the six Mediterranean countries in membership of the Organisation for Economic Co-operation and Development (O.E.C.D.) to relate advance in educational provision with social progress and economic growth. It is based on the realisation that an increase in output depends, apart from any considerations of the physical capital involved, not only on the volume of labour available but also on the quality of its education and training.

The project started from a review of the position in Portugal with regard to the provision of the highly qualified technical and scientific manpower necessary for development. Published in 1960, this review led the Portuguese Government to set targets for educational developments. The other member countries in the Mediterranean Lands (Spain, Italy, Greece, Yugoslavia, Turkey) were invited to see the suggestions and expressed interest in what

Portugal was doing. Then since it was realised that all the countries face a number of common problems the project was envisaged on a regional basis. Two of the relevant common problems immediately apparent were the lower *per capita* income than for other O.E.C.D. countries, and the larger percentage of the labour force engaged in agricultural pursuits. All the countries had ideas, and even plans, for economic growth and industrialisation but all suffered from a shortage of educational facilities when compared with O.E.C.D. countries in northern Europe. Most of the countries showed a shortage of qualified manpower on the scientific and technical sides. (One exception to this was north Italy, which is well developed industrially, though, of course, geographers would argue that north Italy is a sub-region outside the Mediterranean area *sensu stricto* and is, therefore, exceptional anyway.) However, the Mediterranean countries share with the rest of Europe a common cultural and educational heritage with the dichotomy between culture (sweetness and light) and vocation marked out plainly. The abstract has always been of greater importance than the practical, and the education of a few to a high standard rather than of the mass to a reasonable standard has been stressed. To adapt the educational system to the needs of a modern economy, planning is needed to alter many of the structures which have grown up in response to these long held aims.

These problems having been highlighted, what emerged from the discussions between O.E.C.D. and the six countries concerned was the need for a joint research project aimed at assessing the educational needs of each country in the context of economic growth for a target year in the mid-seventies. In particular attention to the problem of producing the required amount of scientific and technical manpower was required. Detailed plans for each country were to be embodied in a report containing a programme of action in the field of education. Each report was to contain:

(a) a complete survey of the present structure of, and recent trends in, the educational system and its apparent problems;

(b) a survey of future needs in education, having regard to demographic, social and economic factors and paying especial attention to the requirements of scientific and technical manpower;

(c) an analysis of changes needed to reach the target;

(d) a costing of the project.

Though each country has a separate report there are certain broad features and conclusions common to all. To quote from the report:*

> If the educational deficiencies of some of the six Mediterranean countries had to be summed up in one sentence, it might be said that they lie somewhere mid-way between those of the more backward countries and those of the advanced countries. In the former it is the absence of universal primary education that is the chief obstacle to economic progress: in the latter, it is usually the lack of higher education which is the chief educational handicap. In most Mediterranean countries neither primary education, nor higher education are anything like sufficient to meet the needs of a modern economy; but the chief obstacle to economic growth lies in the lack of middle-level technicians and skilled craftsmen and workers.

All educational provision has to increase but the largest increases have to come in the age range with which this book is concerned and this can only be achieved on the basis of better lower secondary education. The second problem is to change the proportions of general education and technical and vocational education. Thus it is not merely a large expansion of the present provision which is required but a change in function, and the provision of education of a different kind. Changes in the curriculum will also be necessary. Students must not be prevented from entering the technical branches by knowing that this will automatically bar them from the university. A variety of paths to higher education is desirable. To some extent the problem is psychological: how to give technical studies the social prestige which attaches (and not only in Mediterranean countries) to studies in the humanities.

From these general considerations the discussion can now turn specifically to Spain and sketch out the present pattern of educa-

* O.E.C.D., *An Experiment in Planning in Six Countries,* Paris, 1965, p. 15.

tional provision concentrating on the upper secondary level. In passing, it may be noted that education in Spain already seems to be expanding. In 1964 the school-leaving age was raised to 14 years and in the same year a Technical Education Act was passed regularising procedures at the secondary level and combining and streamlining some of the courses offered.

PRESENT SYSTEM (See Fig. 12)

Primary education starts at the age of 6 and, until the new law of 1964, finished at 11, giving a 6-year course, which has now been extended to 8 years. However, at the end of the primary

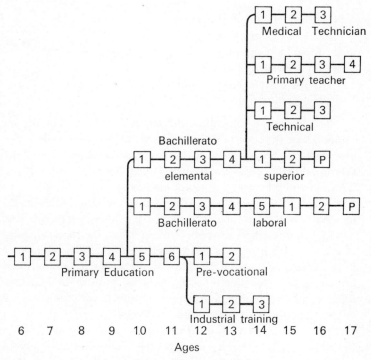

Fig. 12. Spain: the present system.

course is an extension to the age of 14, called preparation for employment.

Secondary education revolves around the *bachillerato general* which is in three cycles. Admission to the secondary school is by entrance examination at 10 years of age. The first 4 years are general in nature and at the end of this section is the elementary certificate (*bachiller elemental*). A further 2-year course, available in two divisions, arts and science with a certain common content, leads to the higher certificate (*bachiller superior*). This is really upper secondary work and for entrance to the university, a further pre-university year is required.

In the pre-university year all students follow certain common courses:

Spanish language and literature	2 hours weekly
Review of modern language	6　　,,
Set topic in geography	2　　,,
Set topic of current interest to be studied from a religious and philosophical viewpoint	2　　,,

The Minister of Education announces the themes for the set topics before the start of the school year. In addition to the common subjects, arts students have 6 hours of Latin and 6 hours of Greek, and students in the sciences have 6 hours of mathematics, 3 hours of physics and 3 hours of biology.

Vocational secondary education, which contains both general education and vocational training, is a relatively new feature. There is in this sector, a 5-year course to reach the *bachiller laboral elemental*, which is more or less equivalent to the lower certificate in the academic school in the basic subjects, but is supplemented by a technical–vocational speciality in agriculture, animal husbandry, mining, fishing, industry or administration gained by the extra year. Students can carry on for two extra years and gain the higher certificate at 17 and then go on to university, or they can be admitted to a variety of upper secondary technical, commercial and professional courses. In these courses there is a good

TABLE 47. WEEKLY ALLOCATIONS IN "BACHILLERATO SUPERIOR"
(HOURS)

	Year 1 (5)	Year 2 (6)
Religion	2	2
Philosophy	—	2
Spanish language and literature	—	6
Cosmology (natural science)	6	—
History of art and culture	—	3
Modern foreign language	3	—
Drawing	2	—
Physical education	3	2
Civics	1	1
Option: arts		
Greek	4	4
Latin	6	3
Option: sciences		
Mathematics	6	3
Chemistry	4	—
Physics	—	4
Total by section	27	23

TABLE 48. WEEKLY ALLOCATIONS FOR A VOCATIONAL
COURSE SPECIALISING IN FARM PESTS

	Year 1	Year 2
Spanish	1	1
French	1	1
Economic geography	1	1
History of agriculture	1	—
Mathematics	1	1
General and applied physics	3	3
General and applied chemistry	3	4
Technology	6	6
Drawing—technical	3	3
Business accounts	1	1
Social law	1	1
Religious instruction	1	1
Development of patriotism	1	1
Practical work	24	24
	48	48

deal of general education which forms a common core for the specialities. Table 48 of subject allocations for a farm pests specialist course illustrates this aspect.

There are other types of vocational provision. Some schools for industry start vocational courses at 12 and overlap the upper secondary level. They award the title "master of industry".

From the general secondary school at the first certificate stage (*bachiller elemental*) it is possible to transfer to commercial schools, technical schools, schools for the fine arts and primary teacher training. All of these are upper secondary provision.

Primary education has little social value and it is possible to go to secondary school without having attended primary school. Thus, as described, from a low age level there are three parallel strands of education and hence decisions have to be taken early. The vocational certificate, from the *bachiller laboral* course, can, it is true, lead to a university course but not to all faculties.

However, since 1950 progress has been made as the following figures show:

ENROLMENT RATIOS (%)

	1951	1960
Primary	60·1	84·5
Secondary	11·0	17·5
Higher	1·5	2·5

Actual figures for 1961 show the strength of the various courses.

TABLE 49. ENROLMENTS IN PRIMARY AND SECONDARY EDUCATION 1961

Level	
Primary	3,830,000
Secondary	667,500
of which *bachillerato general*	474,100
commercial schools	21,700
vocational training schools	63,400
bachillerato laboral	22,200
technical schools	39,800
primary teacher training	43,200

Most of the provision at the secondary stage is in private schools, e.g.:

	State	Private	Unrecognised
Secondary	25%	46%	29%
Primary	76%	24%	—

Unrecognised status at the secondary level means pupils do not have to attend classes but study privately due to the lack of space in official establishments. This description, the figures and Fig. 12 sufficiently explain the present position.

EXTENSION TO THE FUTURE

The report then examines in great detail the occupational structure expected after 15 years of planned economic and social progress. During this period it concludes that a radical transformation in the occupational composition of the available manpower will occur so mere extrapolation into the future can be ruled out. A better way is to examine the manpower structure, and its educational background, in the most modern enterprises and expect this to apply more generally in the future. International comparisons are also useful. As economic growth increases to certain levels, the structure of employment will tend to become equated with that at present existing in other countries which have reached a comparable stage of growth. In 1959 Spain had 15% white-collar workers, i.e. professional and technical workers, senior administrative and management personnel and clerical and sales workers. In 1900 U.S.A. had 18% in this category and by 1959 the proportion had increased to 42%. Because of the advance of technical knowledge the rate of change will be different but figures of this kind can be a guide. Working from these considerations the report demonstrates that it is the middle levels of the manpower structure—technician and managerial levels—which need the greatest increases and it then proceeds to change these into the required educational levels as in Table 50.

TABLE 50. CHANGES IN EDUCATIONAL LEVELS BETWEEN 1960–75 (000's)

	Stock in 1960	Stock in 1975	Index 1960 =100	Annual rate of increase (%)
Higher education	194	349	180	4
Secondary education	415	234	298	7·5
of which:				
general and commercial	225	669	311	7·9
technical	30	148	494	11·2
vocational	50	199	398	9·6
primary teachers	100	158	158	3·1

The increase for higher education does not turn out to be particularly ambitious as compared with plans for other countries but a very great expansion in the upper secondary sector is indicated.

Having analysed these trends the report goes on to consider how the educational system can be organised or reorganised to meet these needs. Once again a mere inflation, an increase in overall size, is not a possible solution because different parts need to expand at different rates. Scaling up is not the answer. One of the drawbacks of the present system is the high rate of wastage, but even with this reduced to more acceptable proportions, the present system could not be expanded sufficiently to produce the required results: the efficiency ratio would still not be high enough. Therefore, along with improvement in quality there must be changes in the basic system. Advances at one level can only be made on the basis of improvements at earlier stages and so primary education must be made as good as possible. At present its status is low and its quality poor. Therefore for those who are to go on to secondary level, primary education has been made as short as possible. This means that secondary education, which is more expensive than primary, starts early and so resources are wasted, and scarce secondary teachers are used on unnecessarily young pupils. Progress can be achieved by improving the top grades of primary education and beginning secondary education at a later age of 11 or 12. Although this may mean a later age for

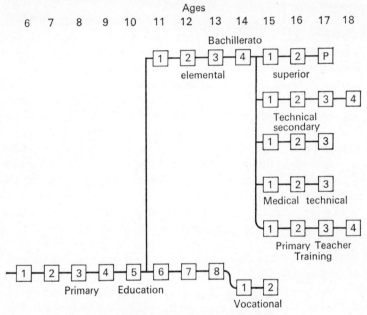

Fig. 13. Spain: proposed reformed system.

completion of secondary studies it would mean a better grounding. At present Spain has the lowest age for completing upper secondary education—17 years of age as against 18 in France and England and Wales and 19 years in Germany.

The first recommendation of the report is for the transfer to secondary education to take place one year later than under the present system (see Fig. 13). However, it does not go on to suggest secondary education for all—evidently a step needing even more preparation—but retains parallel tracking at the lower secondary level. With primary education continuing to 14 years, this will give 8 years of compulsory education, and vocational training can follow this. A 2-year course is suggested on the industrial side, but for agricultural education a more flexible pattern is thought appropriate to allow for regional differences—not only in conditions but also in needs.

Consolidation is recommended for the lower secondary level, leaving one course which will lead after 4 years to the *bachillerato elemental*. For some years commercial schools have tended to integrate with the general course. Now this becomes a firm proposal, and in the same way vocational secondary education leading to the vocational certificate, previously parallel to the general course, should also be integrated with it—the *laboral* strand at the lower level is abandoned. Thus all pupils transferring to secondary education at 11+ will follow a common course to 15 years of age and only then will courses divide. The upper secondary level will provide parallel educational tracks built on the base of a general course without differentiation.

Starting from the age of 15 with the general education certificate there will be two main and two subsidiary opportunities:

1. As at present a further course, 2 years in length, will lead to a higher certificate and for those wishing to proceed to university there will be a pre-university course lasting 1 year.
2. The 4-year certificate will give entrance to the technical school. These schools will correspond roughly with the present schools of the same designation and will prepare for a higher vocational certificate. The course will vary in length, either 3 or 4 years, depending on the speciality involved and the degree of proficiency required. Most present courses are too long and suffer greatly from wastage. Shortening of the course will be possible because entrance is later and based on 4 years of general secondary education.
3. Primary teacher training will start on the basis of the 4-year certificate and will last for 4 years.

4. Medical technicians' training will start from the same base and last 3 years.

The report makes estimates of the numbers likely to be required in the various branches.

In vocational training in 1960 under 6000 were completing courses and the estimate for 1975 is in excess of 100,000 for industry and the service occupations alone. This is a great increase and it may have been wise to base this on primary (or elementary) education only and not attempt to give secondary education for all and mount vocational training on that. Agricultural education will be additional to "the first hundred thousand". Courses here can be of shorter duration and can possibly be seasonal in nature, buttressed by further periodic courses of a refresher type.

In 1962 63,700 were successful in the *bachiller elemental* certificate. By 1975 this should have increased fourfold to a total over a quarter of a million. At the *bachiller superior* level a sixfold increase is required bringing the 26,500 successes in 1962 to about 150,000 by 1975. In that year about half that number will be expected to be taking the pre-university year successfully, a fivefold increase from the 13,700 passes registered in 1961.

Technical secondary education will be expected to show the largest rate of increase, from 4000 in 1961 to about 45,000 in 1975.

Working these figures to give enrolment ratios for the 14–17-year-olds (still rather lower in age than the upper secondary ages that have been considered in other chapters) a figure of 48% is reached for 1975 compared with 15% for 1960. If this can be achieved it will make Spain in 1975 equivalent in the 14–17 enrolment ratio with France in 1958 and rather better than Germany in 1958 and England in 1957.

To attempt in a relatively short time to narrow the gap between Spain's economy and that of the more industrially advanced nations in Europe is the purpose of the ambitious plan reviewed above. Whether Spain can achieve what is envisaged is not within our province to predict. Certainly, as previously noted there has been recent legislation consonant with the ideal of progress contained in the plan. Raising the compulsory school-staying age and reducing technical courses to a viable length are small beginnings. Many social inequalities also need attention: more opportunities for women and the lower income groups generally, the reduction of wastage by reducing drop-out and the need for repetition, and the reduction of regional inequalities. But from the viewpoint taken here the most significant part of the prescription is the breaking up of structures at the lower levels to allow for later consolidation. Geologists studying fossils find it is the undifferentiated forms of life which can go on and evolve, while those forms which have become too differentiated can normally only proceed to extinction. Fortunately, school systems are susceptible to a certain amount of unscrambling and new systems can arise out of the transformation of the old. This is the solution which the Mediterranean Regional Project has recommended in Spain. It still leaves a dual system operating low down in the age groups, so eventually even further breaking down may become necessary, but here, at any rate, is a recipe for progress.

CHAPTER 14

Some Adolescent Attitudes

> I would there were no age between 16 and 23 or that youth
> would sleep out the rest.
>
> (SHAKESPEARE, *A Winter's Tale*, III. 3.)

> From pigtails to wedding veils*
> From pinafores to lace
> And in between are the special years
> Time never can erase.
>
> From play toys to college boys
> From little girl to wife
> And in between are the special years
> You remember all your life.
> . . . So slow up,
> Don't rush to grow up
> You'll be a woman before long,
> Just stay a while in the special years
> Their magic will soon be gone.
>
> (Pop ballad, 1965)

Upper secondary schools only exist to serve pupils or students. These very terms carry in them the idea of an educational institution of some kind. Today, in an affluent society, the youngsters are much more a part of the whole world, and if we think of them only in school terms, the image we get is a partial one. Schools formerly tended to take the limited view as Richard Hoggart in the *Uses of Literacy*† showed for the period between the wars, and Jackson and Marsden have underlined for a later period in *Education and the Working Class*.‡ But this limited view is becoming more difficult to

---

* Copyright 1964, Painted Desert Music Corp., New York, U.S.A. Used by permission.

† Hoggart, R., Chatto & Windus, London, 1957.

‡ Jackson, B., and Marsden, D., Routledge, London, 1962.

sustain. A *Guardian* report of the conference of the Incorporated Association of Headmasters, a mainly grammar school body, on the last day of 1965, headed "Need for schools to come to terms with pop culture", describes a discussion which is very relevant. One contributor said that 10 years before no headmaster would have taken seriously "pop" culture as an educational issue. Now they were obliged to come to terms with it because it could not be kept out of the schools. Another headmaster testifying to his belief in the worth of the young people of today, drew attention to the note of protest in the current pop culture, and thought the criticism of society was taken seriously by the youngsters. The social conscience of the pupils which made them increasingly aware of the needs of ordinary people was the theme that another headmaster pursued. He thought that in the past youngsters had no recognisable culture but today's wide range of culture did not replace better interests. The consensus seemed to be that school had to come to terms with the new cultures. This entails seeing the pupils as rounded persons. Is this change of attitude connected with the crystallisation of the idea of the upper secondary school?

It is a truism to write that life is continuous and all divisions in education are to some extent arbitrary. What was originally "all through" has now been divided into a number of stages—nursery, primary, secondary, higher, further, tertiary and even quaternary are some of the alternative terms. This book has been considering and explaining an even more restricted field—a sub-section of the secondary stage. The justification is the practical one that educational offerings at this stage seem to be differentiated from the preceding and succeeding stages. Some of the research findings which support the divergence of education at this level into separate specialities growing out from a common curriculum in the earlier years have been rehearsed in the chapter on Sweden. This chapter is attempting to review briefly some of the social background to this stage.

Primary education is the essential basic education which everyone needs: secondary education is extra education which is terminal for some, but preparatory for others who are going on to higher education. The minimum of primary education necessary if pupils are to maintain literacy throughout life seems to be 4 years, but many systems regard primary education as of a longer duration than this. This imperfect divide arose because in most countries two systems of education, one for the upper social class, and the other to give the rudiments to a lower social class, developed in parallel, and rarely met. However, when a few of the lower orders were needed to transfer to the upper system arrangements were made at an early age in order to give a sufficiently long secondary course. Anyway, those who were chosen for transfer were sufficiently able to have mastered the primary course in a short span of years. Thus when secondary specialised education was for the few it could begin at an early age, and the common learnings of the primary school needed only a little time. Life has become more complicated: knowledge has proliferated and after a long struggle secondary education for all has been acknowledged as necessary. It has been recognised that primary education no longer subsumes all that the average person needs to know—a longer period of tutelage for all is essential.

A burgeoning economy needs more of its personnel educated to a higher level and at the same time is better able to support them for this longer period. Though the whole community is richer than it was before the war, it is the lower income groups which have, in general, made the greatest relative improvement so they can now more easily support their young people in a longer school life. Earnings of these young people have risen faster than adults and so those who stay on at school have to forfeit more in pay than previous generations, though there is no doubt that the delayed payments are better and those with "more education" do catch up.

Social changes have gone on too. Smaller families make it easier to support children at school, but have tended to make the family less tightly knit. Adolescents more and more, and earlier and earlier, look outside the home and mix with their age-mates. The growth of the mass media of communication has greatly affected the youngsters, and their new found affluence has

1*

attracted commercial interests which have not only satisfied, but also stimulated and even created the teenage market.

Just how recent this change is, can easily be forgotten, but it has been recorded for us by a former H.M. senior chief inspector of schools as follows:*

> After the War, when I was stationed as H.M.I., in the Midlands, I spent many days in the newly created modern schools of Warwickshire and the Potteries and I was deeply impressed not only by the promise of some of these schools but also by their actual performance. Many of the old senior and central schools had been very good places in the five or ten years before the War; and some of these schools with grammar schools as yet un-expanded and the eager spirit of the post-war years still strong and active, took their opportunities with both hands. In cramped and often ancient buildings their work was good in both academic and practical directions; their social life blazed into cheerful activity in many ways seldom before attempted. Their staffing, though short, and more feminine than masculine, was less unstable than now; and the pressure of certain unhelpful forms of public mythology was hardly felt until, at least, about 1950: the word "teenager" had hardly been coined, so far as I can remember—certainly the species in any number, or with any self-conscious group solidarity, was not conspicuous either in the schools, or if my memory is right, in the youth clubs.

It is in societies with a high degree of technological develop-ment that the discontinuity between adolescent and adult roles becomes greater. At less advanced stages of progress the division is less marked. Each advance calls for a longer formal education and work roles become dissimilar from the parental generation. A flexible labour force needs broad layers of knowledge of a general kind with specialised knowledge superimposed upon it. Now the discontinuity has become so great that a subculture or subcultures have grown up with values and norms which differ from the larger society.

These social, economic and technological changes have affected all the age group so that no longer are the larger groups who stay on at school for an increasing time so ready to conform.

Between the wars those who stayed on at school were the chosen few—academically able and willing to conform to the mores of the school. Musgrove, in an interesting and provocative book

* Wilson, P. *Views and Prospects from Curzon Street*, Blackwell, Oxford, 1961.

Youth and the Social Order* (1964), contends that the grammar school reduces its pupils to a seemly subservience and, along with higher education generally, most easily achieves its ends with certain personality types. He affirms that if people are arranged in one continuum from introversion at one end to extraversion at the other, and along another axis from neuroticism at one end to stability at the other, then those who are "neurotic introverts" are better fitted for the grammar school than the "stable extroverts". On the other hand, he finds the products of the modern school suffer less from doubt and uncertainty and identify better as adults. Obviously as more stay on at school, even assuming Musgrove is right in his original contention, a wider spectrum must be admitted, and eventually the growth in numbers must be such that fundamental changes occur. When the enrolment ratio was low, the few who stayed on for upper secondary education could well be accommodated as a special group in a school planned originally for a different purpose. When a majority enters the upper secondary school changes will have to be made for no longer will all be able to follow the same courses as did the *élite* in previous times. A change in the scale of operation will eventually cause a break in tradition.

Can the upper secondary age group be regarded as a unity? Adolescence, however defined, covers a much greater age range and many of the suggested age limits include higher as well as secondary education in their span. Abrams, looking at the group as consumers, based his calculations on the 15–25 age group which is not a much wider range than Shakespeare's 16–23 in *A Winter's Tale*. However, it is not possible to lay down age limits or even to be completely objective about any limits. If the beginning of adolescence is defined as physiological maturity this may be susceptible to fairly precise determination but it will vary much from individual to individual; and, if its end is defined as the attainment of social maturity this is extremely subjective. At the beginning of the century Stanley Hall suggested a period from about 12 or 13 to 22 or 25. The term teenager suggests a beginning

* Musgrove, F. W., *Youth and the Social Order*, Routledge, London .1964.

in line with Hall's figure, and a conclusion at 19, and there are many who would argue that maturation has advanced so far that there is no need to delay legal maturity until 21: it could well be granted at 18. The lowering of the age of franchise from 21 to 18 is, in fact, part of Socialist policy. Upper secondary schooling cannot be contained within very definite limits either, but the years from 15 to 19 seem a sufficient span and it is in this period that the zenith of the maturational and social phase which we call youth or adolescence occurs, not only in our islands, but also in many other cultures, though it is yet too soon to speak of it as universal.

If school is thought of merely in a narrow sense there is perhaps no need to make the upper secondary phase distinct in treatment and accord it a separate institution. But education is, of course, much wider than this and, as with a more complex society, social roles also take longer to learn, so one function of adolescence can be seen as allowing a person to become socially co-operative and responsible. Here the argument for a separate, unique, institution becomes much stronger. As a child, he has grown up in a family which is an age-heterogeneous group. At some stage he will transfer to age-homogeneous groups and in adolescence peer-grouping seems to reach its height. Youth is a period of preparation which, with proper treatment, should enrich personal and social life. Dr. Wall has expressed this cogently as follows:

> It is not fanciful to attribute much of the flexibility and complexity of the modern personality, its cultural possibilities and its variety of adjustments, to the prolongation of adolescence which has come about in the last century and notably in the last fifty years. Not only is adolescence longer even for those who have always been favoured by circumstance; as a period interposed between more or less irresponsible childhood and full adult status, it has been extended to all classes, and it is still for a variety of reasons, growing longer.*

While an entirely separate institution for a few favoured adolescents may have been unnecessary, its usefulness for a stage

* Wall, W. D., *Child of our Times*, National Children's Home Convocation Lecture, 1959.

which is becoming longer and more important for all youth becomes apparent.

Musgrove, in his book already referred to, suggests that adolescence is really an invention of about the last two centuries. He sees young people being more and more excluded from the nation's economic life and segregated in a position of diminished social status. Although this segregation gives a special position, and many would argue that adolescents have "never had it so good", Musgrove is adamant that this is a position of rejection from the true business of life. The young are rejected by adults and, because of this, the youngsters in their turn reject the standards and guidance of authority. Adults, he contends, are in favour of the young living a separate life and are opposed to the earlier assumption of adult roles.

The current adult image of the youth culture of today appears to be one of irresponsibility, hooliganism and disrespect for authority, but this is an exaggerated picture based on journalism. More careful objective studies like that of Veness* on school-leavers have demonstrated how realistic are their aspirations; so realistic and mundane, in fact, as to lead some psychologists to deplore the lack of adventurousness and the growth of conformity. True, delinquency has increased, but it is still only a small minority of the age group who are markedly deviant in this way. Even when the extreme radicals and extreme bohemians are added to the delinquent group it still leaves a tremendous majority who, though they may behave in a distinctively teenage manner, are neither misfits nor criminals. However, helped by a self-seeking commercial stimulation, compounded of disc-jockeys, Carnaby Street and so on, there has grown up a cult which glamorises youth and opposes it to maturity. Rising affluence has done much to unify the teenage group. Originally the teenage culture was largely working class, but with growing affluence and more education, this class has become more assured and other teenagers from other classes have come under the same general influences. Grammar school boys (and public school boys in vacation) favour the same

* Veness, T., *School Leavers*, Methuen, London, 1962.

clothes and the same "pop" music, and between the classes at adolescence there is little difference in the amount of money available for spending. In this way a more homogeneous culture has arisen and it has become sharply differentiated from adult norms. As is well known, there are sub-cultures within this teenage culture. In particular can be contrasted the "rockers", typically wearing boots, jeans and leather jackets (in 1964/5), and emanating, again typically, from the secondary modern C-streams, and the mods, a more open group sometimes categorised as being effeminate. The mods are more academic with a provenance in the C-streams of the grammar school. The rockers are the "Teddy boys" while the mods have a less openly aggressive manner and are usually the more *avant-garde* of the ordinary teenagers. Other countries have similar groups. In the States are the "bop" (the aggressive), the "cool" (the withdrawn), and the "zoot" (the manipulating and exploiting). Various countries have their *halbstarke, blouson-noirs, raggare, nozerno, stiliagi, provos,* children of the sun, and hipsters. When only an *élite* stayed on to the upper secondary level, aggressive behaviour was not unknown. In his autobiography in verse, *Summoned by Bells,** John Betjeman has described his fear of being basketed by "Big Five" when at Marlborough. The whole episode is too long to quote but should be read before condemning modern youth with fewer advantages. Undergraduate rags are much more innocuous and are usually accepted as an amusing kind of craziness. Now with more privileges and generally well-lined pockets the whole age group want the same kind of licence that was formerly granted to the chosen few: and so we find four days of "Rock round the Clock" by youngsters in Copenhagen; 150,000 Parisian youngsters dancing and defying the *gendarmerie* in la Place de la Nation in June 1963; and, fulfilling the same need as these "performance riots", was the pop concert given by the Beatles in the Shea Stadium of New York in the summer of 1965.

Mays, in an important book, *The Young Pretenders,*† analyses the

* Betjeman, J., Murray, London, 1960.
† Mays, J. B., Michael Joseph, London, 1965.

problems of modern youth and argues for a more central and well-defined place for the adolescent in our society. Like many other sociologists and psychologists, he points out that too many arguments concerning teenagers have been built on stereotypes at the extremes. (All stereotypes have been called "false maps of non-existent territory".) Mays sketches out a typology of teenagers to include the whole spectrum and identifies six overlapping groups. (It is interesting here to look back at Chapter 5, p. 83, where Weaver sketched out a typology of teenage groups by educational levels and distinguished six overlapping types.) The first four of the groups that Mays distinguishes are, in greater or lesser degree, deviant; his final two groups include the majority of teenagers. Probably a really positive view would list these first but here Mays's order is taken.

1. In this group are the socially frustrated who react in an aggressive fashion to the limitations of their environment. Generally they are of lower-class origin and have a low status, though their sub-culture gives them a status as "toughs" and "Teddy boys" or whatever term may be fashionable.

2. Separate from this group but close to them is a similar unsuccessful stratum. These youngsters, perhaps because of a different temperament, react not by open aggression, but in a way which indicates dissatisfaction while avoiding violence.

3. This group consists of the socially and psychologically depressed "beats" and "queers" who, more or less, withdraw from society. They are basically inadequate and tend to rely on alcohol and drugs. It is in this group that the sexually deviant are to be found.

4. This is the group of the angry young men, who are often quite well educated. They tend to adopt causes, are usually politically very "leftish" and adopt a well-marked humanitarian approach.

5. The first of the majority groups are the new men of the affluent society, who are largely working class in origin, and because of the good pay which goes with the better-skilled and semi-skilled jobs in the newer industries are able to take a generally

optimistic view of life. Mays instances Arthur Seaton of *Satur-day Night and Sunday Morning* as a member of this group, though to me he fits more closely as a member of group (1)—perhaps on the fringe. True, in the Sunday morning section of the book, he does show signs of settling down to a more socially acceptable role and here he speculates concerning his life as follows:

> Misbegotten into a strange and crazy world, dragged up through the dole, and into the war, with a gas mask on your clock, and the sirens rattling into you every night, while you rot with scabies in an air raid shelter. Slung into khaki at eighteen, and when they let you out, you sweat again in a factory.*

This shows Arthur Seaton as a representative of the specially deprived group growing up during the depression, the years culminating in Munich and World War II and not a typical member of this group.

This group of more affluent working class can be expected to grow with full employment and the large net additions (not merely replacements) which are needed in the craftsmen's ranks. As the end of Chapter 5 points out, the provenance of these new skilled craftsmen must be from the ranks of those previously unskilled or those who would previously have entered unskilled jobs.

6. This consists of those who have made a good adjustment to the realities of life and have accepted the standards of present-day society. Many have a middle-class background but many others from the working class have joined this group via the grammar school.

Resources at the upper secondary level must not be concentrated on one group but spread widely to include them all. It is fairly easy to make opportunities for the conformists in groups 5 and 6, and Chapters 5 and 3 on Further Education and Traditional Schools have shown what is being done. To bring in the more deviant groups is more difficult.

In the final chapter of his book Mays makes a number of suggestions which he thinks could bring progress towards the solution of these problems confronting society at the adolescent stage. In

* Sillitoe, A., *Saturday Night and Sunday Morning*.

essence his ideas can be reduced to two main themes and it is useful to list them and then analyse their relevance to problems of
upper secondary level education as outlined here.

First, he believes it is necessary to decide on the kind of society
towards which we want to work and is emphatic that the present
ills will not be eradicated until we have got our philosophy right.
Concerted action can only follow agreement at the ideological
level. In particular at this level he looks at the position with regard
to competition and co-operation and echoing Horace Mann, who
wrote "of emulation in schools as an incitement to effort beware,
lest the quickener of the intellect prove a depraver of social affec-
tions and we barter morals for attainment"; he makes some suggestions for a decrease in the competitive basis in schools.

Secondly, Mays argues for an honoured place for youth in
society and translates this desire into practical proposals for institutions at the youth level, pointing out how woefully lacking is
adequate provision. Comprehensive education he believes is an
essential basis because it demonstrates at the organisational level,
the egalitarian spirit which is an important social end. Coupled
with this would be the amalgamation of private and authority
schools; the elimination of the pathogenic inequalities of provision
(what the Newsom report called schools in the slums); the elevation of vocational education to a rightful place: the provision of
more guidance at all levels: the abolition of a sudden break between school and work, and the setting up of youth colleges with a
relaxed and permissive atmosphere. Many of these are the familiar progressive reforms and this book has been cataloguing the
progress which is being made towards their realisation. Some of
his ideas have been tried out in other countries. The U.S.S.R. and
China have a consistent ideology which is translated into its
practical outcomes at the organisational level. The U.S.A. has a
comprehensive system of schooling, though it is not without its
pathogenic blackspots; and, for a time, at any rate, John Dewey
supplied it with a *raison d'être* at the philosophical level. Sweden,
and perhaps also France, can throw some light on the competition
versus co-operation issue. Youth problems in these countries may

help us to see more clearly the effects of Mays's proposals and whether they are useful at the upper secondary level here.

Although it is voluntary, the youth movement in the U.S.S.R. is very closely structured and involves at some ages almost all, and at the ages we are most interested in, a good proportion, of youngsters. It is organised in three stages: for younger children there is the Octobrist group from ages 7 to 9, followed by the Pioneers covering ages 10–14 and the Komsomol (short for the All-Union Leninist Communist League of Youth) catering for the ages 15–27. The break at 14–15 is significant in the light of the earlier discussion on the peak age of adolescent activity, and it is, of course, the Komsomol which mainly concerns us here, but a paragraph about the Pioneers will allow some parallels and differences to be pointed out.

Though the Pioneers is a voluntary organisation, almost all children join as soon as they are eligible and the number enrolled is 20 million, a number slightly in excess of the Komsomol enrolment, despite the wider age range of the latter. Very few youngsters do not join the Pioneers which is the organisation through which recreational activities of all kinds are organised. The range of activities catered for, either through schools or through the special Pioneer Palaces and Pioneer Houses, is very great, consisting of all kinds of cultural activities, sporting festivals and out-of-door festivals and excursions. But quite as important as its recreational side is its function as the means by which the moral qualities required by the Communist ideology are transmitted to the younger generation. The Pioneer rules are a code of conduct which can be constantly used to stress the responsibility of the individual member to the brigade. Rule 2 states: "A Pioneer prepares himself to enter the Komsomol organisation."

The Komsomol is less directly linked with school because membership includes upper secondary school pupils, as well as those in higher education, and workers on farms and in industry. Though much of the membership is adolescent, it is essentially an organisation with an adult outlook and much of the stress is on political work. As the membership of almost 20 million shows, it is a mass organisation, but only about one-third of the age group belong. Candidates have to prove their worth both politically and in study or work and behaviour, so entry is not automatic even for those who desire to join and there are some who prefer not to take on the arduous duties connected with membership or attempt to set an example for their peers. As studies in the U.S.A. and elsewhere have shown, in a free and fairly open society the adolescent peer-group is a powerful agency of social control. In Russia the youth programme is very consciously organised by the Soviet government and the Communist Party as an agent of social control. It is not really an agency of and for youth, but of the party and government. Tightly organised and directed from above, it helps to block the formation of dissident youth groups, and by working at the official level discourages the development of a deviant youth culture. Using methods involving the pressure of public opinion and the operation of public shaming, it prevents semi-deviant patterns from coalescing into viable groups. However, from the tally of those enrolled compared with the size of the age groups it is obvious there are many outside the ranks of the Komsomol and in this sense sub-cultures are present. In addition to the apathetic who do not attempt to attain the official norms of active, loyal involvement, there are also the so-called "idlers" who refuse to adopt the production ethic. These are a small minority of the youthful population, but in the late fifties a more general attitude of lack of interest in production by those leaving the 10-year school was sufficiently widespread to help to bring about the 1958 law to put right the divorce between learning and life. Too many Soviet students (and in many cases their parents too) considered that, as Khrushchev put it, "they need not grow potatoes or milk cows". This was the time when some scions of successful families were sufficiently spoiled by their parents to become the "stiliagi"—somewhat equivalent to our Teddy boys. Since 1960 these extreme forms are reported to have declined, but there are still less flamboyant manifestations of the same outlook. Now they are known as "the crown princes", which is a sufficiently descriptive title. In 1961 a decree attempting to deal with anti-social attitudes provides for such members to be sent to special areas for periods from 2 to 5 years.

In China the position is in many ways similar to that in the U.S.S.R. There is only one model for youthful behaviour—a carefully constructed bundle of values and norms acceptable to the Party.* Known as the Wu Hao model it unites the goals of (1) a good worker, (2) a good neighbour, and (3) a good scholar with the advocacy and exemplification of (4) good health and (5) the good life—the true Communist citizen. Without doubt this is a very satisfactory model from the regime's viewpoint and without its Communist overtones it would be almost universally acceptable. In fact, Havighurst's analysis of the ten developmental tasks of adolescence parallels the strands of this Wu Hao model. Listing Havighurst's tasks and appending the numerals from the Wu Hao model as specified above, makes this clear:

(a) achieving new and more mature relationships with age mates of both sexes (2);

(b) achieving a masculine or feminine social role (2);

(c) accepting one's physique and using the body effectively (4);

(d) achieving emotional independence of parents and adults (4);

(e) achieving assurance of economic independence (1);

(f) selecting and preparing for an occupation (3);

(g) preparing for marriage and family life (2);

(h) developing towards civic competence (2);

(i) desiring and achieving socially responsible behaviour (5 and 2);

(j) acquiring a set of values and an ethical system as a guide to behaviour (5).

China is, in fact, aiming overtly at the same ends that more permissive countries hope to reach by less well formulated means. The Communist countries have a clearly stated aim at the normative level, which at the operational level is translated into a

* Hickrod, G. A. and L. J. H., The Communist Chinese and American adolescent sub-cultures, *China Quarterly*, April–June 1965.

straightforward organisation which is sure of its goals. Even so, several possibilities are apparent and also realised. Many accept the model and are motivated to achievement, but there are a minority who reject what is put before them, and more who view the programme with an air of indifference. As might have been expected, it is not merely the provision of a philosophy which will do the trick: the right philosophy has to be found. Mays points to the Christian ethic and suggests that what is easy for the Christian can be arrived at in other ways by the non-Christian who will accept "a religious truth which is sustained even though some of the religious ideas which have been associated with it are no longer tenable". He would put before young people the examples of great lives which illustrate the ways in which the human spirit can triumph. Some of the agreed syllabuses of religious instruction have tried this as one approach among many. Japanese moral education has worked along similar lines. Many would regard this as an emasculated approach to a great end: indeed, Mays's first requirement is a very difficult assignment and something less grandiose than a philosophy may have to suffice. A Bill of Human Rights may be as near an approach as can be achieved.

Some of Mays's suggestions at an organisational level may be less difficult to attain, but their effectiveness is not certain. The U.S.A. has made tremendous provision in high school, junior college, college and university for this age group. American society is, by and large, open, and status is by achievement rather than ascription. Institutions are mainly comprehensive and co-educational. Because the Latin (or academic) school, in a climate of anti-intellectualism, never really got a hold in the western European fashion, a more general school was readily achieved, and around the turn of the century Dewey provided the philo-sophical justification for a proliferation of subjects which gave everyone a chance to continue their schooling so that now one-third of the age group proceed to higher education as against 8% in the United Kingdom. However, the very profusion of choice available and the possibility of unlimited aspiration have made problems for some, and, coupled with this, in a country of overall affluence, there are considerable pockets of poverty and under-privilege giving standards below what would be the minimum in a Welfare State. Currently an income of $2000 is regarded as the poverty line and 20% of families are below this limit. Thus many American youngsters are in a role–conflict situation and some have contracted out of the competitive situation and form a delinquent group which is, however, only sizeable in some of the central city slums. The original "Blackboard Jungle", a vocational high school in New York, taking largely the lower end of the ability range, drew a picture of some of this depressed group growing up. Various writers have sketched out a series of high school sub-cultures. A simple tripartite division is:

(a) the academically oriented, a conscientious and responsible group;
(b) the fun sub-culture concentrating on school athletics and social activities generally; and
(c) the delinquents.

Other, more complicated, typologies are possible and are common in the literature. The details are not important in our context, but what is to be emphasised is that in a society with a high degree of technological development and therefore a great discontinuity between adolescent and adult roles due to the long formal education preparing for work roles dissimilar from those of the parents, sub-cultures grow up with values different from the larger society. Sometimes they come to have an independent force.

Some psychologists have suggested that the generally matriarchal society in the U.S.A., with a concentration on the "good" rather than the aggressive father who opposes at home, has led to more counter-aggression and delinquency outside the family group. America, too, can afford a large leisure class of youngsters, not in the labour force, but yet consumers on a vast scale and hence commercial influences have been very important. The result is that youth has an honoured place in society but it does not carry much real status, and the U.S.A. has problems which are greater than ours.

Racial difficulties; the culturally deprived and underprivileged;

the inequalities of educational provision: these are some of the problems which are inextricably mixed up with the problem of youth which has still to be solved. Is it possible that common learnings go on too long? Already in Chapter 7 it has been seen that some regard the junior college as comprehensive and suggest that common learnings are not complete even at that stage. It is feasible that an inordinate delay in the choice of a definite future role, at least to prepare for, may be the cause of unsettledness. Thus the present trend at senior high school level to a greater degree of depth and academic rigour in contrast to the more general offerings in the recent past must be watched with care for its side effects on the problem.

Mays also deals with the problem of competition and co-operation. Coleman* in his essay "Academic achievement and the structure of competition" makes some important points on this topic, much in keeping with what Mays has in mind, but perhaps his most fertile suggestion is to be found in the appendix to the essay. Coleman, working with American high school pupils, underlines what he calls the paradox of secondary education: there is more to learn in a complex society but the "society of adolescents" takes little interest in learning but more in cars, dates, pop music and sport. He is referring here to the fun sub-culture already mentioned. His investigation showed that good academic achievers in school usually had a low status or were even negatively valued. Most students believe in working below the level they could reach and so hold down the average mark. (In a wider context this attitude is held to be true of workers generally.) Coleman, looking from this viewpoint, distinguishes two groups in the high school—the mass of sociable average students and the academically oriented isolates. It was, he thought, possible to be a good academic achiever or be popular, but it was hardly possible to be both.

This established he goes on to refer to Morton Deusch's experiments on inter-personal and inter-group competition which show

* See Chapter 27 in Halsey, Floud, and Anderson, *Education, Economy and Society*, New York, 1961.

how better results can be obtained by co-operation inside groups which are competing against other groups. Applying the findings to the high school situation, with regard to games and scholastic matters, Coleman shows that while in respect of games and athletics there is inter-institutional competition and therefore no one minds games players practising in the lunch hour, in scholastic matters competition is inter-personal and so studying at lunch time is regarded as queer, and interested academics are ostracised for a too intense effort. What is required, he suggests, is more inter-institutional rivalry and competition in academic matters, so just as congratulations are showered on athletic successes so scholastic achievements should be similarly stimulated.

Having made these suggestions Coleman adds a note contrasting conditions in Czechoslovakia with those in U.S.A. There he finds that academics are less despised and speculates whether this may not be connected with the fact that the syllabus is laid down far away from the school so that all are competing against an impersonal body—the examination setters—rather than against their friends. If this is true for Czechoslovakia it should also be true for France where education is highly centralised. Historically Frenchmen have honoured the intellectual, but the nationwide examination and centralised syllabus could have been a contributory factor. Currently, 30% of 18-year-olds are in the academic school and about two-thirds of them will achieve success in the *baccalauréat*. Is there any connection between the attitude stemming from central control and the reports that the teenager movement in France is less of a problem than elsewhere? Even the chain of teenage fashion shops is called the "Pre-bac" (pre-*baccalauréat* examination).

Compared with England, France's teenager movement was late in coming to a head. There had been earlier outbreaks by the more deviant *blousons noirs*, but not until 1963 was there a massive demonstration. On 22 June (near Midsummer's Eve) a commercial radio station staged an open air "pop" music show in la Place de la Nation, and 150,000 boys and girls gathered to rock and twist, defying the efforts of the police to disperse them. Previously the spending power of the teenagers had helped to make them respectable, but this June evening caused sociologists to begin to pay more attention to the movement. However, it does appear the whole teenage revolt is less extreme than elsewhere. One schoolboy of 14 explained "I'm not really a *copain* (teenager) here yet. It won't happen—going about in gangs—until I'm 15 or 16." Another boy at a *lycée* said French youth had less need to rebel against conventions than the British because schools were less rigid. He thought French youths were more like mods and there were fewer rockers.

When thinking of co-operation it is useful to remember the Scandinavian countries which at an adult level have worked co-operative schemes in agriculture to a greater extent than most countries. In Sweden, the gains to be obtained from growing up side by side is one of the outcomes the authorities look for from their reformed school system which has stressed this aspect. Their expectation of co-operation from private education to attain these aims has also been noted. Growing up together has been thought of as more important than extending the academic schools downwards to include the ninth grade.

Obviously it is impossible here to make a complete comparative analysis of these problems, but enough has been said to show they are widespread and there are no quick solutions which appeal to our ideas. Merely to give youth an honoured place by setting up separate institutions catering for the age range will not be a total answer, though it may be a necessary step on the way. If society requires this age group to have more and more education, and the necessity for this seems incontrovertible, then the institutions must be acceptable to those who will use them. But buildings and establishments alone, nor the education given in them—even when it is broadly conceived—will not be sufficient. Only when the ideals which are required are really supported by the wider society outside, will true progress result.

CHAPTER 15

Circular 10/65
and Upper Secondary Education for All

AT PRESENT, local education authorities in England and Wales are
engaged in the difficult task of reorganising the pattern of educational provision at the secondary level. For many years to come,
perhaps throughout this century, these changes are likely to continue, for, although a final goal has been stated—it is the Government's declared objective to end selection at 11 + and to eliminate
separation in secondary education—this is a broad aim and
interim solutions are to be accepted as a step on the way. As
money becomes available this interim plan will need reappraisal
and definitive schemes may take long to implement.

Viewed in perspective, Circular 10/65 from the Secretary of
State for Education and Science on the organisation of secondary
education only heralds the quickening of a process which has been
going on slowly since 1944. During these two decades changes at
the secondary level have made it necessary for the central authority, in compiling statistics of secondary schools, to change their
classification on several occasions in an effort to describe the available provision. The 1944 Act made secondary a stage after primary and secondary education is defined as full-time education
suitable to the requirements of senior pupils, other than that given
under further education. A junior pupil is one who has not
attained the age of 12 and a senior pupil has not attained the age
of 19. This gives a possibility of 7 years of secondary education,
though this is not compulsory, and not all full-time education between 12 and 19 ranks as secondary: it may be further education.

And the Act is silent about secondary organisation. Obviously there is much room for manœuvre.

In the early years after 1944 grant-aided secondary schools were classified as secondary modern, grammar and technical, but in addition there were a considerable number of pupils of secondary school age in all-age schools. There were also secondary pupils in direct-grant schools, and, outside the grant-aided system, were the independent schools. In 1950 the Ministry extended the classification, and for the next 8 years, beside the headings detailed above, separate numbers were given for three kinds of bilateral school—the three possible combinations of grammar, technical and modern—and for multilateral schools and comprehensive schools. At the outset, none of these individual totals was large and their grand total was only 45, but, by 1957 it had more than trebled to 161. The following year saw another attempt at a rationalisation of the statistics, with a joint grouping of bilateral and multilateral schools still separated off from comprehensive schools, and the introduction of an all-embracing title—other secondary schools—to cover those not amenable to classification. Since 1958 the numbers of schools in these categories have shown a considerable growth, and Circular 10/65 will accelerate this change, for its purpose is to provide some central guidance on the methods by which secondary education can be reorganised on comprehensive lines.

It lists six forms of comprehensive organisation which have emerged from experience and discussion and it gives some appraisal of each. Two of the forms it outlines it regards as not truly comprehensive and only acceptable as interim arrangements. Our main interest here is in the shape of the upper secondary school which will result from the reorganisation. The circular writes in terms of junior comprehensive and senior comprehensive schools and makes it clear that the terms junior and senior throughout the circular refer to the lower and upper secondary schools in two-tier systems of secondary education. Here upper secondary education has been regarded as the education given between the ages of 15–16 and 18–19 in whatever kind of school organisation it has occurred. It is useful now to examine the kind of upper secondary provision which would result from each of the six main forms of comprehensive organisation listed in the circular. Figure 14 will help the written description:

(i) The orthodox comprehensive school with an age range from 11 to 18. The circular states this pattern can provide an effective

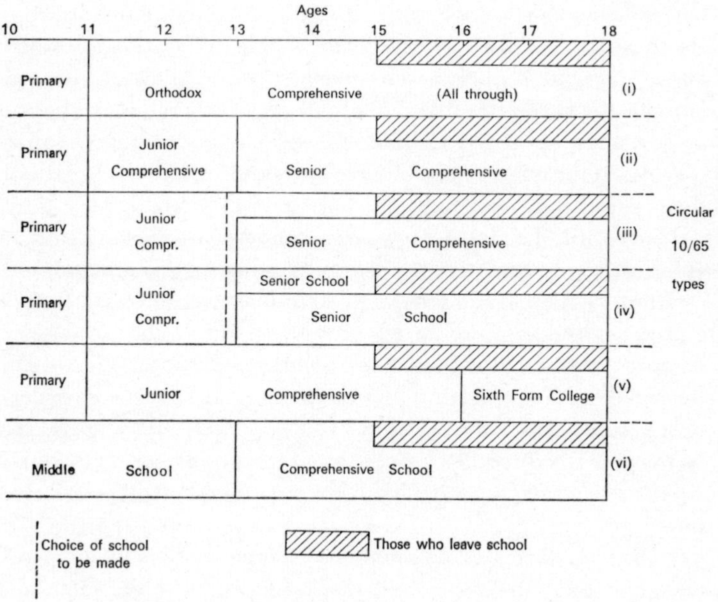

FIG. 14. Possible patterns of comprehensive schooling.

and educationally sound secondary organisation and if it were possible to design a new pattern this would in many respects provide the simplest and best solution. Obviously it appeals to the Department for they say there are strong arguments for its adoption wherever circumstances permit.

Such an arrangement clearly gives an upper secondary department well articulated with its lower secondary counterpart. The circular suggests that a viable sixth form can be produced by a six- or seven-form entry. In making this assumption the argument seems to be thinking of the traditional "academic" sixth form and its orthodox extension and not in terms of upper secondary schooling for all adolescents which would eventually produce a sixth-form year group approaching any other year group in size. At the upper level it is expecting that other institutions will cater for some of the education especially in the vocational–technical sectors. If the school at its highest level is engaged with only the "academic" side, there is a possibility that at lower levels it may overvalue this kind of pupil in preference to those who will continue their education elsewhere. Despite many experiments, and much attention directed towards more general and vocational studies, this is a criticism which has been made of existing comprehensive schools of this type and as yet this charge has not been satisfactorily refuted.

(ii) A two-tier system. At 11 years all pupils transfer to a lower school where they remain for 2 or 3 years depending on the size of the available buildings, for this is a scheme designed to make use of existing accommodation. Then at either 13 or 14 years all pupils transfer again to the upper secondary school which provides all kinds of courses for the whole ability range up to the age of 18. This gives a rather lengthy upper school course, but the size of school is much reduced as compared with the orthodox all-through comprehensive school.

(iii) A two-tier system with some pupils remaining in the lower secondary school until the compulsory leaving age while others transfer at 13 or 14 to the upper secondary school. Transfer is by pupil and parental choice and in practice this works to give a restricted grouping in the upper school, weighted towards higher ability and superior socio-economic status, even in the years below the compulsory leaving age. Again it is a scheme designed to make use of existing buildings. In essence the Leicestershire Plan is a scheme of this type with the lower school called a high school and the upper school retaining the status name of grammar school. While the upper school caters for a wider ability range than the normal grammar school, it is not fully comprehensive. From 14 to 15 years two schools exist in parallel and cater for a different clientele and therefore segregation continues. The Secretary of State is only willing to consider this as an interim solution. In Leicestershire, when the leaving age is raised to 16 years, the intention is that all pupils shall transfer to the upper school and then the Mason (Leicestershire) Plan will become a truly comprehensive two-tier solution identical with type (ii) above.

(iv) This is a variant of the above. At 13 or 14 years a choice has to be made for entry, either to an upper school with a short course leading, probably beyond the compulsory leaving age, to C.S.E., or G.C.E. O-level, or to an upper school with a longer duration including, of course, traditional sixth-form work. Again this gives segregation in parallel schools.

(v) This is another two-tier system. At 11 years all transfer to a comprehensive school which caters for all abilities to the age of 16 years. Following this age is a sixth-form college for the 16–18-year-olds. It is a two-tier variation with a higher age of transfer. The circular notes two conceptions of the function of the upper tier:

(a) a college which caters for the educational needs of all young people staying beyond the age of 16 (this is sometimes called a junior college and would in some respects resemble the senior high school in the United States);

(b) a sixth-form college more oriented to academic work and requiring entrants to have achieved a certain standard in O-level examinations and be preparing for specified examinations or other goals at the end of the course.

As a further variation, the upper secondary stage, either junior college or sixth-form college, may be attached to a single school and adolescents from other schools may be allowed to transfer to it. An arrangement of this nature has one well-marked drawback. A recent article* dealing with the environmental effects on

* Eggleston, J., Environment and comprehensives, *Education*, 28 January 1966.

comprehensive schools shows that when the decision to continue at school also requires a decision to transfer to another school there is an unnecessarily large fall-out, and suggests situations involving such double decisions should be eliminated. Under the Leicestershire Plan pupils of all social backgrounds have tended to stay on more than in areas with tripartite arrangements.

Eggleston has, of course, been studying instances where some pupils transfer to join others who are continuing in an all-through institution, e.g. pupils leaving modern schools to join grammar schools or comprehensive schools at 16 years, and his findings do not necessarily (and are not likely) to hold good for situations like the true sixth-form college where all transfer together. These would appear to offer an attractive new start in a fresh well-planned environment with old acquaintances, and everyone making a new beginning. Critics have suggested that settling down in a 2-year institution would take up too much of the available time. The rapidity with which most pupils settle in a new school at the age of 11 can be truly amazing. In this country there is little experience of a similar process at 16, but the answer to an inquiry concerning the settling-in process at Atlantic College (the international sixth-form boarding school in Glamorgan) suggested that boys were working well and happily on their second day at college.

(vi) An organisation which involves middle schools with an age range from 9 to 13 years, straddling the present primary–secondary divide, followed by an upper school to which all transfer at 13 years. In effect this gives a two-tier system at the secondary level and a fully comprehensive upper secondary portion with a restricted age range. The ages chosen mirror those which have existed for many decades in the preparatory–public schools of the independent system. Only a limited experiment with this solution, in a part of the West Riding of Yorkshire, was originally sanctioned by the Secretary of State, but in Parliament on 25 April 1966 he relaxed from the extremely cautious approach in the circular and promised a willing consideration of such schemes if clear advantages were demonstrated.

This brief commentary concerning the present proposals for secondary education has aimed to set the current situation in perspective. It will now be followed by an equally brief summary of the arrangements and plans in the other countries dealt with in this book, expressed as far as is possible in the terms of our Circular 10/65. Comparisons can be full of pitfalls: countries with very ambitious plans may not be able to achieve their targets completely; but the exercise will throw into relief the difference of approach at the upper secondary level between most other countries and ourselves.

FRANCE

The eventual French plan is a two-tier system with a first tier from 11 to 15 followed by a variety of provision and opportunities above this age. Sixth-form colleges will cater for the academically oriented, but there is full-time provision of technical and vocational education. At present, during the changeover there is a good deal of variety of structure and it will take some time to establish the plan. In fact, for the foreseeable future it is envisaged that the pupils who will leave at 16 will spend their last year in the *collèges d'enseignement général* which cater mainly for the 11–15 age-group. This is type (iii) of Circular 10/65 something like the Leicestershire arrangement. But the percentage expected to do this is small and the large majority will transfer to other specialised institutions at the end of the orientation period at 15.

The whole arrangement is comprehensive or multilateral to 15 with parallel tracks (a quinti-partite system) beyond.

U.S.S.R.

The Soviet Union has a two-tier system. Compulsory schooling, with a common curriculum and time allocation, ends at 15 years, and after this age there is a tripartite system. Each branch combines general and vocational–technical education but in different proportions. For students going on to vocational education proper or taking a secondary specialised course, transfer to another institution is necessary, but general academic education after the age of 15 may carry on in the same school or may require transfer to another school of the sixth-form college type. In fact, some schools in the U.S.S.R. provide all the 10 years of education under one roof. From 7 to 17 years, it may not be necessary to change school though the breaks in the course are still present.

Beyond compulsory age there is a good deal of part-time provision both in evening or alternating shift schools or by extension–correspondence courses. The part-time provision is well organised and leads to qualifications identical with those attainable in full-time courses.

SWEDEN

The Swedish plan is a definite two-tier system with the comprehensive provision continuing up to the age of 16 years. At 14 and 15 years there is a large common core to the curriculum and a small amount of differentiation, but in the final ninth year of the comprehensive school nine major branches are available. After 16 there is to be a definite break to autonomous institutions, and movements to attach the final year of the comprehensive course to either the academic upper school or a technical school have been rejected. The 9-year school at the primary and lower secondary level is an entity with a unifying aim. After 16 years a wide variety of provision is available in the academic schools (*gymnasier*), continuation schools or vocational schools.

U.S.A.

The preferred pattern in the States is for 3 years of junior high school to 15 years followed by 3 years of senior high school from 15 to 18 years with a wide range of opportunities. In some large urban areas there is a certain amount of specialisation between schools, e.g. New York has a number of vocational high schools but generally the norm is a separate upper secondary school catering by means of optional (elective) subjects for the whole ability range. The enrolment ratio for the 15–19-year age group in 1960 was 65%.

It is in this pattern of one institution offering a variety of academic courses alongside vocational education that upper secondary provision in the U.S.A. differs from France, Sweden and the U.S.S.R., which separate the academic streams from the technical and vocational at this level. The presence of these manifold courses and the broad ability range in the senior high school has caused some British educationists to regard the comprehensive system with something approaching horror. The Spens report of 1938, interested particularly in technical education, thought (using American experience transmitted by Professor I. Kandel) the multilateral school would tend to favour an academic type of course, but most critics have highlighted the dangers which could result from students of high ability choosing the easier options which must be readily available for the wide ability span. In many cases, these critics failed to allow for the effect of indigenous traditions on seemingly similar institutions: our tradition would not allow for the under-valuing of academic approaches, as the comprehensive schools established so far have shown. In this decade the American high school seems to be adopting an approach more like ours: it is certainly turning more definitely towards greater academic rigour.

The system in the States, then, is a two-tier one with a good articulation between the tiers and an all-purpose upper secondary school which in Circular 10/65 terminology approaches type (v) mode (a).

JAPAN

After the war Japan adopted the junior–senior high school pattern from the U.S.A. and though it has since adapted the curriculum to suit its indigenous traditions, the pattern of schooling has been retained. In the two-tier system the upper secondary school offers a wide diversity of courses of both an academic and vocational–technical nature in the same building and caters for a large percentage of the age group. It approaches the type (v) mode (a) pattern.

In addition it makes part-time education and correspondence education available: these routes can lead to qualifications identical with those obtained full time.

FEDERAL REPUBLIC OF GERMANY

The present system does not provide secondary education for all, and the Rahmenplan still envisages parallel tracks at the lower secondary level and makes no attempt at fusion at the upper levels. Although an advance, the plan is not very forward looking, and has been criticised inside Germany for its lack of vision. However, the inclusive nature of the part-time requirement to 18 years, already working well for a long period, is a mitigating factor.

SPAIN

Compared with the other countries considered here, Spain has a low level of educational provision and the plan for the future does not envisage secondary education for all.

The consensus of opinion from abroad favours a two-tier system with some kind of sixth-form college as the upper tier, starting often at the age of 15. At the upper secondary stage there is a divergence of practice between one institution at this level catering for the educational needs of all young people, as in the U.S.A., and Japan, and parallel institutions specialising in one type of education, as in France, Sweden and the U.S.S.R.

The problem of England and Wales is complicated by the ordinary level examination of the G.C.E. at the age of 16 years, which is used by about one-quarter of all pupils. Soon the C.S.E., which will cater for even a higher percentage eventually, will be an added difficulty. The existence of these examinations makes transfer at 15 years quite out of the question. Germany manage with one external examination at the end of their long course. Even so it is largely internal and moderated. The examination at 16 years is based entirely on teachers' assessments. France, which had two parts to the *baccalauréat*—12 months apart—has abandoned the first. The U.S.A. has a credit system differently organised and Japan has followed suit. The U.S.S.R. has an examination at 15 years. It is of a lower standard than G.C.E., and almost everyone is expected to pass it. None of these countries has a problem similar to ours. Transfer at 14, as in Leicestershire, giving a 2-year course to O-level, is regarded by some as giving too short a period of examination preparation. Apart from the provision of buildings, one of the main arguments used for the Hemsworth (West Riding) plan, with transfer at 13, is that it keeps examination pressures out of the middle school. In effect, the timing of our examinations means that if we are to have an upper school of the sixth-form college type it must start at 16 years.

Circular 10/65 indicates a definite preference for the all-through 11–18 solution—"there are strong arguments for its adoption wherever circumstances permit", whereas for the sixth-form college solution "the Secretary of State believes that the issues have been sufficiently debated to justify a limited number of experiments". When the two short paragraphs setting out the pros and cons of the sixth-form college are examined the lack of depth in the arguments advanced is apparent.

"Children may lose from a lack of contact with senior pupils" (para. 17) but lack of contact with sixth-formers may be outweighed by greater opportunities for leadership which younger pupils themselves will have in the lower school (para. 18). They may lose or they may not lose!

"Some teachers may find unattractive the prospect of teaching the whole ability range in a school offering no opportunities for advanced work" (para. 17). In primary schools and in secondary modern schools many teachers have found a worth-while teaching career with a restricted age range. The latter may welcome the whole ability range—and many are well qualified to teach it.

"Many teachers express a preference for work in schools catering for the whole secondary range" (para. 17). How many have
experience with a restricted upper range? Public schools have
dedicated teachers with the lowest secondary age groups excluded
from their schools. Anyway, can preferences be allowed to decide?

The circular goes on to speak of the gain to sixth-formers from
attaining something of the status and freedom of students. Although biological maturity has advanced, social maturity has
probably advanced even more rapidly. Small privileges are no
longer satisfying and sixth-formers are now more like under-
graduates a quarter of a century ago. And, of course, with increasing enrolment ratios sixth-formers are no longer a small privileged
élite.

The method of organisation of orthodox comprehensive schools
could present some evidence on the separate upper secondary idea.
In large schools there are two main forms of social organisation—
a vertical division into houses and a horizontal division into lower,
middle and upper schools: some subdivision seems necessary to
prevent the large school becoming too impersonal. Actual schooling, in the strict sense, is almost wholly given in groups which are
homogeneous in age. A house system cuts across the teaching
groups and mixes the age groups from 11 to 18. Lower, middle and
upper divisions tend to keep the age groups together. Some schools
have been built on a house plan which entails that the administrative and social arrangements in school shall be organised on this
basis, whereas other schools are built so that more flexible arrangements can obtain. It would be interesting if we knew whether the
house plan made rigid by buildings, is in any way inhibiting, and
whether in practice heads are favouring one kind of arrangement
more than another. Schools of reasonably long standing are reported as changing from a vertical to a horizontal system, and
increasingly there are accounts from more traditional schools of
arrangements whereby sixth forms are separated from the main
school to give more privacy and freedom. Only the passage of
time and a research project (the N.F.E.R. are to study the comprehensive school) can quantify this feeling. Sixth forms have

always had a special position, but in these days it seems to be even more special. If there is really a trend to a separation at the sixth-form level, Circular 10/65 could be pressing a wrong choice.

A recent article from the further education side* has argued along these lines, pointing out that, although further education and schools are both administered from the town hall by separate departments they are growing together at the upper secondary level, for if few schools as yet have vocational courses, colleges of further education have many A-level students. (An interesting development is the provision of day-release arrangements for over 100 students at the Holyhead Comprehensive School under the administration of the headmaster. Anglesey, already a pioneer in comprehensive organisation, may here be fostering another progressive step.) Upper schools could meet the developing personal and social needs of the increasingly mature adolescents and provide economically for the fullest range of opportunity, and lower schools from 11 to 16 could be of less than mammoth size.

This still leaves the problem of unity or diversity of institution at the upper secondary level to be solved. The circular speaks of the need to prevent duplication of resources and unnecessary overlap, but whether there should be complete integration, with the establishment of a unitary or comprehensive institution at this stage is less easy to decide. Comparison with other countries gives no unequivocal answer. Europe seems to have chosen one route (France, Sweden, U.S.S.R.): the "new" countries another (U.S.A., Japan). If parallel arrangements are introduced at 16 will they soon be overtaken by the tendency for comprehensiveness to move further up the age range and in 20 years will another circular similar to 10/65 be necessary? Pedley, in *The Comprehensive School*, and Elvin, in *Education and Contemporary Society*, have argued for a comprehensive education at this level with one institution catering for full-time and part-time students side by side. Caution, and the working out of evolutionary processes, suggest a more pragmatic approach, with a variety of opportunities beyond

* Mumford, D. E., Implications of reorganisation for further education, *Education*, 4 February 1966.

16, not all in one stable. But everything seems to point to the wisdom of a separate institution for these older adolescents.

With the growth of more automation and the onset of the cybernetic revolution, an era of more leisure for all is confidently promised. When this millennium arrives, and we are often assured it will be sooner than we envisage, we may find our planning wrong and have to recast it to provide general offerings to a later stage. Over a century ago Matthew Arnold came back from France with the injunction "organise secondary education". Since 1902 organisation and reorganisation has been an accelerating process and there is no real reason to believe the definitive plan has yet been drawn up. With the growth of knowledge of experiments elsewhere, the volume of experience on which planners can draw increases, and just as Matthew Arnold brought back, not a detailed prescription but a general principle, so today, out of a detailed study of foreign education may emerge more general insights that we cannot afford to neglect.

Bibliography

REFERENCES are cited as they occur but the following works are also useful:

The three volumes of the *UNESCO World Survey of Education*

Vol. 1 *Handbook*	1955
Vol. 2 *Primary Education*	1958
Vol. 3 *Secondary Education*	1961

are a mine of information.

The publications of the Council for Cultural Co-operation of the Council of Europe especially Education in Europe (Section II, *General and Technical Education*) and particularly II, *5 School Systems—a guide* (Strasbourg 1965) contain much useful material.

In addition to works cited in the chapters may be noted:

Chapter 5. *British Technical Education*, P. F. R. Venables, Longmans, London, 1959.

    The Evening Institute, H. J. Edwards, National Council for Adult Education, London, 1961.

Chapter 8. *Education in France*, G. A. Male, U.S. Dept. of Health, Education and Welfare, Washington, 1963.

Chapter 11. *Soviet Education*, N. Grant, Penguin Books, 1964.

Chapter 12. *Schools of West Germany*, T. Heubener, New York Univ. Press, 1962.

Index